Commitments
of Traders

Founded in 1807, John Wiley & Sons is the oldest independent publishing company in the United States. With offices in North America, Europe, Australia, and Asia, Wiley is globally committed to developing and marketing print and electronic products and services for our customers' professional and personal knowledge and understanding.

The Wiley Trading series features books by traders who have survived the market's ever-changing temperament and have prospered—some by reinventing systems, others by getting back to basics. Whether you are a novice trader, professional, or somewhere in-between, these books will provide the advice and strategies needed to prosper today and well into the future.

For a list of available titles, please visit our web site at www.Wiley Finance.com.

Commitments of Traders

*Strategies for Tracking the
Market and Trading Profitably*

FLOYD UPPERMAN

WILEY

John Wiley & Sons, Inc.

Published by John Wiley & Sons, Inc., Hoboken, New Jersey.
Published simultaneously in Canada.

For general information on our other products and services or for technical support, please contact our Customer Care Department within the United States at (800) 762-2974, outside the United States at (317) 572-3993 or fax (317) 572-4002.

Wiley also publishes its books in a variety of electronic formats. Some content that appears in print may not be available in electronic books. For more information about Wiley products, visit our web site at www.wiley.com.

Library of Congress Cataloging-in-Publication Data:

Upperman, Floyd, 1966–
    Commitments of traders : strategies for tracking the market and trading profitably / Floyd Upperman.
        p.   cm.   (Wiley trading series)
    Includes bibliographical references and index.
    ISBN-13: 978-0-471-71965-6 (cloth)
    ISBN-10: 0-471-71965-X (cloth)
    1. Commodity exchanges.   2. Stocks.   3. Investment analysis.   4. Portfolio management.   I. Title.   II. Series.

    HG6046.U66 2006
    332.64—dc22

                                                                                                    2005023676

Printed in the United States of America.

10 9 8 7 6 5 4 3 2 1

Contents

Preface

This book describes and explains my proprietary trading strategies, indicators, and methods developed over the past decade. Among my most treasured proprietary indicators are those derived from an obscure weekly U.S. government report, called the *Commitments of Traders* (COT). My approach to incorporating this data into my trading is the main topic discussed in this book.

As insightful as I have found this data to be, there are limitations to its use, and more importantly, there are proper and improper ways for a trader to act on it. Traders need to recognize and understand the limitations of any indicator or data when making financial decisions; it is absolutely crucial to interpret the COT data properly and incorporate it into a complete trading system that also uses traditional technical analysis. My own position trading approach includes statistical indicators derived from the COT combined with unique price patterns, price structures, and price-derived indicators based on traditional technical analysis.

A common misconception with the COT is that the commercials always represent the "smart money" and that they are always or almost always right in the market. This is not entirely true, as I illustrate in this book, but there is more to it. To unlock the potential of the COT data as a tool for trading, the user must dig a little deeper into the data instead of simply honing in on the net-commercial position.

The commercial data can be examined more thoroughly by separating it into its two entities (commercial producers and consumers) and by applying unique indicators to each component. This is discussed in detail in later chapters of this book.

Most of the COT indicators I have evaluated over the years focus primarily on the net-commercial position. However, additional insight can be gained by looking at the two individual entities that make up that position. There is a balancing act going on here between the two commercial entities. One is the consumer of a certain commodity and the other is the producer. In a perfect world, the producer produces just enough to supply the demand of consumers, and the consumers always have enough to keep them happy.

As we know, it is not a perfect world. Sometimes there is not enough supply to satisfy all the demand, or there is oversupply and not enough demand to consume all the supply. By monitoring the positions of these two entities, we can gain insight into this crucial balancing act and watch it unfold.

The individual positioning of the commercial consumers and producers can provide a valuable glimpse of the true supply and demand in the underlying cash market where the physical commodity exists. And herein lies the real benefit of incorporating this data into a position trading system. No group understands the fundamentals (supply and demand) in a market better than the producers producing the supply and the consumers consuming it.

A mistake traders often make when looking at the COT reports is to assume that if the commercials are holding a large net-long or net-short position in the market, the prudent thing to do is to immediately establish a position with the commercials. That is untrue and can result in a fast loss. It is essential to use the COT in conjunction with traditional price-derived technical indicators, not in place of those indicators.

The COT, or indicators derived from it, does not provide adequate data to establish a position in the market. When establishing a position, several factors must come into play, and of course, the price behavior is a big part of this.

The COT is only one factor, one measure. I have developed specific criteria that combine price-derived indicators with the COT and specific price patterns to help identify the optimum and proper entry points when using the COT as a guide. By leveraging the COT in this way, we can take advantage of the insight it provides under the right technical conditions that might warrant a technical trade even if we did include the COT in the analysis.

My strategy is to monitor the COT activity across multiple markets. When both the COT and the technical conditions concur in a specific market (once the market begins moving in the direction of the COT), a specific entry can be established. This usually doesn't happen right away. Most of the time there is a setting-up period where the COT begins exhibiting notable conditions but price has not yet responded. It is during this period that traders should closely monitor the price structure using traditional forms of technical analysis in order to make the entry at an appropriate and optimum time based on the price structure as well as the COT (the two together). If there were ever a Holy Grail for position trading, this is one of the closest things to it.

The biggest mistake traders make when using this data is simply following the net-commercial position and entering the market as soon as the commercials are holding a large position on one side. If you learn one thing from this book, it should be to never enter a position solely on the net-commercial position. Timing, as mentioned, is the main reason that this doesn't work. Furthermore, a net-commercial position can reach and stay at an extreme level for months before anything happens in the market.

In fact, the existing trend may very well accelerate when the net-commercial position reaches an extreme level. This is because of the various trend phases, which I also discuss. My methods include monitoring the net-commercial position; I want to be clear on that, too, because it is a critical measure. However, it is essential to monitor it using the right kind of indicators (e.g., I use statistics). Further, the net-commercial position should be examined in the context of both entities composing the net-commercial position—the producers and the consumers—and also in conjunction with price behavior.

The real key to being able to incorporate the COT into a trading strategy resides, first, in having a thorough understanding of the data—knowing what its limitations really are and how to use the data within the confines of its limitations. Second, this data must be used in conjunction with other appropriate methods, including traditional technical analysis of price and efficient position management indicators.

A trader must be doing everything right essentially to produce repeatable successful results. There are many other influences on the markets to consider (such as seasonal influences), but the COT is among the most underrated and least talked about data in the financial community today.

Important Note: The charts and graphs in this book have been produced from my web site, www.upperman.com. Many are examples of components of actual trade setups. Production considerations required converting the color graphics in the charts to black and white for this book. This takes away an important visual aid in the charts: the differentiation among the various lines and points on a graphic (e.g., price, net-commercial position, moving averages), which are displayed in color on a computer monitor. Therefore, I have set up a special section on my web site, enabling readers to view the charts in color as they would normally appear. To access these charts, visit www.upperman.com and click on the link titled "View Book Graphs." Access to these graphics is free.

For more information about my trading strategies, services, and proprietary market information, I can be reached via e-mail at floyd@upperman.com or please visit www.upperman.com.

BACKGROUND INFORMATION

I first became interested in the markets during the 1980s after receiving some shares of stock from a company I worked for at the time. The company provided an employee stock ownership program that, even as a young man, I could appreciate. You really could not lose with this program. Every six months, the company would evaluate the price of their stock and allow employees to purchase shares at a price 15 percent below the lowest price during the previous six-month period (they allow a certain percentage of an employee's salary to be used for this purpose).

After the shares were purchased, they were yours to keep. This was before electronic trading, and the certificates were actually mailed to you. You could take the certificates and deposit them at a brokerage house, cash them out at a local bank, or just hold onto them. I chose to simply hold onto the certificates.

After having acquired a decent number of shares, a bull market erupted and the price began rising. Suddenly I had made more money in a short time doing nothing (remember this) than I had ever made working for the corporation in that length of time. Since I was busy with other priorities, I just held onto the shares. The price continued to increase as a trend had taken hold. This was my introduction to the markets and their possibilities.

As a result of this introduction, I would learn one of the most powerful money-making secrets to investing I'd ever learn. The lesson was twofold: Although I did the right thing initially by sitting and doing nothing while my profits grew, years later I would discover I did not sit long enough. I would remember this just as all traders and investors are reminded about leaving money on the table at some point. I've done it in every market I have ever participated in—equities, options, futures, real estate, business, you name it. There is a trail of money behind me sitting on a trail of tables. Still, doing the right thing for part of the time has always paid off.

By sitting and doing nothing with those shares, I had made more money than some of my astute colleagues who had more experience with this sort of thing. Being naive sometimes does have its advantages. Some of my colleagues deposited their shares with brokerage houses. This gave the brokerage the ability to jump in and out of the market with their shares by simply making a phone call. During the day while I focused on my work priorities, I noted their roller coaster emotional swings as they jumped in and out attempting to capture the market swings. After all their hard work, however, not one of them did any better than I did. My secret was that I did nothing at all. I sat on my shares and did nothing while the market continued to rise. By doing nothing, I made more money with my shares than my colleagues who jumped in and out. Later I would discover that several colleagues actually lost money. This experience had a profound influence on my early investing and trading career and to this day still has an influence. My main focus is still on position trading, not day trading, and I trade in all kinds of markets.

Now to the leaving the money on the table part: Being the young single man I was back then, after my shares had increased so much, I could not resist the temptation to cash out and treat myself to something really spectacular: A Corvette!

This Corvette still sits in my garage, and you can be assured that it is one of the most expensive Corvettes in the world! Not because it is a rare, fancy model. It is just a regular Corvette, nothing special. However, the shares I sold to purchase this car went on to increase in value more than 100-fold after I sold them. So goes the saying: If we only knew yesterday what we know today! And that is the real basis of this book and my studies of the markets.

In *Commitments of Traders*, I discuss some of the most sensitive data available, along with the proprietary techniques I have devised to provide valuable insight on what tomorrow may bring. In addition, having access to certain data can provide a trader with the confidence to do one of the most important things a trader can do in an ongoing profitable position—*and that is to do nothing.*

In the many years that followed my introduction to the markets, I have learned the power of doing nothing in terms of execution, while doing plenty in terms of being patient, observing, and monitoring both price structure and fundamental data. Years of observation and countless hours of data analysis have enabled me to devise and develop unique strategies and techniques that can provide insight into where the market may be headed and how we can determine when it is there.

My ongoing quest to identify high-probability situations and efficient money management techniques has led me away from everything the masses use and toward developing my own charting software. I have implemented unique proprietary measurements and models that are composed and derived from nontraditional sources such as the COT data.

To a trader, the power of compounding profits is as big as the power of compounding interest. And in today's world of fast-moving derivatives, the early lessons I learned still hold true. Like many other professional position traders and investors who have come before me, I still make the most money from sitting and doing nothing. From my experience and observations, I have concluded that no person will ever outsmart the market. It is true that some traders can beat the market some of the time, but no one beats the market all of the time. Furthermore, every good trader leaves a little on the table most of the time. That's one of the telltale signatures of a profitable trade.

RISK DISCLOSURE

Hypothetical performance results have many inherent limitations. No representation is being made that any account will or is likely to achieve profits or losses similar to those shown. In fact, there are frequently sharp differences between hypothetical performance results and the actual results subsequently achieved by any particular trading program.

A limitation of hypothetical performance results is that they are generally prepared with the benefit of hindsight. In addition, hypothetical trading does not involve financial risk, and no hypothetical trading record can completely account for the impact of financial risk in actual trading. The ability to withstand losses or to adhere to a particular trading program despite trading losses can also adversely affect actual trading results. Numerous other factors related to the markets in general or to the implementation of any specific trading program cannot be fully accounted for when preparing hypothetical performance results. All of them can adversely affect actual trading results.

The risk of loss in trading commodity futures contracts can be substantial.

You should, therefore, carefully consider whether such trading is suitable for you in light of your circumstances and financial resources. You should be aware of the following points:

- You may sustain a total loss of the funds that you deposit with your broker to establish or maintain a position in the commodity futures market, and you may incur losses beyond these amounts. If the market moves against your position, your broker may require you to deposit substantial additional margin funds, on short notice, to maintain your position. If you do not provide the requested funds within the time your broker specifies, your position may be liquidated at a loss, and you will be liable for any resulting deficit in your account.
- Under certain market conditions, you may find it difficult or impossible to liquidate a position. This can occur, for example, when the market reaches a daily price fluctuation limit (limit move).
- Placing contingent orders, such as stop-loss or stop-limit orders, will not necessarily limit your losses to the intended amounts, since market conditions on the exchange where the order is placed may make it impossible to execute such orders.

- All futures positions involve risk, and a spread position may not be less risky than an outright long or short position.
- The high degree of leverage (gearing) that is often obtainable in futures trading because of the small margin requirements can work against you as well as for you. Leverage (gearing) can lead to large losses as well as gains.
- You should consult your broker concerning the protections available to safeguard funds or property deposited for your account.

All the preceding points apply to all futures trading whether foreign or domestic. If you are contemplating trading foreign futures or options contracts, you should be aware of the following additional risks:

- Foreign futures transactions involve executing and clearing trades on a foreign exchange. This is the case even if the foreign exchange is formally linked to a domestic exchange, whereby a trade executed on one exchange liquidates or establishes a position on the other exchange. No domestic organization regulates the activities of a foreign exchange, including the execution, delivery, and clearing of transactions on such an exchange, and no domestic regulator has the power to compel enforcement of the rules of the foreign exchange or the laws of the foreign country. Moreover, such laws or regulations will vary depending on the foreign country in which the transaction occurs.

   For these reasons, customers who trade on foreign exchanges may not be afforded certain protections that apply to domestic transactions, including the right to use domestic alternative dispute resolution procedures. In particular, funds received from customers to margin foreign futures transactions may not be provided the same protections as funds received to margin futures transactions on domestic exchanges. Before you trade, you should familiarize yourself with the foreign rules that will apply to your particular transaction.

- Finally, you should be aware that the price of any foreign futures or option contract, and therefore the potential profit and loss, may be affected by any fluctuation in the foreign exchange rate between the time the order is placed and when the foreign futures contract is liquidated or the foreign option contract is liquidated or exercised.

This brief section cannot disclose all the risks and other aspects of the commodity markets:

- No trading system can guarantee profits.
- Hypothetical trading results can be unreliable.

- Futures contracts are volatile and risky.
- Past performance is not indicative of future results.
- You should not trade with money you cannot afford to lose.

No representation is being made that any account will or is likely to achieve profits or losses similar to those shown in this book. Trading is not Floyd Upperman's only source of income.

Acknowledgments

I t has been said that we build on the knowledge and experiences of past generations until we arrive at the truth. Einstein could not have discovered his theories of relativity without the formulation of Maxwell's equations or Newton's laws. Einstein, although a genius, was still building on past discoveries.

I, too, am building on past discoveries about the COT data and price behavior. And I, too, have learned from others. Larry Williams has been using the COT data and sharing its potential with others for many years. I have gotten to know Larry over the years and have grown to respect and appreciate his great passion for understanding market behavior. It was through his work that I first learned about the obscure government report called *Commitment of Traders.*

Walter Bressert, who has been working on market cycles for over 30 years, has been a good friend for many years now and we have shared our ideas as well. I also want to acknowledge the work of the late Bruce Babcock. Bruce was there to answer my most amateur questions when I first began seriously studying the markets. He taught me that all traders are amateurs at some point and that successful traders are not born with all the skills and knowledge needed to succeed; traders can only obtain this information and knowledge by doing the necessary work to obtain it.

I would also like to thank my editor, Kevin Commins, at John Wiley & Sons, for his assistance and dedication in seeing this project through.

Finally, neither this book nor my professional career would be possible without the unconditional love and support of my family and especially of my dear wife and partner Kimberly, who has been a great source of strength for me over the years.

Commitments of Traders

## CHAPTER 1

The Commitments of Traders Report

In today's computer-driven world, futures traders have access to hundreds of technical indicators. Most of these indicators, however, share a common origin. The majority are derived from old prices, volume, and open interest. While these indicators have important uses, traders should also understand they have limitations as well.

All price-derived indicators are limited in their ability to anticipate significant future turning points precisely because they are derived from past data. Some indicators that are widely followed, however, will often work well over a short-term period. This may occur because many traders are using them. Thus, acting on them generates a self-fulfilling prophecy over the short-term. In the longer-term however, the market will go where the fundamentals allow it to go, because changing fundamentals drive market participant activity.

Price behavior is a reflection of market participant activity. Thus, another way to track and measure price activity is to track and measure the participant activity. Since the price of a futures contract moves up and down based on the buying and selling by market participants, indicators derived from the participant activity can provide insight into the future direction of price. I characterize these as "leading indicators." A detailed study of the market participant activity can also reveal how specific market participants view market fundamentals. The size of their position and whether they are accumulating or liquidating positions can at times reveal how they perceive future market conditions. The data contained in the

Commitment of Traders (COT) report, which is compiled every Tuesday and released every Friday by the Commodity Futures Trading Commission (CFTC), allows traders to track and study the activity of individual market participants in a given futures market. Indicators derived from this information can provide traders with a unique market perspective that is unobtainable through traditional price-derived methods. The lagging characteristics of most price indicators are also a good match with leading COT indicators. A combination of leading and lagging indicators can be extremely helpful in both anticipating major turning points and confirming them.

The CFTC, which oversees all trading activity in U.S. futures markets, requires that all U.S. futures exchange clearing members, futures commission merchants (FCMs), and foreign brokers report daily positions that meet or exceed specific reporting levels, as determined by CFTC regulations (see Table A.1, CFTC Reporting Levels, in the Appendix). The reporting levels vary from market to market, and can change from time to time. On average, the current levels capture roughly 70 to 90 percent of the total open interest in each market.

The CFTC compiles and sorts the data in markets in which 20 or more traders hold positions equal to or above its reporting levels. This data is subsequently sorted by market and released on the CFTC web site (see http://www.cftc.gov/cftc/cftccotreports.htm). There are two classifications of the COT report: The first is "futures only" and the second is "futures and options." Most of the discussions in this book focus on the futures only report.

LOOKING AT COT DATA

The COT data, as provided by the CFTC, is broken down by longs and shorts (see Table 1.1). Looking at Table 1.1, you can see a single snapshot of the long and short positions held by commercials, as well as the positions held by noncommercials and those in the nonreportable category.

Although the COT report is readily available, many traders do not understand the data, or do not have the capability or resources needed to fully exploit its potential. One of the reasons for this is that the data is not easy to work with in its raw published form. It is almost impossible, in my opinion, to gain useful insight from the data by simply reviewing the raw numeric changes from week to week. One of the first steps toward making use of the data is to place the data in a graph so that changes can be monitored and examined along with price activity. This allows a trader to observe some of the general relationships between price activity and the COT. However, much more work is required before we can begin to unlock

TABLE 1.1   COT Data Showing Wheat Futures Positions as of May 3, 2005

```
WHEAT - CHICAGO BOARD OF TRADE
FUTURES ONLY POSITIONS AS OF 05/03/05                              |
---------------------------------------------------------------| NONREPORTABLE
         NON-COMMERCIAL       |   COMMERCIAL    |     TOTAL      |   POSITIONS
-------------------------------|-----------------|----------------|----------------
-
  LONG  | SHORT  |SPREADS |  LONG  | SHORT  |  LONG  | SHORT  |  LONG  | SHORT
-------------------------------------------------------------------------------
-
(CONTRACTS OF 5,000 BUSHELS)                         OPEN INTEREST:     195,264
COMMITMENTS
  30,927   48,301   8,791  135,815  103,039  175,533  160,131   19,731   35,133

CHANGES FROM 04/26/05 (CHANGE IN OPEN INTEREST:      -7,243)
  -5,601      609    -548      563   -8,811   -5,586   -8,750   -1,657    1,507

PERCENT OF OPEN INTEREST FOR EACH CATEGORY OF TRADERS
     15.8     24.7     4.5     69.6     52.8     89.9     82.0     10.1     18.0

NUMBER OF TRADERS IN EACH CATEGORY (TOTAL TRADERS:       192)
       42       80       29       39       50      106      140
```

Source: CFTC.

its full potential. My background in engineering, statistics, and programming has enabled me to create and develop custom statistical studies and charting programs that allow me to examine the COT from every angle. I have developed numerous computer programs and unique trading methods that use a combination of leading COT indicators and lagging price indicators to identify specific market conditions. Many of these methods are discussed in this book. I have also developed a proprietary, automated computer program for analyzing COT data, which is also available on my web site (www.upperman.com).

It is important to understand not only the insights that can be gained from the COT data, but also the ways that this information can be used with other trading indicators to enhance any trading system. As I illustrate through trading examples, the COT data can be used in *any* commodity—agricultural, natural resources, or financial market. For example, analysis of COT data in the financial markets, such as Standard & Poor's 500 (S&P) futures or Nasdaq 100 futures, can enable you to measure and track the level of hedging or speculating taking place in the stock indices. Large shifting of hedged or speculative positions in the futures often leads to sharp rises or declines in the individual stocks that make up the indices. This information can be used to help manage stock portfolios.

When analyzing COT data in any futures market, consistency is paramount—using the same study week after week, with the same parameters, to obtain important knowledge and understanding of the unique behavior of market participants. Because each market is unique, market behavior in one market may mean something entirely different in another. Thus, within the context of a particular market, the objective is to search for and identify *predictive patterns of behavior.*

The first step is to understand who the market participants are, how they are categorized in the COT report, and how they typically operate in the market.

COT AND MARKET PARTICIPANTS

The COT data, as provided in the weekly report, is essentially a numeric snapshot of all holdings that meet or exceed the specific reporting limits of a particular market. Those positions that do not meet or exceed the specific reporting limits are also in the COT data, but they are not separated by participant type. All positions that meet or exceed the reporting limits in each market are identified and separated by market participant type. There are two distinct types of market participants, and three categories that are tracked in the report. The two types of participants are commercials and noncommercials. The three categories of participants are commercials, noncommercials, and nonreportables. Positions in the nonreportable group are not sorted by type. Understanding how the data is divided is an important first step in developing various ways to exploit and use the information as an aid from a trading standpoint.

The three categories of the COT report are:

1. Large commercial positions (Producer and Consumer Hedgers)
2. Large noncommercial positions (Funds and Large Traders)
3. Nonreported positions (Small Speculators and Small Hedgers)

Of the three, the large commercial category is widely considered to be the most important group. It comprises commercial producers and commercial consumers of a particular commodity. The COT report identifies commercial traders based on two factors: (1) Their position must be large enough to be reported and (2) they must be classified as a *hedger.* This classification is determined when the account is first established—as either *speculative* or *hedging.* This classification also has certain tax benefits or consequences. When opening a hedging account, additional documentation (Forms 102 and 40) may be required by the CFTC to verify a participant is engaged in a business activity hedged by use of the futures or options markets.

Commercial participants are considered the most knowledgeable in each market because their very livelihood depends on their determination of future prices. Although commercial producers and consumers have different reasons for being in the market, they share a common goal: to reduce their risk in the cash market. For producers, this may mean locking in a particular price using futures contracts to reduce the risk of being forced to sell at lower prices in the cash market. Hence, producers will establish a short position in the futures market to reduce or contain their exposure if cash prices fall. Commercial consumers, on the other hand, are concerned about the possibility of rising raw commodity prices and use futures to contain that risk. Thus, the commercial consumer may buy futures contracts to lock in the future price of whatever commodity it needs.

The noncommercial category represents large trader positions and funds that are large enough to be reported, but are not classified as hedgers. Commercial interest can also be included in the noncommercial category, however, because the category is determined solely by account type. There is no rule that states commercials can open hedging accounts but cannot open speculative accounts. Therefore, it is quite possible (and probable), that some speculative accounts are actually controlled by commercial interests. However, this is likely to be minimal because the tax benefits associated with hedging accounts are an incentive for commercial hedgers to open hedging accounts versus speculative. Most of the time, commercials are going to take advantage of the tax benefits of being classified as a hedger when appropriate (but the CFTC will always have the final say here). Keep in mind that commercials are not required to take advantage of the tax benefits of being classified as a hedger. Furthermore, a large participant could be classified as a commercial hedger in one market and noncommercial in another. Because of these complex issues, it is likely that some level of "cross-contamination" exists between categories. The commercial category, however, widely regarded as the most important category, is likely to contain the least amount of cross-contamination, since it is more difficult to be classified as a hedger and verification is usually required. Thus, I regard the commercial category as the most pure of the three.

HEDGERS AND SPECULATORS

An important aspect in understanding commercial hedgers is to realize that they are involved in the underlying cash physicals in some way. There are many ways a market participant or entity can be involved in the underlying cash markets. However, there are basically two types of commercials: commercial producers and commercial consumers. To meet the definition of hedging, a commercial hedger should be taking positions in the futures market that somehow offset their exposure to risk in the physical commodities, from either a producer or consumer standpoint. In other words, their futures position should not increase their exposure to risk, otherwise they are not hedging. Let's look at some possible examples.

A commercial airliner is a consumer of jet fuel. Rising fuel prices may adversely impact a commercial airliner's business. To offset this risk, the airliner may choose to enter long positions in a fuel market. The airliner should not be in the fuel market selling short, however, because this would simply increase their exposure to the risks of rising fuel prices. To reduce this risk, they should be buying futures contracts to lock in prices. If long fuel contracts and fuel prices rise, the gains in the long positions should offset some or all of the higher fuel prices in the cash market.

A commercial producer, on the other hand, is concerned about falling prices. For example, a grain producer is exposed to the risk of falling grain prices. To manage this risk, the grain producer may elect to sell short grain contracts as a hedge against falling grain prices. The grain producer should not be buying long, however, because this would simply increase their exposure to the risks of falling grain prices. Based on these beliefs, two important assumptions can be made regarding the two types of commercials and the commercial data. Since a commercial producer should always be short to be hedging, we can assume the commercial short positions in the COT data largely represent the commercial producers. Since a commercial consumer should always be long to be hedging, we can assume the commercial longs primarily represent the commercial consumers. These assumptions are not perfect, but they can provide a means for measuring and tracking specific commercial perceptions regarding the future supply and demand in a market. For example, when the net-commercial position is extremely one-sided in a market, this indicates an extreme difference between the number of commercial longs and shorts. Using the assumptions discussed previously, we can examine the data to see which side is leading the net-commercial position higher or lower. If the data shows the commercial longs are at a statistical extreme, while the commercial shorts are inside their normal distribution, we might assume the commercial consumers are the force behind the extreme one-sided position—which is usually bullish. If the data shows that the commercial short position is at a statistical extreme, while the commercial long position is inside its normal range, then we might assume the commercial producers are the force behind the extreme one-sided position, which may be bearish. Examining the data in this fashion can enable a trader to obtain better clarity and specific insight into commercial hedging, which at times may reveal important clues about future supply and demand, which drive prices longer term.

The commercials are also the primary participants in the exercising of futures contracts. If they so choose, the commercial hedgers could make delivery against their short positions and take delivery to settle long positions, thereby fulfilling their contract obligations. They may also exit out of established futures positions by buying back shorts or selling longs, versus taking or making delivery. Most of the time this is what happens since, in fact, only a few contracts, representing a small percentage of open interest, actually go to delivery. The majority of contracts that trade never go to actual delivery for physical commodities. The commercials often exit their positions, or they may roll them into the next month. They may also allow the contracts to expire because many markets have a cash settlement, requiring no physical delivery of commodities. If the contracts are cash-settled, a commercial hedger holding long positions may also receive the cash settlement in U.S. dollars at expiration.

The noncommercial category is made up of large individual traders and trading funds, which may have positions in one or several markets. In this regard, they are not unlike large mutual funds in the equities markets that generally trade multiple markets. In addition, activity in the noncommercial category includes spread trades among large speculators and funds.

All other open positions that do not fit into the commercial and noncommercial categories fall into the *nonreportable* category (which is often referred to as "small speculators"). It is important to understand that the small speculator category can contain both small commercials and small speculators. All participants holding nonreportable positions share a common trait: The number of contracts held does not meet the reporting limits set by the CFTC for that particular market or commodity.

In this book, as well as in my own trading systems, I focus on the commercial data as being primarily "commercial interest," and the noncommercial as being composed primarily of "noncommercial interest" (although this category could have some cross-contamination). All the studies I have done on this data show that each category has a unique signature. They tend to move independently of one another, which also suggests and confirms to some extent the purity of the participant groups.

Trading Behavior—The Producer

The standard approach to using COT data has been to focus primarily on the net-commercial position. This approach has been useful, as long as it is used in conjunction with price-based indicators and measures. The analysis of the commercials can also be taken a step further by separating the commercial data into two entities: producers and consumers. The exact commercial details are not provided in the COT report. Therefore, certain assumptions have to be made as already explained. Logically, the assumptions add up nicely. Again, these are the assumptions: There are two kinds of commercials—producers and consumers—and their contrasting activities in the cash markets require opposite tactics in futures trading.

Simply stated, commercial producers produce the commodity. They understand the fundamentals of production very well; they know how much it costs to produce a commodity, and probably know how much money they can get for it too. They also know what their supply is, and they know what market demand is. They may be very good at locking in high prices for their raw product, but they are not perfect; no one is. To hedge, they short futures, with the option of offsetting their positions by delivering against the shorts rather than buying them back. If the commercials are producers of the raw commodity and have established a futures trading account as a hedger, then by law they are required to show that they are involved in the cash market.

Commercial producers of the underlying raw commodity should always be short the futures (opposite of the commercial consumer) when hedging, because this reduces their exposure to the risk of falling commodity prices. By shorting futures, commercial producers can lock in a price for their product.

In the agricultural commodities, it is easy to identify a producer (e.g., an oat farmer or a soybean farmer). But what about the financial markets such as currency futures? A commercial producer of, say, Canadian dollars would be a U.S. corporation that does business in Canada. It produces Canadian dollars as a result of its sales in Canada.

Let's take the hypothetical example of XYZ Corporation, a U.S. company that sells goods and/or services outside the United States. XYZ needs to convert the foreign currency it receives (produces) from its sales into U.S. dollars. For XYZ to control and manage the risk associated with varying exchange rates and the prices of their goods and/or services, XYZ would use the futures market to lock in a predetermined exchange rate. This limits XYZ's exposure to risk due to unforeseen fluctuations in currency rates between the U.S. dollar and the foreign currencies involved.

In this example, XYZ sells goods in Canada and receives Canadian dollars. To limit its exposure to exchange rates, XYZ (being a producer) would sell short a certain number of Canadian dollar futures contracts traded on the Chicago Mercantile Exchange (CME), thereby locking in an exchange rate for the physical Canadian dollars (CD) received. Let's assume XYZ sells short at a price of 6400 (or 64 cents U.S. for every $1.00 CD). This also equates to $1.00 U.S. for every $1.36 CD collected as a direct result of sales in Canada.

With the exchange rate locked in, XYZ Corporation has removed its exposure to risk of changes in the currency market that could adversely affect the corporation's compensation for the goods and services sold in Canada. Moreover, XYZ knows for sure exactly how much it will receive— in U.S. dollars—for its goods and/or services sold in Canada. XYZ likely would have taken into account the current exchange rate available through futures, which would be used to help determine the pricing of their goods and services in Canada. The prices paid in Canadian dollars would then be converted to U.S. dollars at a predetermined conversion rate, as set by the short sale of Canadian dollar futures.

Subsequent delivery of the agreed payment in Canadian dollars could be used to meet the delivery obligations of the short futures position. At delivery, XYZ would receive U.S. dollars at a rate of $1.00 for every $1.3600 delivered in Canadian dollars, based on the entry price of the short sale of futures.

To recap, XYZ essentially produced Canadian dollars in the United States, as a result of its sales in Canada. It used the futures market to hedge currency risk that could negatively impact its bottom line. And, no matter what happens to currency prices, XYZ delivers Canadian dollars at the predetermined exchange rate of $1.00 U.S. for every $1.36 CD collected.

Trading Behavior—The Consumer

The commercial consumer consumes the raw commodity. These entities, which may include corporations and large businesses, understand the fundamentals of supply, and therefore they understand price very well. They know how much of the raw commodity they need, how much their competitors need, and what they should be paying for it. They tend to be very good at buying low, but may continue to buy even when prices appear high. This does not mean that they are always bullish. They buy futures to hedge their cash (spot) purchases of the raw commodity.

An example would be an airline that purchases energy futures to hedge its fuel needs out into the future. They may be aggressive buyers in the futures market if they believe that prices are cheap and will rise in the future. They may hedge more aggressively if there is a current supply problem in the cash market, and they need to lock in and secure delivery. (When demand outpaces supply, prices in the front months may become higher than those in the back months. Normally, the back months are higher due to carrying charges.)

If commercial consumers are in dire need of the raw commodity, they will pay virtually any price to get what they need. This is not a position in which any business wants to find itself. Thus, these big consumers manage their purchases well so that they have adequate supply and pay less than retail prices. Thus, it makes sense to monitor their trading activity!

Another example of a commercial consumer is a cereal maker (such as Quaker Oats) that makes and sells oatmeal. To do so, they need the raw commodity, oats. In this case, the commercial consumer hedges against the risk of rising oat prices by buying oat futures, which are traded on the Chicago Board of Trade. The long position essentially locks in a price for oats, and gives the cereal company the option (but not the obligation) to take delivery at the entry price of the long futures position. Deliveries take place during the delivery period of the contract, which tends to occur after speculators have moved to the next month.

By hedging in the futures market, rising or falling oat prices will no longer affect the cereal company's cost for producing oatmeal. They also avoid any short-term capital gains tax implications because of their hedger classification.

FUNDS AND SMALL SPECULATORS

The two other groups within the COT data are the *funds* and the *small speculator*. They typically buy and sell for the purpose of speculation only. They do not deal in the cash market, but instead use futures to trade, whether with the trend or countertrend. Many funds are major trend followers and trend contributors. The majority of large commodity funds tend to follow the same strategies and benefit from trending markets. They are trend contributors because they maintain and add to their positions as a market trend continues.

The funds speculate in the futures market, taking measured risks, in hopes of making a profit. The commercials, on the other hand, do not solely engage in futures to make a profit (although they do not want to lose money either). Commercials do not profit in the same way a speculator does because of their cash positions. Further, commercials do not necessarily exit all positions in the same way as a speculator. This is where a key difference lies. In addition to the commercial's ability to take or make delivery of the underlying commodity, the commercial may also retain the same amount of hedging by rolling losing positions from one month to the next. Speculators, however, do not tend to roll losing positions. This is important to understand because of its potential impact (or lack thereof) on the market.

Small traders have some advantages in the market. Being small, they can get in and out of positions without being concerned about how the market may react. Large traders, on the other hand, have accumulated a large position in the market (as reported in the noncommercial category of the COT report), and everyone who looks at the COT data knows about it. They can't hide it. Since they are speculative traders, they have to liquidate their positions to realize a profit (if they have one) at some point. Price slippage during that liquidation process may also cost them much of their profit, given the size of the position.

Large traders and large trading funds are at a disadvantage in this area. Most individual traders are below the CFTC's reportable levels and can get in and out of the market without reporting their positions and without much slippage overall.

FUNDAMENTAL VERSUS TECHNICAL ANALYSIS

As the discussion of the players in the market—the commercials, noncommercials, and nonreportables—shows, much information and insight can be derived from the COT data, once it is dissected and understood, with reasonable assumptions applied. The problem many people have with the COT data is that they try to apply or use it as if it were a traditional price-derived technical indicator. It does not work that way.

Commitment of traders data is only useful when combined with other indicators and measures, particularly those that lag the price trend. Most price-derived indicators are lagging and some are sharply lagging. The commercial element of the COT, however, is a *leading indicator.* By combining the two—lagging and leading indicators—a fairly timely market indicator can be obtained.

The majority of traders use technical and fundamental analysis to determine their trades. In general, small, individual traders rely on technical analysis, whereas large commercial institutions tend to focus on fundamentals. The reason for this is clear: Commercial producers and consumers of commodities are in an advantageous position to understand the fundamentals since they are directly involved in the production (supply) or consumption (demand) of a particular commodity.

Small individual traders, who are below the reporting limits of the COT, usually rely on sources such as government reports for their fundamental information. The fundamental information the public receives in these reports usually originates from the commercial producers and consumers. Thus, the trading activity of the commercials—as evidenced in the COT report—is particularly valuable in understanding the underlying fundamentals of a particular market.

For example, by the time a U.S. Department of Agriculture (USDA) report on the supply-and-demand situation in a particular commodity (such as corn, soybeans, etc.) is made public, the large commercials may already be aware of the tone, if not the content. Therefore, they may already be positioned before the report is made public.

Technical analysis, on the other hand, is derived from price data. Since the pool of data is the same, there are inherent similarities in technical systems. In fact, there are seven universal data points (opening price, high price, low price, closing price, net price change, volume, and open interest), from which all popular technical indicators are derived. Although these technical indicators (stochastics, MacD, moving averages, Relative Strength Index, and so forth) are great tools, and I use them as well, they should not be used alone.

Given the popularity and proliferation of technical systems, it is easy to understand why individual traders gravitate toward price-based, technical analysis, as opposed to fundamental analysis. Dozens of popular charting programs are available for individual traders to chart prices and apply popular technical indicators, but very few software programs allow users to chart the fundamentals. Even fewer indicators are derived from fundamental data.

Most speculative traders start out knowing very little about the fundamentals that influence and drive commodity prices. (Their choice to ignore the fundamentals is also a leading reason why they will never see a profit, either.) Fundamentals are crucial to the markets. Although prices may reflect the fundamentals, price behavior alone does not always show the direction of the market. Only the fundamentals can reveal this. The price structure and technical analysis of price data can only provide a view of where the market has been.

Using technical analysis is like looking in the rearview mirror of your car while you are moving forward. Fundamental analysis is the proverbial view out the front windshield at what is ahead. Whereas the analogy is easy to understand, fundamental analysis is not so simple. Each market is unique and has its own set of fundamental influences that are specific to it. (For this reason, I usually recommend that new traders select one market and become an expert in its fundamentals before moving on. Individual traders often become overwhelmed by fundamentals when they attempt to learn the fundamental influences that affect *all* the markets.)

BALANCE AND MARKET EQUILIBRIUM

In a perfectly balanced market, supply and demand of a particular commodity would be in equilibrium. Commercial producers' output of a particular commodity would be just enough to meet commercial consumers' demand. Prices would be stable. In the real world, however, the market gets out of balance due to disruptions in supply or demand, and prices become unstable, rising or falling depending on market conditions.

As this price action begins to unfold, speculators come into the market, buying or selling depending on the perceived imbalance, which may cause prices to rise or fall further. Eventually, this activity will help bring the market back into balance, because prices will either rise high enough to generate additional production (thus easing supply shortages), or they will fall far enough to generate additional demand or curtail production.

This ebb and flow in the fundamentals can be seen with careful study of the COT data as it relates the activity over time. Because it reveals what large commercial players—the key producers and consumers in the underlying physical commodity—are doing, it is essential to understanding the dynamics of a particular market.

USING COT DATA

In my study of market participants, I have found that the large moves occur when there are imbalances in supply and demand. The current activity in the market (buying and selling) sets the price. The market tends to discount current conditions and adjust for future conditions. It can be anticipated that the large users and producers of the underlying commodities begin making adjustments to offset perceived changes in supply and demand ahead of time. These adjustments may become evident in the futures market prior to shortages or gluts in supply, as well as before unusual changes in demand.

The large users or producers can often identify deteriorating conditions in the physicals *before* any real deterioration in demand or supply is noted publicly. This lack of public notice is more or less due to a lack of interest at the right time. Why? The public tends to follow rather than lead. By the time the public finally reacts, a good bit of the move in the market has often already occurred.

The public (by way of the media) tends to focus on current events and not on future perceived conditions. The news is always focused on what is occurring *right now*. Today's news, however, isn't going to help anyone identify trends in the futures markets because the large commercial participants in the market are focusing on *future perceived conditions*. In fact, once the actual disruption in supply or demand has occurred and hits the news, commercials may have already adjusted their positions on paper.

Indeed, those paper adjustments need to be closed out to fully offset the initial preparation for whatever the current disruption. Hence, the trading adage: "Buy the rumor, sell the news." The public is usually there, ready to take the other side of the trade, when it is time for the initial adjustments on paper to be closed out by the commercials.

Tools such as COT data, my Upperman Analysis, and IMPA trade set-ups make it unnecessary to trade based on current news, price activity, or the herd mentality. Instead, by pinning down the action of the market participants, identifying trends, and putting them into historical context, traders can position themselves in front of trends and ahead of the news!

## CHAPTER 2

Trading with COT Data

When tracking commodity prices, there is a simple, yet important truth to keep in mind: *Commodity prices do not fluctuate like stocks.* At a recent workshop, I put up a price history chart for soybeans going back to 1969 and a chart of General Electric (GE) stock for the same period. I asked the crowd: "Which would you have rather owned?" The answer was unanimous. Everyone would have rather purchased GE in 1969, not soybeans (see Figures 2.1 and 2.2).

This illustrates an important difference between stock prices and commodity prices. Stock prices on average tend to rise or fall over time as a function of corporate profits. If a corporation stays in business, does well, and manages to grow profits, over time the public's confidence in the corporation increases and shareholders benefit from the rising share prices. This can be seen in the price history of GE shares. However, you must also keep in mind that there is no intrinsic value for a piece of paper that says you own shares in a corporation. The value of that paper is in the complete control of the corporation. If the company goes bankrupt, the paper becomes worthless. This is one of the key differences between commodities and stocks. Commodities have intrinsic value. An ounce of gold, for example, will always be worth something. Its value, however, is not in the hands of a corporation, rather, collectively, people from all over the world determine the price of gold based on what they are willing to pay for it. You could claim that stock prices are determined the same way, but the fact is

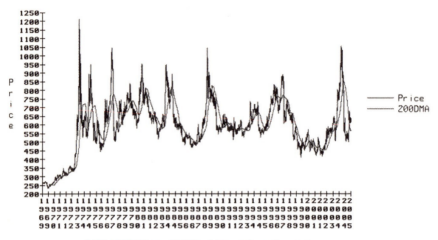

FIGURE 2.1   Historic soybean prices, 1969–2005.

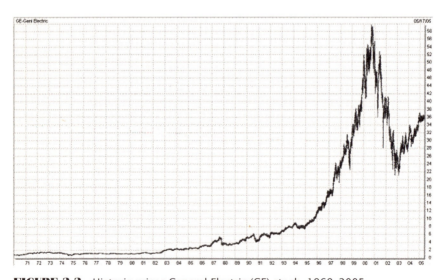

FIGURE 2.2   Historic prices General Electric (GE) stock, 1969–2005.

that the world is full of bankrupt companies whose stocks are now totally worthless. Commodities never become worthless.

The other part of the equation is supply. Supply and demand go hand in hand with each other in determining price. Ultimately, commodity prices are determined by supply and demand factors. When supply and demand are in balance, commodity prices are stable. When supply and demand get out of balance, prices react and may go through a period of boom or bust. There are numerous fundamental influences that can impact the supply and demand for a particular commodity. Many such influences cannot be controlled and may be difficult to predict (such as the weather). Because of this, many individual commodity traders feel the playing field for commodities is more equal than for stocks. We don't have to worry about corrupt corporate insiders manipulating weather, for example, because no one can control the weather. Adverse weather conditions, such as hurricanes, droughts, and so on, can be a big influence on commodities. There are numerous other fundamental influences on commodity prices that are beyond the control of individuals. In addition, commodity prices tend to cycle through boom and bust periods. As of the writing of this book, for example, crude oil prices are going through a major boom period. The price of crude oil futures reached all time highs recently. However, just six years ago the price of crude oil was extremely low. At that time, the supply outlook reported in the news was bearish (outstripping demand). Soon, however, this perception changed and prices more than quadrupled! But who knew? There were no corporate insiders with inside information, but there were clear signs in the behavior of some market participants, that indeed, demand was increasing! The price cycles in soybeans can also be seen in the previous history graph of soybean prices. While commodity prices clearly go up and down, experiencing periods of boom and bust, one other important fact should be noted. Commodity prices have a strong tendency to eventually regress back to long-term means. This is something stock prices simply don't do. This occurs as disruptions in supply and demand are eventually resolved one way or the other. There are only a few cases where this has not occurred, and in those cases the reason it did not occur is because of changes in government policy. Governments always have some controls at their disposal (such as releasing strategic oil reserves, gold reserves, currency reserves and so on) to manipulate the market for the better good as they see it. Many of these controls are short-term, however, except for one. And that is permanent changes to policy. For example, the U.S. government set the price of gold for years. The U.S. government also has certain tools such as farming programs, rationing, and so forth, that it will use to bring supply and demand back in balance and thus prices back to their longer-term means. The government may even give away commodities (wheat, for example) when supplies become too plentiful, thereby reducing supply. Governments have had these tools available to them for years. However, as the world becomes more connected and the markets more liquid, the leverage governments have may very well become less and less.

Thus, another fundamental difference between equities and commodities is that the commodity market exists in a more price-controlled environment, whereas equities exist in an environment in which prices are expected to rise.

Why would someone prefer to trade commodities to equities? For me, the answer is a personal one, but it is worth sharing to illustrate the potential for profiting in the commodities market as well as how to systematically analyze and trade these markets.

STATISTICAL ROOTS OF THE COT DATA ANALYSIS SYSTEM

My background is in engineering, and I held a number of positions in the semiconductor industry for 10 years, including three years with Intel Corporation in New Mexico in the 1980s, and seven years with Motorola. Although I enjoyed working with these prestigious firms, my dream was to be financially independent, my own boss. As I weighed my opportunities, nothing excited me more than the markets.

While working as an engineer, I spent a great deal of spare time and money researching the investment world. One of my first discoveries was that it is impossible to become self-sufficient by working for someone else and investing on the side. I had already started trading stocks by this time; I had experienced some success with it and knew that others were making money as well. But stocks, at the time, were slower, and I did not want to wait 10 years for a stock to go up or recover, nor did I have hundreds of thousands of dollars for adequate leverage. Next, I invested in stock options, which certainly provided the opportunity to multiply one's money in a short time. I made some money, and I lost some money. Without a system, I relied on information from the media, friends, and gut instinct. All these sources proved to be inconsistent and unreliable. I needed an approach and a system.

Finally, I decided to try commodities. Not knowing much about them at the time, I started out like everyone else: reading the *Wall Street Journal* and *Barron's* religiously, studying charts for hours, and reading books. As a result, I made some money and I lost some money. Then I made one of the worst mistakes of my trading career: I allowed a so-called expert—a broker—to show me how to trade. The broker did worse than I did. Discouraged, I thought seriously of giving up. Yet, I believed I could make money at trading commodities; I just needed to be patient and wait for the right opportunities.

When opportunities presented themselves, I pounced on them and often made money quickly. But I also saw that even the best-looking opportunities do not always yield a profitable result. This taught me the valuable lesson of combining risk containment with patience. By this time, I had spent a small fortune on software packages, systems, and programs. None of them provided me with consistent results or the clarity I was seeking. After trying all the software on the market, I finally realized I had to develop something on my own to gain an edge over the majority of traders who rely on the same software, the same indicators, and the same data. I needed a different approach, with unique measures and indicators.

I began filling up my computer hard drives with all the commodity price data I could get—historical daily price data, intraday tick data spanning decades, and so on. I used my knowledge of statistics and engineering, combined with my programming skills, to design a trading system based on repeating patterns and conditions that were characteristic of each commodity. Computer back testing yielded an amazing discovery: There is an underlying order in commodity markets that is not found in the historic price movements of individual stocks. Certain price patterns are highly correlated to positions held by the participants in the commodity markets.

As an engineer and a lifelong student of mathematics, I have a deep appreciation for and understanding of statistics. In fact, I trace the paradigm roots of my COT data analysis to significant statistical studies of the past. Among them is the work of Dr. W. Edwards Deming.

DEMING'S STATISTICAL APPROACH

In the post-World War II global economy, Deming taught Japanese businesses how to greatly improve their products using statistics to monitor their manufacturing processes. The Union of Japanese Scientists and Engineers instituted the "Deming Prize" in his honor. It is awarded each year in Japan to a statistician for contributions to statistical theory. Curiously, Deming first attempted to teach these advanced ideas on data analysis in the United States, but American businesses at that time didn't believe any other country could compete with their products.

In 1946, Deming became a professor at the Graduate School of Business, New York University, and a year later was invited to Japan by General Douglas MacArthur to work with his economic and scientific staff in the survey of the housing, agriculture, fishing, and industry, and in the conduct of a population census. He also began his interaction with Japanese statisticians and scientists. In 1950, Deming was invited by the Japanese Union of Scientists and Engineers to return to Japan to teach his methods for the achievement of quality. This changed Japanese products in the years that followed, and the United States fell behind on quality. By the 1980s, the United States was scrambling to catch up.

From 1980 until 1993, the year he died, Deming held his legendary four-day seminar 10 times a year in every corner of the world, reaching over 200,000 manufacturing managers. Top managers in the United States from companies such as General Motors, Ford, AT&T, and Xerox attended. Fifteen universities granted him *Honoris Causa* degrees. In 1985, he became a Distinguished Lecturer in Management at Columbia University; in 1986, Cambridge University Press published *Out of the Crisis*; and in 1992, the MIT Center for Advanced Engineering Studies published *The New Economics*, in which he presented his theory of profound knowledge.

What does this have to do with commodity trading? I am proud to say that I have developed my market studies and trading systems from and around the same principles pertaining to data analysis and charting that I found in Deming's work. With my engineer's mind-set and love of statistics, I know the power of this approach: to analyze a market on a consistent basis over a period of time, using rigorous rules and exacting standards. This is the discipline I bring to my study of COT data.

While others concentrated on traditional technical analysis of price and the pursuit of price-derived indicators, I developed a unique and proprietary market tracking system that combines the important elements of price behavior (based on sound statistics) with the behavior of the market participants provided through the COT data. The end result is an entirely proprietary trading system, complete with unique indicators derived from the COT data and further supplemented with more traditional, but proprietary, price indicators. At this point, I was ready to make a career change, quitting my corporate job permanently to spend my time doing what I love: tracking, studying, and trading the markets.

The lessons of my own experience, may be meaningful to other traders. I found commercially available charting software and price-tracking systems are neither versatile nor complex enough to do the kind of statistical studies on fundamental market data and comparison correlations that are necessary to gain a unique perspective on the market. It stands to reason: If you use the same software, methods, and indicators that everyone else uses, you will have the same results as everyone else.

SOLVING THE PROBLEM OF THE MARKET

Traders often look at the market as a single entity—"the market." The market, however, is really the result of all participants and the actions of each one. To achieve success on a consistent basis, traders must step outside the realm of common perception and tackle the markets as if they were a problem that needs to be solved. Solving the challenging problem of the market is not easy. The driving forces in the market are human emotion and irrational behavior that reflect the actions of people under pressure. There are certain traits, habits, and behaviors that all people possess, and under certain conditions, all people will react in largely the same way. This understanding should become part of the trader's market analysis.

In addition, certain patterns signal when crowd behavior is extreme or overwhelmingly one-sided. This is something that I have learned to track and measure. Make no mistake: Tackling the challenges in the markets is complicated; it requires following trading disciplines and rules to contain risk and avoid one's own human weakness.

COT DATA AND PROPRIETARY INDICATORS

Commodity trading is often viewed as a zero-sum business. Essentially, that means each time a trader makes money on a trade, someone somewhere has lost money taking the other side of that position. While that is true, it is important to understand that for a commercial participant who is using the commodity markets to hedge, losing on a position may be acceptable. In fact, with their hedging activities, they often *expect* to lose.

Producers who want prices to go higher in the cash market will hold a short position in the futures market as insurance against prices going down. If prices rise, producers will lose money on the futures/hedge position, but will more than make up the difference in the cash market. They may carry out this type of hedging activity again and again, with the same losing result on paper, as they fade the trend higher. To reiterate, the commercials do this because they need the insurance that hedging with futures contracts provides, not because they are seeking an opportunity to profit from the trend.

Individual traders may be on the other side of this hedging activity, and they may profit from that trend. The market may continue moving higher, and they may continue to profit by buying into it. The ones who are selling into the rising trend are the commercial entities, especially producers who are happy to sell short in a rising market because, as hedgers, they are locking in at a higher price. If the market drops sharply, they have their insurance, which is what they were seeking in the first place. So is this really a zero-sum game? It can be seen as such; but both parties may be perfectly happy with the result: the speculator who made a profit and the commercial who successfully hedged.

The speculator who engages in trading actually takes on the risk that the commercials are trying to guard against by hedging. In a sense, what is really being traded is not just soybeans, crude oil, or some other commodity; what is being traded is *price risk*. The futures markets were originally created for two purposes: to allow commercial consumers to guard against rising prices in the future by locking in a price *now*, and to allow commercial producers to guard against falling prices in the future by locking in a price *now*. An example is a farmer who locks in a high price for soybeans in July by selling short November soybean futures contracts. When he brings his crop to the market in November, he may make delivery to fulfill his obligations on the short November futures contracts at the price he initially sold short in July. He benefits from the higher July prices in November, which is the harvest period when much supply is hitting the market and driving cash prices lower.

In both cases, risk is transferred to speculators, both large and smaller market players, who take on risk in exchange for the potential opportunity to realize a profit. The speculators provide the liquidity in the market that allows commercials to guard against adverse price swings. This is also how prices for physical commodities are maintained or kept stable over long periods, even while short-term disruptions in supply and demand may cause prices to fluctuate wildly at times. The markets were not created primarily to give people an opportunity to speculate. Speculators make it work, but the real function is to provide a service for commercials. That service cannot function without speculators.

The functions of the market are also important to society because of the price stability over time that ultimately benefits the end users. The price of unleaded gasoline futures traded on the New York Mercantile Exchange quadrupled from January 1999 to January 2005. During this time, unleaded gasoline prices at the pump also increased, but by no means did they quadruple. Even though the cash market price of crude oil has risen dramatically during the past five years, these price increases have been mitigated by the commercial consumers' ability to hedge, which lowers the cost of raw materials and ultimately benefits the consumer.

Speculators play an important role in the futures market, taking on the risk from commercial participants who need to hedge. When the prices move in their favor—rising when they are holding long positions and falling when they are short—they stand to make a profit in exchange for that risk. But what happens when the market moves against them? In the example of speculators going long in a rising market and a commercial producer selling short into the trend, who is really at risk if prices fall? Not the commercial who is short, but rather the speculator who has taken on the price risk with a long position. The speculator takes on the risk, which can be very great, in exchange for the opportunity to profit.

Commercial participants do not just hedge at any price. They have access to vast amounts of data related to their field of business and the markets they deal in. They can and do analyze the markets very closely and make calculated decisions on when exactly to hedge for insurance purposes, how many contracts to enter, how much they should pay, and so forth. As the commercial participants look out in the future and make their hedging decisions, I monitor their activity—as revealed in the COT data—using a forward-looking "leading" indicator to determine where they believe prices are moving in the future.

Funds, meanwhile, are simply speculating on the direction of prices based on other information, including price behavior and fundamental analysis. But the funds do not have access to all the information that the commercials do, and the decisions that funds make are not as crucial to their business as the commercials' need to hedge their cash positions. That is why we often see the funds flipping positions, from net long to net short and back again, more quickly and more actively than the commercials overall.

In addition to the commercials and the funds, there are other participants in the market. They are the small speculators who are looking to make a profit on price movement. In commodities trading, it is said that roughly 80 percent of all small speculators lose money trading futures. All small speculators typically use the same software packages, the same indicators, and make the same mistakes. Thus, the average trading life of a small speculator is about one year. New ones come in as others give up and quit. If you want to differentiate yourself from the pack, you have to step outside the norm and be willing and able to look at the markets differently, and approach your own trading in a unique fashion.

To take a unique view of the futures markets, I have devised a forward-looking indicator that I call the *Individual Market Participant Analysis* (IMPA). The IMPA methodology is based on in-depth COT analysis and is the core of my longer-term position trading system. The IMPA contains indicators and charts with forward-looking indicators derived from data that is unrelated to historic price. This is a sharp contrast to traditional technical analysis, which relies on historic price data. In essence, IMPA combines lagging price-derived indicators with forward-looking proprietary indicators derived from the weekly COT data.

HOW DOES INDIVIDUAL MARKET PARTICIPANT ANALYSIS WORK?

Individual Market Participant Analysis measures and monitors the activity of market participants (meaning the actions of all traders), combined with price structure. This careful mix can provide a "virtual" window into the future. Monitoring the behavior of some traders and understanding what normal behavior is compared with abnormal behavior among market participants is the key to the IMPA strategy. To do this effectively, one needs to understand normal reactions to market fluctuations versus extraordinary reactions. This can be accomplished using COT data, which reveals not only where the market has been, but also where it is likely to go based on the current positions held in the market (the number of shorts and longs), and who is holding the majority of positions (hedgers, speculators, and so forth). Monitoring this behavior week to week and relating it to price fluctuations provides valuable market insight. Over time, you can see the behavior and reactions of the various participants as they prepare or position themselves for certain situations. Ultimately, the participants drive the price in the futures market. Therefore, understanding their behavior is essential.

Individual Market Participant Analysis Position Trading comprises two key components: fundamental analysis and technical analysis. The fundamental analysis is used to select the markets that may have a unique, underlying fundamental condition that is bullish or bearish. Not all the markets will have the right fundamental conditions. Most of the time, the markets are in balance and trade in a range. My analysis includes tracking the supply-and-demand balance using the COT data to break down the open interest (open positions) by individual participant type and then tracking each participant's behavior using statistical analysis.

The fundamental portion of the IMPA system tracks the relationship between the three participants in the COT data: commercial hedgers, funds, and the public. The COT data allows us to track the activity of these individual market participants, recording and measuring their trading (long, shorts, and delta) on a week-to-week basis. Then, using a proprietary statistical formula, I am able to determine when the dominant market participants (the commercials) are building statistically significant positions. The commercials, which normally represent the largest single component in each futures market, accumulate or scale into large positions over time, ranging from weeks to months. I then track this behavior and study the relationships between their actions and the behavior of the market as a whole.

The IMPA system identifies markets that have a high probability of breaking out to the upside or downside and trending. I do not care if the commercials are long or short. They can actually be net-short and bullish (which we have seen in silver several times in the past). What I do care about is the size of their net position and to a lesser extent the direction and how this compares statistically to past positions. During normal market conditions, the size of their net-position is expected to fluctuate inside a "normal" range. When the net-position moves outside this range, a statistically significant event is triggered. That essentially alerts me to focus more attention on a particular market. I determine the normal range using a weighted mean (weighted toward the most recent years) and a proprietary number of standard deviations from this mean. This creates the upper commercial limit (UCL) and lower commercial limit (LCL) lines. This approach alone can enable you to anticipate many major reversals. It should be noted, however, that this is a forward-looking "leading" measure and it must be combined with other forms of traditional technical analysis.

The heart of the IMPA analysis is the UCL/LCL trigger graphs. The UCL and LCL are proprietary indicators derived from commercial position data and represent my core indicators. Similar individual calculations are also performed on the commercial producer and commercial consumer positions, as well as the fund positions to create additional statistical tracking studies that are used in conjunction with the UCL/LCL.

The IMPA analysis will only work when combined with the appropriate price-derived technical indicators. When either the LCL or UCL is triggered, a statistically significant event has occurred indicating the net-commercial position is outside the normal range for that particular market. Once this component is in place, I know conditions are ripe for a significant turn in the market. At this point, I begin examining the technical conditions of the market for a potential buy or sell, based on my other criteria. *I never buy or sell based on the net-commercial position alone.* Understanding this is crucial.

IMPA UPPER AND LOWER COMMERCIAL TRIGGER LINES

By monitoring, tracking, and developing indicators based on the behavior of "expert" market participants, I am able to decipher *their interpretation* of the fundamentals and incorporate this interpretation into a trading system. This trading system also features unique technical analysis of price and correlates price structure with the positioning of these experts. This technique provides a superior assessment of current market conditions, as well as an assessment of the likely direction ahead. This approach is much more thorough than simply relying solely on price-derived indicators.

One of the big issues with using fundamental analysis alone is that of *position management.* If a market is bullish based on the supply/demand fundamentals, yet the price continues to fall, the overall supply/demand situation may continue to get *even more bullish.* Yet, the price may continue to fall. Thus, traders must incorporate some technical analysis into their strategies to properly manage positions and achieve their trading goals. Key points of a strategy would include:

- *Loss control and loss containment:* Technical analysis enables traders to identify specific price stops.

- *Position management:* Technical analysis allows positions to be managed using specific price behavior, and price patterns for entry and exit.
- *Timing:* The most important benefit from technical analysis is the timing factor. However, unless the right fundamental conditions exist, a trader doesn't even need to begin looking at the technical conditions.

When position trading, my first focus is on the fundamental analysis of the market. If a fundamentally bullish or bearish condition exists, I will then begin looking to exploit those conditions using traditional technical analysis, price structure analysis, pattern recognition, and even seasonal price behavior. To successfully incorporate COT data and indicators derived from COT data into a trading strategy, it is also necessary to combine some popular traditional price-derived indicators as well. Tracking and observing popular technical indicators is helpful in anticipating and determining the actions and opinions of the crowd. Keeping this in mind, traders can learn to anticipate crowd reactions to popular indicators. In addition, I have found patterns to be useful when combined with the COT. I use patterns not because they provide insight on turning points, but because they provide logical locations for stops.

My overall trading strategy consists of the following:

- Price trend versus UCL/LCL penetration: I go with the trend until the trend has ended or changed. The IMPA can become bullish or bearish long before an existing trend ends. A large buildup of commercial positions does not necessarily indicate a change in trend is imminent. This may take weeks or months, and in that time the data may also change. Thus, where the commercials were once excessive, they may no longer be so. A large buildup of opposing commercial positions can occur, and the existing trend can continue. However, a large buildup of fund positions almost always must be liquidated at some point.

Commercial positions, as stated previously, can be liquidated in the cash market or in the futures. (Only a small percentage of all commercial positions will be delivered upon or go into delivery. However, commercial participants have the option to take or make delivery to settle their contract positions.) Furthermore, a commercial entity can also have some speculative positions. And, it is not always easy to differentiate commercial hedges and commercial speculative positions. (In fact, most of the time it is not.) Just because a position falls under the "large trader" (noncommercial) category is no assurance that it is not a commercial position. It might very well be a speculative commercial position.

Some assumptions must be made pertaining to this data. Because all the facts are not provided, I have to fill in some blanks using experience, instinct, and observation.

• *Purity of commercial positions:* As noted in Chapter 1, the commercial category tends to be the most pure. Commercial positions cannot possibly be fund positions because of the legal requirements. Since the commercial category tends to be the least contaminated, much of my focus is on this category for initial monitoring. Hence, I use the UCL/LCL tracking of net-commercial positions.

Once an excessive commercial position is noted, it is important to begin monitoring the commercial and fund graphs, as well as the commercial producer-to-commercial consumer relationship for imbalances. This helps in understanding the potential demand versus supply relationship with price.

EXTREME COMMERCIAL POSITIONS AT MAJOR TURNING POINTS

One of my trading rules is that *extreme commercial positions almost always are present at major turning points.* However, not all extreme commercial positions lead to significant changes in trend. I began to see this in the 1990s, which led me to pursue other price-derived indicators and measures to combine with the UCL/LCL. Many factors influence major conditions and the market rarely ever responds to COT data alone.

The COT report must be looked at as a snapshot of the internal makeup of each market. This picture reveals the positions of the major market participants at a specific time only (usually Tuesday's close). Again, the market does not necessarily respond to this (although it can), but it is a picture of the market that shows the longs and shorts held by each category of market participant. If a rally happens, one can look at the most recent COT data to see which participant category may have benefited the most or was positioned the best to benefit. Generally, the large trader or fund category (noncommercial) and the commercial category are the most important to monitor and measure.

The net-commercial position—made up of commercial longs and commercial shorts—is a "net" of what the commercials are doing as a category. It is the difference between the longs and shorts. Generally speaking, I conclude that the commercial consumers—who are attempting to hedge against higher prices—hold a significant portion of the commercial longs (as discussed in Chapter 1). The commercial short positions are held by the commercial producers who are attempting to hedge against falling prices for their products.

Although the COT data is not enough by itself to formulate a trading strategy, it can provide an assessment of the overall fundamental conditions. But this is not based only on the net-commercial positions. When examining the COT, it is important to take in the whole picture of producers, consumers, funds, and so forth.

Looking at price structure, there is no question that it provides some insight into the market direction. It is limited, however, to where the market has just come from, and whereas that direction may have been up or down, this is not necessarily where the market is going next. Old prices, whether two minutes, two hours, two weeks, or older, can only tell us about the past. Using this or any trend that is in place, traders may try to ascertain where the market is headed. But if you only look at price for insight, you can be blindsided by fundamental changes in the market that alter future price and trend.

This change could occur with the next tic in the market. If you are trading S&P 500 futures using a technical-based system on the day the Federal Reserve announces a decision on interest rates, you may be completely caught offguard when the market whipsaws at 2:15 P.M. EST immediately following the Fed's announcement. To avoid that, you have to know at least a little about the fundamentals—in this case, the date and time of the FOMC meetings, what is expected, and how it will likely influence the market. That is just the basics. You would probably also want to do some research ahead of time to have an opinion on what their decision is likely to be.

Beyond the Fed example, many other fundamental events occur regularly and at specific times. Each market has its own fundamental influences and reports. Grains are influenced by the March 31 *Planting Intentions Report* and other crop reports released by the USDA throughout the year (also at specific times).

By becoming an expert in one market at a time, you can focus on learning all the different fundamentals that influence prices in an individual market. I took this approach years ago, choosing soybeans as the market I wanted to become an expert in—and it paid off. I learned about the fundamental reports, weather and seasonal factors, supplies, and demands that influence this market. This knowledge has enabled me to trade this market successfully.

Fundamental-based position trading in one market can be very slow for a speculator. There isn't always a strong fundamental reason to take a position, and even when there is a strong fundamental reason, the technical picture may not be favorable.

Since it is practically impossible to become an expert in all the markets, another method I have devised for tracking the fundamentals is to follow the COT and let the real experts show me what they believe are the fundamentals. The large market participants, who have the resources and the means to track all the data and evaluate fundamental reports very carefully, will adjust their positions accordingly. That is where the COT shows its true value. Instead of attempting to become an expert in all the fundamental influences of every market, one can track the COT data carefully.

By doing so, you will be able to monitor the activity of the large participants and ascertain their assessment of fundamental conditions.

I have been studying and working with COT data for over a decade; I
believe it is among the most underrated financial data available today. In
the following chapters, I explain, step-by-step, my methods for analyzing
this data and incorporating it into a position trading system. I discuss and
demonstrate the techniques I have developed to unlock its potential and
leverage its value as a trading tool. My approach to analyzing this data, in
fact, enabled me to avert a major market decline in the U.S. equity markets
in early 2000 through 2002; and in early 2003, the same approach provided
a strong buy signal that indicated it was time to get back into U.S. equities
for awhile.

## CHAPTER 3

Understanding Net-Commercial and Net-Fund Activity

The data in the COT report is a good leading measure of the market because the commercial participants are the best source for fundamental information. In fact, the producers and consumers provide much of the information that ends up in government reports on specific commodities. But the raw commercial data in each weekly *Commitment of Traders* (COT) report is not enough. Each weekly report is only a snapshot in time of holdings among the market participants. What makes this data meaningful to a trader is the perspective it provides about market fundamentals. To evaluate this effectively, one needs to look at the commercial data from two perspectives: First by focusing on the net-commercial position, looking at the net of commercial longs and shorts; second by focusing on the individual long and short positions that are believed to correspond to consumers and producers, respectively.

The trigger is the net-commercial position, specifically when it is at an extreme level. This goes back to the issue of balance: In a perfect world, producers would produce just enough of a commodity to meet consumer demand. Under this ideal situation, the commercial producer and the commercial consumer would hold exactly opposite positions. When the positions held by producers and consumers are out of balance to a degree considered statistically significant, it often reflects that supply and demand are also out of balance (or will be in the near future).

When there is a supply-demand imbalance, the market price will eventually help adjust that situation. Here is how it might unfold: Assume there is a supply shortage in a particular commodity because the output from commercial producers is not enough to meet the demands of commercial consumers. As that imbalance occurs, the funds (speculators looking to make a profit in a particular market) will become aware of it.

When an imbalance begins to occur, the funds generally take the other side. As they do that, their buying or selling also influences the prices. For example, if they perceive a shortage in supply, these speculative participants will buy in anticipation that prices will rise. This will help fuel a price rally in the market. Now, what happens? Prices may rise enough to actually reduce demand. It may become too expensive for some consumers to use the commodity, and so they reduce their demand or find a substitute to meet their needs. This decrease in demand will lead to the imbalance subsiding or reversing. Or, prices may rise enough that additional production comes onto the market from new sources. This increase in supply will also help to bring the market back into balance. These are the typical mechanics of a market cycle of a commodity.

NET-COMMERCIAL DATA

With this understanding, it may be tempting to view the net-commercial data—the net positions of all commercial participants based on the outstanding longs and shorts—as the "smart money." After all, the commercial participants are the closest to the fundamentals. This is generally not the case, however, when it comes to their market participation as reflected in the COT data because commercial participants are hedging. They are active in the market seeking insurance from the unexpected. From a producer's viewpoint, this would be a dramatic drop in market prices; from the consumer's perspective, this would be a dramatic increase in prices. Therefore, the commercial participants are buying on the way down and selling on the way up. This usually results in an inverse correlation between the net-commercial data and price trends.

At the same time, commercial participants also speculate. Their speculative nature often comes through when their *collective combined position* is at an extreme level. When this happens, the commercial position appears to be the "smart money" in the market, buying the bottom or selling a major top. The signature for this exception is an *extreme collective position*. This position is defined as being completely outside the normal distribution of recent and historical positions. I use statistical models to identify this. When the net-commercial position has exceeded the normal variation by a statistically significant degree (e.g., a certain number of deviations), I know that this position is highly unusual. It is a rare occurrence. A plus-or-minus ($\pm$) 3 standard deviation boundary would only be penetrated 0.27 percent of the time.

I created the UCL/LCL (upper commercial limit/lower commercial limit) statistical indicator to help identify the extreme net-commercial position. Through the UCL/LCL indicator, the COT data are brought together, providing an excellent leading gauge. It allows the commercial participants to speak with one voice composed of many collective voices about the fundamental conditions of the marketplace.

Figure 3.1 illustrates my net-commercial UCL/LCL control indicator identifying a change in the equities market in April 2000—which signaled the ending of a major bull market.

As Figure 3.1 shows, the net-commercial position (top line) was showing successive increases through early 2000 and then dropped sharply by April 2000, which generated a major sell signal on April 7 in the Nasdaq 100 futures.

In another example of the UCL/LCL statistical indicator in action, Figure 3.2 shows the position of commercials in soybean futures. Notice their extreme position in the market.

The UCL/LCL is only one gauge out of many that a trader must understand and focus on. Each gauge provides specific information about the market. Just as the various dials and gauges in an airplane cockpit help the pilot stay on course, market indicators give traders a broad array of measures to navigate in the market.

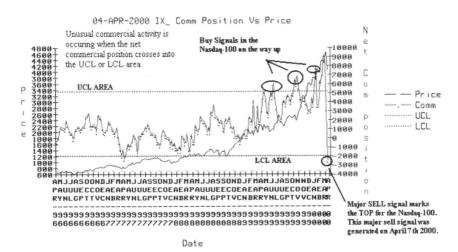

FIGURE 3.1 Commercial activity in Nasdaq 100 futures versus price, showing buy signals on the way up and major sell signal generated when commercial position declined sharply.

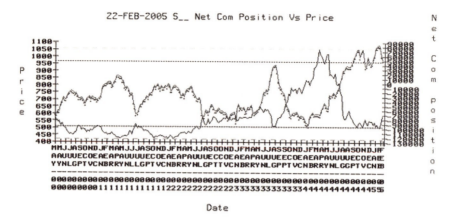

FIGURE 3.2 Soybean futures, showing net-commercial position versus price.

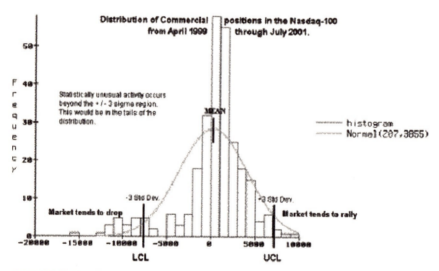

FIGURE 3.3 Illustration of distribution of commercial positions, showing lower commercial limit (LCL) and upper commercial limit (UCL), based on –3 standard deviation and +3 standard deviation.

Traders need to differentiate among their indicators to access and assess as much relevant information as possible. The inherent problem with relying only on price-derived indicators is that they tend to be redundant; after awhile, you are looking at the same thing, just in different ways. The COT data, however, can provide a new source for unique measures and indicators.

Figure 3.3 illustrates how the UCL/LCL lines are calculated. The exact placement of the lines is proprietary but this shows how the basic concept is applied to the COT data. The upper and lower net-commercial limits (UCL/LCL) are calculated using a proprietary formula based on probability distribution analysis. The purpose of these studies is to alert traders when certain internal data (unrelated to price) are outside normal historic distribution patterns. When this occurs, it is a significant statistical event.

All the upper and lower participant position limits are derived from the same statistical measurement based on the historic distribution of market positions for each category. The graphic shown in Figure 3.4 is the basis for this statistical assessment and measurement.

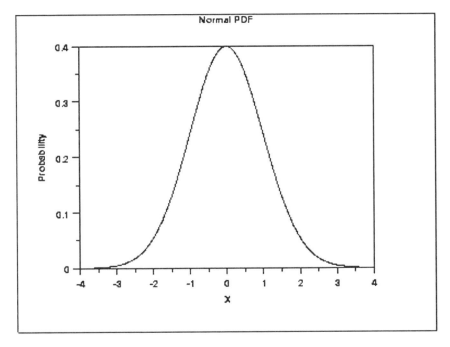

FIGURE 3.4 Illustration of historic distribution patterns.

BACK-TESTING THE CORE UCL/LCL INDICATOR

In 1998, I wrote a computer program to test and measure the effectiveness of the net-commercial UCL/LCL trigger selection in identifying previous major turning points. The same test was performed the same way in 38 different markets to verify consistency. My main goal with this study was not to generate a system performance record, but to test and measure the effectiveness of the UCL/LCL in identifying significant turning points across a number of markets. This test was done on past data but the program was not built around the data for the purpose of producing results. That practice is called *curve fitting* and obviously that kind of information would not be useful. Thus, I took special precautions to ensure the results were not curve-fitted. Nonetheless this was a computerized hypothetical measure at best since the trades were not actually executed.

A complete trading system needs to contain many elements, not just an entry and an exit, although they are important steps. To evaluate and illustrate the potential value of this data as well as its effectiveness in a system with an entry and an exit, I added a couple of basic price-derived indicators to determine where to enter and when to exit following a UCL/LCL buy or sell trigger selection. The indicators used for this study were simple moving averages—the 18-day moving average of closing prices and the 10-day moving average of closing prices—for all 38 markets.

In all 38 markets tested, the UCL/LCL trigger selections identified the largest percentage moves *before* they happened. When the UCL/LCL buy and sell trigger selections were combined with the moving averages, the result was a net profit in every one of the 38 markets tested. In addition, the UCL/LCL trigger selections provided accurate leading insight on the large moves. In many cases, several losses occurred due to early entry points, but that is to be expected because UCL/LCL is a true leading measure and the only technical indicators applied were simple moving averages. This factor also affirmed the importance of combining the COT data analysis with other measures such as technical indicators, price patterns, and seasonal behavior.

Using the basic moving averages contained the losses in both size and frequency. This is a noteworthy advantage of using moving averages. These are excellent indicators to add to a COT-based system because they lag. Adding the lag of a moving average with the lead of the UCL/LCL trigger has proven to be a powerful combination.

The 1998 studies provided proof that the net-commercial position was, indeed, a good leading indicator of commodity prices. It does not work 100 percent of the time in every single market tested; nothing ever does. However, the overall results were impressive (for back-testing results, see Appendix on p.153).

NET-FUND POSITIONS

From the COT data perspective, the commercials have the inside scoop on the fundamentals. However, we often see the commercials moving countertrend, scaling in and out of positions. The funds, meanwhile, are primarily trading with the trend. There are times, however, when the fund activity deviates from the price trend. This can be seen when looking at the net-fund position, which is the net of the longs and shorts among the funds. This is particularly significant when net-fund positions meet or exceed what I have identified as the upper or lower statistical reference points. When the net-fund position is at an extreme, it is time to pay attention to this activity too because the collective position of these participants may be providing insight into market direction. I view the funds as the fuel for the market, propelling it in one direction or the other. When their collective position is extreme, I know an extreme amount of "fuel" exists because their position eventually must be liquidated.

In general, I measure fund activity in the same way that I do the commercial positions. The fund position is examined and plotted on a net-fund basis. Statistical reference lines are then added so that I am aware when the funds have an unusually large net-long or net-short position. Similarly, the net-fund position can be analyzed much in the same way that I break down net-commercial positions.

In the case of the funds, I am looking at two different opinions held by trading interest, instead of two objectives held by hedging interest (producers hedging by selling short and consumers hedging by buying long). The net-fund activity compares the opinions of two opposing camps: the bulls and the bears.

In a market that is trending higher, the net-fund position will be long most of the time, although there are always a certain number of fund shorts or spreads. I monitor the relationship between the fund longs and fund shorts in much the same way as I do the commercials. Using statistical analysis of the data, I am comparing the two opposing fund populations. This is a very useful tool.

Keep in mind that, unlike the commercial participants that are active in the market primarily to hedge, the funds are in this to make a profit. They are not hedging or attempting to manage physical positions in the cash market. Therefore, when the funds have a statistically large net-long or net-short position, I know that this also indicates a large amount of fuel is available to power a trend in the opposite direction.

Watching the activities of the funds and large traders, I can see why this group tends to have the smartest speculators. Although they do not have firsthand access to fundamental data (they are relying on the same government reports and data as everyone else), in general they have an edge: They have expertise in analyzing the fundamental data once it has been released and they have deep pockets that enable them to ride trends out.

At some point after a large net-fund position (short or long) has been built up, the funds will have to exit, buying back shorts and selling longs. As they do, the market must absorb this activity. When they buy back shorts, this will provide momentum to the upside and prices will likely rise. When they sell long positions, it will pressure the market to the downside and prices generally fall. This is why I refer to the fund positions as fuel.

Something interesting that I look for is the exiting of funds from long positions while prices are still going higher. This happened in soybeans in 2004 as the market was topping (see Figure 3.5). During the spring of 2004, the net-fund long position was observed declining while soybean prices continued pushing higher. Within weeks following this divergence, the top was put in the soybean market for 2004.

On Figure 3.5, the point marked "X" indicates where the large net-fund long position began declining, which was shortly before the soybean market topped in 2004. An incident such as this is often a good leading indicator, particularly when the size of the net-fund position is statistically

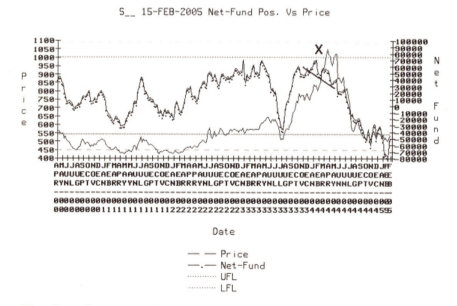

FIGURE 3.5 Soybean futures from April 2000 to February 2005: Net-fund position (darker top line) versus price.

significant. This type of occurrence is *not* a fundamental leading indicator because it does not reflect the behavior of the fundamental experts (producers and consumers). Rather, it focuses on the noncommercial participants, which is the large trader category. Again I view this position as fuel for a trend.

COT and Trading Systems

The COT data and the net-commercial and net-fund analyses provide meaningful market intelligence. By themselves, they are not enough to trade the market, but they provide the heads-up that a market bears watching or that further analysis is warranted. Put another way, COT triggers an early warning that it is time to apply technical analysis to a market. In fact, COT can be combined with virtually any other trading system as a complementary strategy to enhance performance. The reason is most trading strategies are based on historic price data, pricing patterns, and other technical indicators. Given the similarity among most technical systems (which rely heavily on the seven universal points mentioned in Chapter 1—opening price, high price, low price, closing price, net price change, volume, and open interest), one way to differentiate your trading strategy is to combine a completely unique approach that is *not* derived from price. This is precisely how I use the COT data.

In addition, many technical systems generate false signals. Using the COT data as a leading indicator can eliminate many of these false signals. The COT data can alert you to rare or unusual conditions in a specific market. Then you can turn your attention to that market and really hone in on it, incorporating other technical indicators to help you assess when conditions indicate a favorable trade setup and when to buy or sell.

In my own trading, this is how I use the COT data. It flags unusual market conditions that bear my careful attention and analysis, including my Individual Market Participation Analysis (IMPA) approach.

Entry into Trades

Many important elements play a role in determining which markets to enter, where and when. There are systems and indicators that define the mechanics of establishing a position, and personal observations and experiences guide traders in making judgments. Trading is a very personal business, requiring individual judgment and decision making.

Experience is your best friend in this effort. Carefully and dutifully observing and logging patterns in price behavior over time will shape your understanding of market behavior and help you become aware of subtle changes that take place in a market *prior* to a significant change in price or trend.

All entries should start with some level of mechanics as the foundation for the trade. Certain predetermined conditions should exist before you consider entering a trade. The entry itself requires a combination of mechanical input and logical judgment, based on observations and experience with each individual market.

All markets possess elements of randomness. No single entry stands out as superior under all conditions. One thing is certain, however: Some traders are better at determining optimal points of entry than others. Some are able to buy the lows and sell the highs (swings or otherwise), with a relatively high level of consistency. They do this through a combination of market feel, perception, and intuition by observing and tracking price movement with the aid of graphs and technical indicators.

Over time, making these observations will train your mind, giving you an edge over new traders who are unaware of the power of such observations and what they mean to the trained eye. This sense of the market is something every successful trader develops to some degree. Eventually, you must be able to implement trades based on independent observations in conjunction with mechanical signals from a system (such as IMPA, discussed in the following section). Acting successfully on this information and making good decisions will build your confidence. In the beginning, you may have issues with second-guessing or hesitating, but with time and experience, you can overcome this timidity.

When trading a longer-term system, such as IMPA, many entries are often available or acceptable once a market is set up or meeting the minimum required criteria. With my system, if I miss an entry at the turning point, other entries may still exist in the future as the market corrects, pulls back, or bounces to areas of neutrality—most notably the key 18-day moving average. However, because of the leverage involved and the risk associated with trading futures contracts, optimum entries are always highly desirable and frequently play a crucial role in determining whether a trader is stopped out prematurely.

So how, then, do you know when to place a trade? In the IMPA system, the answer is a series of triggers that combine the power of the COT data analysis with technical indicators to determine what market to trade and when.

IMPA TRADING SYSTEM CRITERIA

The IMPA system uses a "trigger selection" indicator based on the net-commercial position, specifically when the net position meets or exceeds certain control limits. This extreme condition in net-commercial positions indicates that the opportunity exists to trade this market. Once that trigger selection is activated, it is time to focus on more traditional forms of technical analysis to identify favorable price areas where significant market turns may occur. In addition, experienced COT traders may want to examine the individual commercial longs and shorts to better understand the cause of the trigger selection or imbalance and to try and determine its origin (commercial producer supply or commercial consumer demand).

The net-commercial trigger signals the strong likelihood that a large net-fund position also exists. The net-fund position is the fuel for starting a new trend. The significance of the net-fund position can be measured using the same statistical analysis methodology used to measure and detect extreme commercial positions.

Here is a breakdown of the four criteria that must be met to complete the IMPA setup:

1. Trigger Selection. Commercial institutions holding an extreme position.

2. Public and/or funds holding an extreme (excessive) opposing position.

3. Proprietary Relative Strength Index (RSI) Indicator diverging in the direction of the IMPA selection.

4. Price structure showing signs and indications that a new trend is beginning.[1]

Identifying IMPA Criteria: Entry and Exit Points

There are seven basic steps to identify market conditions for the IMPA trade setup, using the graphs and charts in my trading system, and for managing the IMPA position trade once action is taken. In Chapter 4, I discuss each of these steps in depth to more fully explain the IMPA criteria and show its usefulness in a dynamic trading system:

Step 1: Examine commercial graphs (UCL/LCL).

Step 2: Examine daily price graphs for RSI divergence, price behavior, and patterns.

---

[1]This is recognized using a rule called the 18-day moving average two-day rule. This rule states the closing price must close over/under the 18-day moving average for two consecutive days to confirm the breakout. Traders may also require that the second consecutive close over/under the 18-day moving average exceed the first (higher high or lower low). In addition, specific price patterns can be used to enter a position early, before the 18-day moving average breakout. The patterns provide the logical stop requirement. The logical stop therefore defines the entry. Without a logical stop, it is very difficult to have any kind of valid technical entry at all.

Step 3: Examine technical data for raw price activity and other characteristics and information.

Step 4: Examine open interest and volume graphs for direction of open interest and volume levels.

Step 5: Examine various supporting graphs for additional IMPA information and price data.

Step 6: Enter the IMPA trade based on the price behavior after the four setup criteria (previously described) are met.

Step 7: Exit the trade using initial predetermined stops, 50 percent rule, and trailing stops.

Overall, the IMPA system seeks to determine when the commercial positions are extremely one-sided, using graphs that contain the UCL and LCL trigger selection indicators. When these lines are penetrated, they indicate a statistically significant position in the market. This signals a fundamentally bullish (UCL) or bearish (LCL) condition may be developing.

As I explain in Chapter 4, I also incorporate two main technical indicators in my IMPA system: a *proprietary RSI* and *two simple moving averages.* My RSI looks at the total sum of points gained on up days versus the total sum of points lost on down days over a specified number of days. The data is then weighted using a proprietary weighting system. I use this RSI, plotted with price, to detect divergence between this indicator and the price. The RSI is plotted concurrently with the price so that I can visually detect divergence when and as it occurs. I do not monitor or use the RSI as an oscillator for detecting oversold or overbought conditions. I have developed a unique oscillator using detrended analysis to identify oversold and overbought conditions that I discuss later.

The moving averages used in my daily price graphs are based on 10- and 18-day periods. My weekly price graphs contain longer-term 4- and 9-week moving averages. These produce results similar to a 20- and 45-day moving average. Finally, my history graphs contain the longest moving average I use: 200 days.

With an understanding of what the COT data are communicating about fundamentals, market intelligence provided by fund activity, detailed technical analysis, and a feel developed through experience over time, a trader can move more confidently into the commodities markets. In Chapter 4, we explore the individual steps in making, managing, and exiting a trade using the IMPA system.

The IMPA Setup Trade

The Initial Steps

The purpose of the Individual Market Participant Analysis (IMPA) system is to identify markets that have a high probability of breaking out to the upside or downside and trending significantly. These opportunities are identified through in-depth analysis of the COT report (as explained in previous chapters), looking for those times when the net-commercial position has reached a significant—or extreme—level. This then becomes a leading indicator, alerting us that the market conditions are such that a significant new trend may develop.

As stated, the COT data alone is not enough to trade on. The seven steps of the IMPA setup trade outline specific criteria that must also be satisfied—including criteria derived from traditional price-derived indicators—before placing an order for a trade:

Step 1: Examine commercial graphs (UCL/LCL).

Step 2: Examine daily price graphs for Relative Strength Index (RSI) divergence, price behavior, and patterns.

Step 3: Examine technical data for raw price activity and other characteristics and information.

Step 4: Examine open interest and volume graphs for direction of open interest and volume levels.

Step 5: Examine various supporting graphs for additional IMPA information and price data.

Step 6: Enter the IMPA trade based on the price behavior after the four setup criteria (described in Chapter 3) are met.

Step 7: Exit the trade using initial predetermined stops, 50 percent rule, and trailing stops.

In this chapter, we review the first four steps of the IMPA setup trade. The remaining three steps, which include placing and managing the trade, are covered in Chapter 5.

STEP 1: EXAMINE COMMERCIAL GRAPHS (UCL/LCL)

The upper commercial limit (UCL) and lower commercial limit (LCL) graphs form the core of the IMPA trading system. Both the UCL and LCL lines are calculated with each new release of the COT data. The calculation is weighted toward the most recent data and takes into account a portion of the entire history. When the UCL or LCL is triggered, it indicates the commercial hedgers are holding an unusual and statistically significant one-sided position.

The UCL/LCL penetration provides the statistical evidence that an imbalance does indeed exist. That means the market is at the very least vulnerable to a price correction and possibly a significant trend reversal. Based on the UCL/LCL price relationship, the statistics favor the possibility that the price will begin a new trend—upward with a UCL trigger or downward with an LCL trigger. This may correct the imbalance of positions between the two assumed commercial entities, producers and consumers. In my studies of price behavior versus net-commercial positions, I have found a strong statistical correlation between *price extremes* and *extreme net-commercial positions*. (The term *extreme* is defined by penetration of the UCL/LCL areas.) In this regard, the UCL/LCL act as a guide to tell us when current prices may be out of whack with evolving fundamentals. These conditions commonly exist prior to all large moves.

Examining the UCL/LCL graph for excessive commercial positions is one of the most important parts of the standard IMPA system. This is the *core indicator.* These indicators must be updated with every release of the COT. This data should be reviewed weekly. The markets in which the commercials are currently holding positions at, near, or exceeding the UCL/LCL indicator lines represent the best candidates for longer-term position trades. Identifying these markets is the first step of the IMPA position trading system. Once identified, these markets are flagged and monitored on a day-to-day basis using traditional forms of technical analysis and specific proprietary price-derived indicators.

Standard required criteria are also key in maintaining consistency for determination of when to enter and how to manage the initial risk. After entering a position, the COT becomes less important as the focus turns to managing the position using predefined logical stop, the 50 percent rule, and my trailing stops methodology (see Chapter 5). As explained in this and upcoming chapters, an entry should only occur after all the required criteria have been satisfied. The criteria represent the mechanical portion of the IMPA position trading system. Further analysis of price behavior, seasonal characteristics, risk exposure, and traders' instinct play a role in determining which setup markets to enter and which ones not to enter, as the system tracks several markets at once. This part of the procedure is not mechanical in nature.

In Figure 4.1 of commercial positions in Australian dollar futures in April 2002, the letters *EUCL* and *ELCL* stand for *extreme upper commerical limit* and *extreme lower commercial limit.* These lines are rarely penetrated. The EUCL and ELCL are calculated much like the UCL and LCL. They are, however, wider than the UCL/LCL and therefore encompass a wider portion of the total distribution. Whereas the UCL/LCL generally encompass 95 to 99.7 percent of the total distribution, depending on the number of outliers, the EUCL/ELCL may encompass closer to 99.9 percent of the total distribution. When the data does not contain any extreme outliers, the UCL/LCL calculation is slightly modified to fit a perceived

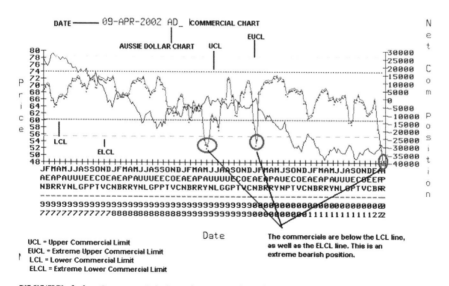

FIGURE 4.1 Commercial chart for Australian dollars.

tighter distribution and the EUCL/ELCL is open to plus or minus three full standard deviations.

As with most data populations, outliers do exist from time to time. Statisticians often exclude them from normal populations to reduce or remove undesirable skewing or noise. Since the markets are prone to occasional unusual conditions, it makes sense to include this data as part of the analysis. The way I handle it is by including them in the wider calculation for the EUCL and ELCL, but I remove the most extreme outliers from the standard UCL/LCL. Removing the extreme outliers from the data results in a smaller standard deviation, thus tightening the upper and lower limits.

If I left the extreme outliers in the standard UCL/LCL calculation, this would reduce the number of UCL/LCL events over time (thus reducing the number of trades). The studies I have done indicate that it is better to remove them from the UCL/LCL calculation and leave them in the EUCL/ELCL calculation. This achieves the optimum number of IMPA trading opportunities without compromising the benefits of the statistical analysis.

When the net-commercial position approaches one of the extreme lines, it triggers a significant statistical event, alerting me to the presence of an extremely one-sided commercial position. Generally, at least the UCL/LCL lines need to be crossed, but there are times when it is not a requirement. You will learn this as a result of experience in a particular market. Each commodity has its own unique characteristics and the commercials are better at forecasting some markets than others.

Using the UCL/LCL measure as my *core indicator* and starting point, I am focused on the right markets ahead of time—before the next potential big move unfolds. As a leading indicator, the UCL/LCL is a powerful tool for anticipating significant trend reversals. The fact that this indicator is not derived from any price data makes it the perfect core indicator for the IMPA trading system and an excellent addition to traditional price-derived indicators.

The UCL/LCL and EUCL/ELCL lines are warning flags that "something is up" in a particular market. Such was the case in March 2005 when the current IMPA data in the 10-year notes and U.S. bonds showed a net-commercial position at extremely high levels (reaching the EUCL). The level of EUCL penetration in the 10-year notes was astonishing. This led me to become bullish on bonds and notes, an opinion I held well into May—even though the Federal Reserve was expected to announce a 25-basis point hike. Keep in mind that when rates go higher, the prices of notes and bonds typically fall. The yield (interest rate) of these instruments always moves in the opposite direction of their price. When the price rises, the yield drops; and when the price drops, the yield rises. However, the net-commercial data penetrating both the UCL and the EUCL indicated higher bond prices, which was contrary to the prevailing opinion of most popular analysts at the time. The Fed remained poised to continue ratcheting the Fed funds rate higher during the first half of 2005. As this occurred, however, it did not have the widely anticipated influence on the 10-year notes and U.S. bond markets.

Alan Greenspan, the chairman of the Federal Reserve Board of Governors at the time, described this unusual behavior as a "conundrum" during his testimony to Congress in early 2005. And even though the analysts were right in anticipating the Fed would continue raising rates through the first half of 2005, they were wrong about the short-term impact this would have on the yield of both 10-year notes and U.S. bond markets. These markets continued to move higher during this period, which is precisely what the IMPA system indicated they would do. This again was opposite of what most popular analysts and economists were projecting. Nevertheless, the trade opportunity was there because bonds did go higher. In just one week in early May, the 10-year note gained $953 per contract, and the U.S. bonds gained a whopping $1,656.35 per contract.

In the wake of the Fed announcement of higher interest rates, I was advising traders on my web site that they should be heeding the 50 percent rule, scaling out of their positions and taking profits. In my May 22 report, I noted a pullback in 10-year notes and bonds below the 18-day moving average for two days in a row. This was my cue to exit remaining long positions. This market had a very nice run from the March 2005 IMPA buy setup, and although this might not have been the absolute top, my strategies managed to take a decent-size chunk out of a decent-size trend. This IMPA buy occurred in March 2005 when virtually everyone in the media was expecting rates to climb (and 10-year notes to fall). The opposite happened and rates actually fell while the Fed continued raising the interest rate of the Fed funds. Nevertheless, it was the UCL and EUCL that once again accurately anticipated the direction the market would take.

Once the UCL/LCL have identified a large buildup in the net-commercial position, I may take my analysis a step farther by reviewing the relationship between the commercial producers and consumers to measure the size of the imbalance that may exist. At this time, I may also measure the size of the net-fund position. A net-fund position that exceeds the UFL/LFL (upper fund limit/lower fund limit) is also very supportive. If the funds are holding an unusually large position, I know the market must absorb the position as they must liquidate or unwind the position eventually.

STEP 2: EXAMINE DAILY GRAPH FOR RSI DIVERGENCE

Relative Strength Index (RSI) is a measurement of the overall strengths of up days versus down days in the market. The traditional RSI formula is:

RSIndex (RSI) =

au = Sum of points gained on up days for last X days divided by X

ad = Sum of points lost on down days for last X days divided by X

Relative Strength (RS) = au/ad

Relative Strength Index (RSI) = $100 - [100/(1 + rs)]$

100 is added to the formula to keep the RSI oscillating between 1 – 100.

The RSI used in my proprietary daily price graphs is a modified version of the traditional RSI. The most important difference is a proprietary weight placement toward the more recent data in the 14-day period used in the calculation. This weighting allows more emphasis to be placed on the most recent market activity and gradually less on the older data. I use this indicator primarily to uncover hidden strength or weakness in a market. I am able to achieve this by comparing the RSI with prices side-by-side.

This side-by-side comparison makes my daily price graphs unique. Most charting programs plot the RSI in a separate window and as a separate entity from price. I have found it to be more useful and enlightening to plot the RSI and the price in the same charting window. This allows the two to overlap and intertwine as market activity unfolds daily and new prices and RSI results are obtained. To achieve this, I had to modify the formula for the RSI slightly so that it tracks along with prices.

This proprietary modification enhances my ability to spot divergences between price and RSI, providing a slight edge over RSI indicators tracked in separate windows. Basically, I am looking for clues about the true strength or weakness of a market. If a market is strong, the RSI should track right along with the price changes. Typically, in strong markets, you will observe my RSI plotting above the prices and diverging higher, appearing to lead the market. As the market trades higher, it could be weakening internally. This can be identified when the market makes a higher high, but the RSI fails to do so as well. As the market trades higher, while the RSI starts to diverge downward and away from the price, it indicates weakness. At that point you would have *negative RSI divergence.*

One of the most important things to remember about my RSI is that I tend to use it as a *leading indicator* and I always use it in conjunction with other indicators. I do not care about the actual value of the RSI, rather I focus my attention on the relationship between the RSI and the price structure (looking for divergence between the two). As Figure 4.2 illustrates, the RSI diverges when the RSI makes a lower high at the same time that price makes a higher high (or a new high for the move). RSI simply doesn't follow suit with a higher high as well. In this example, the RSI has begun diverging from the price structure and fails to make a higher high with price. This occurred at the top of the market (when the market was making

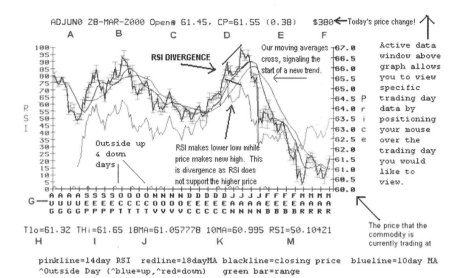

FIGURE 4.2 RSI divergence. *Notes:* A = Commodity, month, year of chart; B = Latest trading date; C = Opening price; D = Closing price; E = Points up/down for day; F = Dollar amount gained/lost for the day; G = Time history; H = Low price of the day; I = High price of the day; J = 18-day moving average; K = 10-day moving average; M = RSI number.

a new high) and was therefore an indication the trend higher was weakening (versus gaining in strength).

STEP 3: EXAMINE THE TECHNICAL CHARTS

On my web site, I track daily technical charts each day, providing a technical overview of the market based on a five-year and 161-day history. The charts also include the current 20-day history of open, high, low, closes, changes, 18-day moving average, and volume/open interest. I use these charts to help determine specific entry points, protective stops, and trailing stops.

The top portion of the chart (see Figure 4.3) contains unique day-of-week price characteristics and statistical information. This information can be used in swing trading (see Chapter 8) and is occasionally useful in assisting with IMPA position trades. Sometimes certain days of the week may exhibit more strength or weakness than other days of the week. As of this writing, the data currently show the S&P 500 futures have been

```
HUT  27R x 8C                                           28-MAR-2000 16:22 Page 1

Day      %Up     AveR    AveG    AveL    Trend    Period    MA        StDev

----------------------------------------------------------------------------
Mon      49 %UP  1.74    1.17   -1.08   63 %UP   10Day     86.88       1.44
Tue      49 %UP  1.71    1.43   -0.82   53 %UP   14Day     88.25       2.59
Wed      52 %UP  2.01    1.27   -1.58   61 %UP   17Day     88.83       2.92
Thu      53 %UP  1.95    1.21   -1.44   56 %UP   21Day     89.14       2.85
Fri      52 %UP  2.00    1.13   -1.14   60 %UP   45Day     82.92       6.89
 A        B       C       D       E       F        G        H           I
20D_Hist Opens   Highs   Lows    Closes  Chg      18DMA    Vol         O/I
3-1      87.95   92.55   87.70   92.43   5.38     80.79    47312.00    98676.00
3-2      92.35   93.25   89.95   91.85  -0.58     81.63    40416.00    98850.00
3-3      93.55   94.55   90.35   90.66  -1.19     82.48    39012.00    99580.00
3-6      91.05   91.65   89.45   91.30   0.64     83.42    33033.00    98313.00
3-7      92.55   95.55   92.15   94.96   3.66     84.45    47754.00   102481.00
3-8      92.05   93.40   87.65   88.23  -6.73     84.98    43547.00   104657.00
3-9      89.30   92.05   86.85   91.85   3.62     85.76    37072.00   103357.00
3-10     91.05   93.05   90.80   92.47   0.62     86.43    32237.00   104717.00
3-13     92.20   93.20   91.60   92.16  -0.31     87.08    28409.00   104236.00
3-14     92.10   92.20   89.80   90.25  -1.91     87.56    36922.00   104668.00
3-15     89.70   89.80   87.10   87.34  -2.91     87.96    32970.00   106620.00
3-16     86.50   88.90   86.20   88.00   0.66     88.49    49730.00   108258.00
3-17     87.75   89.35   87.55   87.76  -0.24     88.91    32223.00   108884.00
3-20     86.90   86.90   83.90   84.64  -3.12     89.11    43101.00   110006.00
3-21     85.20   85.80   84.75   85.57   0.93     89.30    30118.00   109220.00
3-22     85.10   87.40   84.00   85.10  -0.47     89.34    45143.00   112224.00
3-23     85.50   86.10   85.10   85.86   0.76     89.30    36935.00   112007.00
3-24     86.50   88.40   86.30   87.78   1.92     89.34    42328.00   111767.00
3-27     87.00   89.30   86.00   88.40   0.62     89.12    30069.00   111512.00
3-28     88.10   89.60   87.60   88.38  -0.02     88.93    30069.00   111512.00
```

Daily Technicals by Floyd Upperman & Associates; All Rights Reserved

FIGURE 4.3 Example of technical chart. *Notes:* A = 20 trading days; B = Opening price; C = High price of the day; D = Low price of the day; E = Closing price for the day; F = Points changed for the day; G = 18-day moving average; H = Volume traded for the day; I = Current open interest. Volume and open interest are reported by the exchanges one day behind.

strongest on Mondays and Thursdays and weakest on Tuesdays and Fridays. This is not always the case, but over time and through observation I have learned how to identify emerging patterns using this data. The data is designed to spot emerging day-of-week patterns by tracking the percentage of up closes over a short-term 161-day period and over a longer-term five-year period. Anytime a bias is identified and confirmed in both periods, it can be a useful tool for short-term swing trading. As of this writing, the S&P 500 has closed up 56 percent of the time on Mondays over the past five years, whereas over the past 161 trading days (of which at least 30 are Mondays) the S&P 500 has closed up 65 percent of the time on Mondays. Thus, the pattern here is that Mondays are comparably strong (compared with other days of the week) in both the recent 161-day period and over the past five years.

The daily technical chart provides access to the raw daily price data and statistics. Every trader analyzes this data differently. You will develop your own style of trading and analyzing this data once you become a more seasoned trader. Just because one trader uses the 18-day moving average as the entry point, does not necessarily mean that it has to be yours. Analyze the data, and paper-trade a system for a while. It is important to determine the best method for you. What is good for one person might not be good for your purposes. It all boils down to your style of trading and the amount of risk capital that you have in your trading account, as well as your trading goals and market experience.

The notation across the top of the chart shows the following unique day-of-week characteristics and statistical information:

$AveR$ = Average range for that particular day based on the past 30+ trading sessions for that particular day of week

$AveG$ = Average gain for that particular day based on the past 30+ trading sessions for that particular day of week

$AveL$ = Average loss for that particular day based on the past 30+ trading sessions for that particular day of week

$percentUP$ = Five-year bias for that particular day of week

$TREND$ = 30+ day bias for that particular day of week (last 161 trading sessions)

$Period$ = Time period

MA = Associated moving average

$STDEV^*$ = Associated standard deviation (STDEV is the average range [distance] of all data points from the mean.)

It is important that I have at least 30 data points before I can take any kind of meaningful statistical measurements; thus, all my daily graphs are based on the 161-day price history. This ensures they contain at least 30 data samples for each day of the week (at least 30 Mondays, 30 Tuesdays, 30 Wednesdays, and so on).

STEP 4: EXAMINE OPEN INTEREST GRAPHS

Following open interest and being able to forecast future prices and commercial activity from changes in open interest will certainly take time and practice. Even then, it is not always clear. Open interest is a subjective and intuitive indicator that requires skill for efficient interpretation.

Trading is not all science. If it were, we could easily have computers do all the work for us. To understand how to comprehend what is going on with changes in open interest, let me first explain the rules:

Rule 1: When the market is moving sideways and open interest declines, this is considered *bullish* because it is an indication that the commercials may be covering short positions.

Rule 2: When the market is moving sideways and open interest increases, this is considered *bearish* because it is an indication that the commercials may be adding to short positions.

Figure 4.4 shows open interest in the Australian dollar. The bars at the bottom show up and down volume (color-coded on the screen, although displayed here in black). The larger dots placed periodically along the "open interest line" represent when a COT report is released. The dots were added for the purpose of tracking changes in open interest between COT reports.

I used to focus closely on the changes in open interest when the CFTC released the COT data every other week or once a month. Now that the

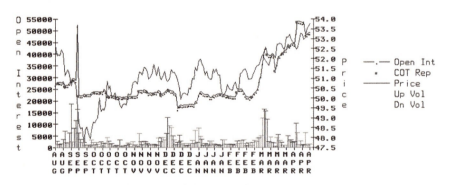

FIGURE 4.4 Open interest graph in the Australian dollar.

data is released every week, it is unnecessary to track changes in open interest as closely because we now have access to the COT (which is a breakdown of the open interest) on a week-to-week basis. The open interest graphs can be used to help determine what the various participants may be doing on a week-to-week basis before the CFTC releases the data on Fridays; however, tracking is not as crucial as it used to be.

In Chapter 5, I discuss Steps 5 through 7 in the IMPA setup trade.

IMPA Setup Trade

Placing the Trade

I n Chapter 4, the first four steps of the IMPA setup trade were discussed. These are as follows:

Step 1: Examine commercial graphs (UCL/LCL).

Step 2: Examine daily price graphs for RSI divergence, price behavior, and patterns.

Step 3: Examine technical data for raw price activity and other characteristics and information.

Step 4: Examine open interest and volume graphs for direction of open interest and volume levels.

Once steps 1 through 4 are completed and we have identified a list of markets with the potential for a successful IMPA setup trade, using steps 5 through 7 we then examine these candidates more closely. These last three steps of the system focus on the details of the participant activity and price structure. I use supporting data and graphs to pinpoint and filter trading opportunities, place the trade according to specific criteria, manage the trade, manage the initial risk using predetermined stops around logical price points, and later manage profits using trailing stops:

Step 5: Examine various supporting graphs for additional IMPA information and price data.

Step 6: Enter the IMPA trade based on the price behavior after the four setup criteria (described in Chapters 3 and 4) are met.

Step 7: Exit the trade using initial predetermined stops, 50 percent rule, and trailing stops.

STEP 5: EXAMINE ADDITIONAL SUPPORTING GRAPHS

As part of the IMPA system analysis, we also examine certain additional supporting factors:

- Commercial net position is at or around the historic extreme.
- A large speculative fund bubble, or media frenzy.
- Prices are at or around the historic high or low.
- Historical performance of each commercial group (producers and consumers) is examined. This includes examining the performance of the commercial producers and commercial consumers independent of the net-commercial position.
- A commercial bull market exists.

Other supporting graphs and data (including producer and consumer graphs) are studied. This includes analysis of the fund activity, including fund long positions, fund short positions, fund spread positions, and net-fund positions.

These additional supporting factors are important, but they are not part of the core criteria. These are things that I investigate closely when a market is meeting the core criteria. Observing changes in these variables over time can improve understanding of the market behavior on a participant level and thus sharpen traders' instinct, an important factor in trading. The instinct of traders is driven by what they observe taking place in the market. Most traders focus entirely on the most common observations (price behavior, price-derived indicators, and news). To improve your instinct and gain an edge, you need to look at unique inputs (as discussed in Chapter 7). The following subsections describe some of the unique things I look at and track. By monitoring these items, I can recognize the conditions that often lead to profitable trading opportunities.

Each of these factors will be examined individually.

Commercial Net Position at or around Historic Extreme

Commercial history graphs display prices and the entire COT spectrum of participants, including commercials, funds (noncommercials), and the public or small traders. Figure 5.1 gives a broad perspective on whether the current commercial position represents a record size net-long or net-short position, and how that corresponds to price. The commercial history graph not only allows us to see the current commercial position, it also contains the fund history and small speculator history. This shows how the fund and small trader categories fits in the complete history. In addition, the graph contains real price data (not back adjusted) dating back to the beginning of the COT, which provides a quick look at price history.

The lines on Figure 5.1 represent commercial, noncommerical (NC), and small trader (SM) activity, along with price, going back to January 1983. (Dates on the charts are displayed vertically, and on the computer screen, the lines appear in color.) The high peak that is circled at the top of the graph shows where the fund position was a record size net-long. The corresponding low spike that is circled at the bottom of the graph shows where the commercial position was a record net short. The price line in the middle was not at historic levels, although it was at the higher end of historic prices going back to 1983. This is all visible when you look

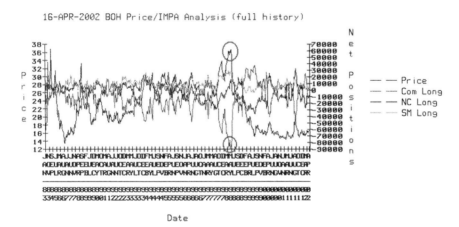

FIGURE 5.1 Commercial history graph showing activity of all three market participants: commercials, noncommercials, and nonreportable (small trader) positions.

at the colored graph, which is extremely telling (see the colored graphs on my web site, www.upperman.com, and click "View Book Graphs"). Sometimes this kind of analysis is all that is needed to spot an unusual condition. However, more detailed work is required before establishing a position.

Large Speculative Bubble or Media Frenzy

If the fund bubble is excessive, it can be observed in the commercial history graph. Other times, the large speculative position may not be a record-size and cannot be easily observed in the commercial history graph. This is when I would use my COT Profile graphs, which dis-play all three categories and price going back about five years (see Figure 5.2).

In Figure 5.2, notice the line that drops off sharply at the far right, plummeting straight down between March and April 2002. This is the commercial position. The other line at the bottom right of the chart is the price. It is interesting to see how the commercials always tend to be on the right side of the market before major trend changes.

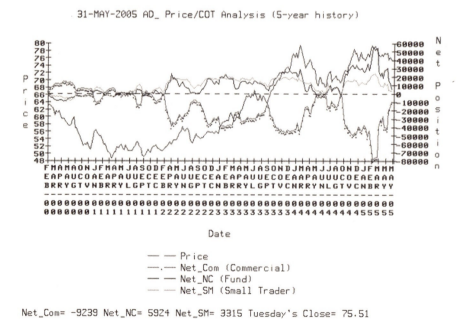

FIGURE 5.2 Activity of three groups of market participants, along with price.

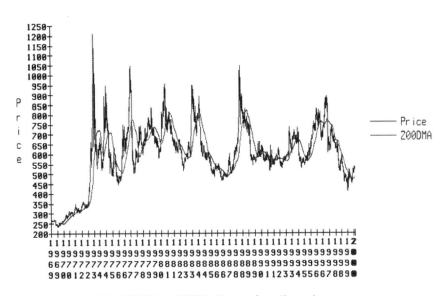

02-JAN-1969 to 28-MAR-2000 Price chart w/200 DMA

⟨DATE HISTORY in YEARS⟩ (Vertical on X axes)

Last updated on 28-MAR-2000 closing= 526.5 200DMA= 481.7

FIGURE 5.3 Price history graph showing history prices (top line with spikes) and 200-day moving average (smoother line).

Price at or around Historic High/Low

For an up-to-date historic price graph on a commodity, I view history graphs with a 200-day moving average. Figure 5.3 is an example of soybean prices dating back to 1969. Viewing prices this way provides, at a glance, the correlation between the current price and the historic highs and lows. This is the "big picture" overview of the market.

Examine Historical Performance of Commercials

In some markets, I've noted the commercial consumers may be a little better at anticipating buy swings, whereas the commercial producers are better at anticipating sell swings (or vice versa). Both groups hedge, but they tend to do it oppositely: Consumers buy futures to lock in future prices, and producers sell futures to protect their business from the risk of falling prices. Buying and selling between the two groups can be observed fairly clearly in the consumer/producer (CP) graph (Figure 5.4), which shows consumer activity at the top, producer activity at the bottom, and the price line gyrating inbetween. Again, however, the two commercial entities must be assumed since these details are not provided in the COT report. I am making an assumption as explained in the first two chapters.

Once the net commercial position is at an extreme or penetrating the UCL or LCL, a more in-depth examination of the commercial positions should then be performed. By breaking the commercials down into producers and consumers, we can obtain insight into the supply and demand and achieve a more thorough analysis. We gain insight from the behavior of the opposing commercial participants. This data is derived from the weekly COT report, but as mentioned earlier, the data in the report is not broken down like this. We have to make certain assumptions in order to break the data down in this fashion. Once broken down into individual consumer and producer entities, I apply the same method of statistical controls to track, measure, and monitor the positions. Accurate interpretation of the individual commercial participant positions is crucial at this step. It takes time to learn how to equate changes in participant positioning to changes in supply and demand and, ultimately, rising and falling prices. For example, I have found that some trigger selections are more significant than others, and not necessarily because of the depth of the penetration, rather because of the relationship between the two opposing commercial forces—commercial producers and commercial consumers.

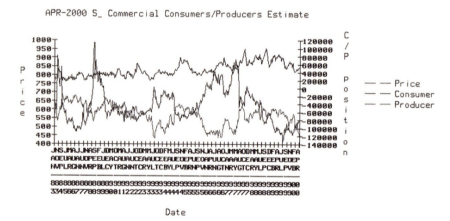

FIGURE 5.4 Consumer/producer graph showing estimated positions in market.

Most of the time, we do not want to hastily follow the net-commercial position once it's reached an extreme level. And unless the commercials are at an extreme (which only occurs a small percentage of the time), we really don't want to follow the commercials at all. In fact, we want to follow and trade with the price trend most of the time. The price trend is the dominant market force the majority of the time. The price trend is usually supported by the large traders and the funds, however, not the commercials. Now when I say follow, what I am saying is that we should be taking positions (longer-term position trades) in the direction of the price trend, as the funds generally do most of the time. The exception to this is when the commercials are holding extreme positions (by historic measures). There are opportunities to swing trade with and against the trend using both swing "A" and "B" approaches, but right now I am referring to long-term position trading only.

After an initial selection has occurred, I look at the individual commercial components (producers and consumers) to see which side is driving the imbalance and, more importantly, to see how the other side is responding. This is really important, particularly today because of the commodity funds.

Ideally, I want to see the following: During net-commercial UCL penetration, the UCL trigger selection indicates the commercial consumer's hedged demand is out of balance with the commercial producer's hedged supply. This is a sign that the consumers may be demanding more than what the producers are willing or able to produce. The closer the commercial producer position is to its UCL during a net-commercial buy selection, the better. However, the individual commercial producer position does not have to be at its UCL to be bullish. Most of the time it won't be and only has to be off its LCL to indicate a really bullish situation.

However, we don't want to see the commercial producers deep inside their LCL or ELCL during a net-com buy. We want to see the commercial consumer positions at their UCL or near it while the commercial producer positions are inside their normal distribution. Again, the further they are from the LCL and toward their UCL the better. This would indicate the commercial producers are not able or willing to meet the commercial consumer demand. If they are deep in the tails and not meeting the demand, the reason may simply be because "they can't." In other words, they may not have the capacity or the supply. But when they are off their LCL and toward the center of their distribution or close to the UCL, this is often indicative of an entirely different situation. What this often means is that they simply are not willing to meet the demand. That is quite different from not being able to meet demand. We have to ask: Why aren't they willing? The answer usually relates to price. In this case, they simply may be holding out for higher prices.

During net-com LCL penetration, the LCL trigger selection indicates the commercial producers hedged supply is out of balance with the commercial consumers hedged demand. This can occur when the producers have more supply than the consumers are consuming. This could be due to excess supply from around the world or weak demand or both. This is usually a bearish situation. The fix for this situation is lower prices. Lower prices will eventually bring in more demand and also reduce new production (new supply). These fixes are what keep the cycle going as eventually supply gets low again and prices move up. We can usually count on the cycle overshooting quite often, too. What we want to see in this case is the commercial producer position at or exceeding its LCL while the commercial consumer position is inside its normal distribution (not in the UCL part of the tail). However, the ideal setup here is when the commercial producer positions are at or exceeding the LCL at the same time that the commercial consumer positions are in the center of their distribution or down around their LCL as well.

In both cases, we must wait for all our criteria to be satisfied and look toward our technical indicators for our entry and management of the position once a bullish or bearish selection (trigger) has occurred. However, when these ideal conditions are present, this can "turn on" or activate our price-derived indicators, too. Many good technical indicators work 50 percent of the time. If you want them to work better than 50 percent (say 80 percent or 90 percent of the time) then wait for the most powerful underlying or ideal trigger selections. I provide an example of this in Chapter 9 via the June 2005 hog trade example. The actual individual commercial producer and commercial consumer graphs are shown.

Commodity Index Funds

In recent years, we have heard a great deal about commodity index funds. There is no question that index funds are gaining in popularity, and commodities are going to be part of that. There is concern, however, that the commodity index fund positions are finding their way into the commercial participant data. I believe this could be the case. However, whether or not they really should be counted as traditional hedgers is unclear. The CFTC will have to figure out how to deal with this issue at some point. For now, however, this is not impacting my strategies at all. That's because I look at all participants and am constantly monitoring all the relationships. Since I already monitor the individual commercial positions, I have a good handle on this. Based on the data, it appears the commercial commodity index funds primarily favor the long side of many of these markets, which makes sense because many of these funds represent alternate investments to stocks and hedges against inflation. If inflation occurs, you don't want to be short a commodity index. You generally need to be long commodities to profit from an inflationary environment. And for the commodity index to profit during inflationary periods, the index needs to be long commodities not short. Thus, I am finding the commercial producer positions (shorts) to be even more important today than ever before. These represent the purest commercial data in my opinion because producers really must produce something in the traditional sense to be hedgers. Commercial consumers have to consume something to be hedgers and this can include a great number of possibilities with all the different derivative scenarios in the market today. The net-commercial position remains my trigger selection but as these index funds enter the mainstream and increase in numbers, we have to be very observant and pay attention to *all* of the individual participants. Breaking down the commercials into individual commercial consumer (longs) and commercial producer (shorts) is crucial now. Many who look at the COT remain 100 percent focused on the old way of looking at the net-commercial position only. In my opinion, however, one cannot solely look at the net-commercial position anymore and expect to observe the same familiar behavior.

Commercial Bull Markets

A traditional commercial bull market is easy to identify due to the inverted price structure across the contract months (from the front lead month out to the distant back months). In a normally structured market, prices in the distant months are slightly more expensive than the front months due to time-sensitive costs referred to as *carrying charges*. The carrying charge includes insurance, storage, and other related costs such as interests on loans. These costs accumulate over time, which is why the back months are typically more expensive than the front months.

In an inverted market, the front months will be more expensive than the back months. The price structure becomes inverted when consumer demand for a particular commodity is out of line with available supplies. This can be a temporary condition or an extended one. It all depends on the need for the commodity, when or if new supplies will be available, and whether other commodities can be substituted.

The distribution of commercial positions varies from market to market over time. In some commodities, there is a tendency for the net-commercial position to remain net-short for long periods of time. An extreme example is silver. The net-commercial position in silver has varied from extremely net-short to barely net-short, but it has been net-short since 1983. This highlights a few important points.

The commercial structure is not the same in all commodities, although most have seen some net-long commercial positions at some point in the past.

This also illustrates the importance of using a statistical method to measure the meaning of the commercial position, rather than assuming that the commercial data must be bearish if the position is net-short. That would be a very wrong assumption to make in silver. The degree of the current net-short position in relation to the historical net-short positions is what I focus on using our UCL/LCL distribution indicator lines.

The IMPA system has had many successful buy setups in silver since 1983, and every instance occurred with a net-short commercial position. Whether the commercials are net-short or net-long isn't nearly as important as is the size of their net-long or net-short position in relation to all their previous positions. More active commercial producer hedging than commercial consumer hedging is likely the reason the net-commercial position on average tends to be net-short slightly more often than net-long (across the commodities markets that I track). The commercial consumer will hedge as well, but the commercial producer tends to be the most active overall. Furthermore, it appears the commercial producer has a tendency to hedge in the back months while the commercial consumer tends to focus more attention on hedging in the front months than in the back months. However, this is not real clear and most certainly varies.

Other Supporting Graphs and Data

I look at other supporting graphs and data as well, including an equity graph, weekly graph, commercial open interest graph, and activity report.

My equity graph is unique in that it helps me determine the day-to-day dollar volatility or monetary risk of a market. This graph shows how much the market fluctuates on a daily basis in dollars not points. By reviewing the graph, I can determine whether I can trade a certain market using our "10 percent rule," which states that no more than 10 percent of available trading capital should be at risk in any one trade—and a smaller percentage for larger accounts (see Money Management section at end of this chapter and Risk per Trade Tables in the Appendix, p. 192).

Defining the location for the stops is a crucial part of my trading. In recent years, I have refined my methodology for defining stops. First of all, I no longer use intraday stops for any position or swing trades. Today, I use only the closing prices for all my position trading and swing trading stops. Switching from intraday (resting) stops to end-of-day (closing) stops has improved the overall performance of my trading. It has eliminated all the false intraday stop-outs that used to occur because of stop running by pit traders or sharp short-term movements during lunch hours or during large orders. Many times I would be stopped out using intraday stops only to see the market reverse minutes later and close in the opposite direction or unchanged on the day. I am sure many readers can recall being stopped out at or near the high or low for the day, only to have the market turn around and move back in your favor by the close. Once you are stopped out, it is difficult to get back in from both a psychological and a practical point of view. You don't want to be hopping in and out of position trades during the day.

Stops are a critical component of a position trading or swing trading strategy. In general with the IMPA, the wider the stop the better, although we must also control risk and contain loss. After years of research and testing, I finally figured out how to achieve an optimum stop. I now focus on the closing prices for the stop because the close represents the most important price of the day. The market can spike up or down sharply during the day for many reasons such as thin trading around lunchtime, news including reports and rumors, and other variables that basically result in noise. The closing price is free of most of this noise. Wherever the market settles at the end of the day is its fair value. And I strongly believe this is the only price that should matter for your stop, and for determining your entry as well. That is why I focus on the closing prices for both entries and exits (stops). Intraday spikes or dips are not all that important to a position trader. What is important is where the market closes however. For example, one of the things I watch closely is the closing price in relation to the 18-day moving average of closes. I will discuss this further in subsequent chapters. When entering using my 18-day moving average 2-day rule, the market must close above or below the 18-day moving average for two or more consecutive days. Likewise when exiting a remaining 50 percent on a stop, using this same rule the market must close above or below the 18-day moving average for two or more consecutive days. Using this method, everything that happens intraday is automatically filtered out. There is a downside and an upside to most everything. The downside with using the closing price for the stop is the fact that occasionally the market may continue moving past the stop intraday and close further away from it, thus creating a larger loss. While this is true, the upside still outweighs this downside based on my testing. When using closing prices, you reduce the number of times you are stopped out on stop running, noise, or any other temporary intraday disturbances.

It is simple to use the closing price for your stop. You do not need to place any fancy orders (stop close only orders, which are not even accepted in all markets). All that you need to do is review the closing price, and if it is through your stop, you simply exit the next day. Second, deciding what price to use in comparing the closing price is an important aspect of defining the stop. Up to this point, all I have discussed is the reference point (closing prices) for the stop I select to use. The selection of the initial protective stop is based on logic, which is why I call my stops *logical stops.*

Various pattern formations provide logical stops. If the pattern is going to be successful, it should not be violated. A "W" or a forward plunger pattern consists of clear lows. If these lows are penetrated on a closing basis, the pattern is violated, and the market is telling us that it is going in the other direction (in this case down). Logic dictates that if the market is, indeed, going higher—not lower—then the price should be going higher. It should not break down to new lows nor should it push through the bottoms of various patterns. When trades have matured beyond the initial entry to the established point, I begin using a different kind of stop that focuses on the trend.

To summarize, there are two key points to my stop methodology:

1. All my stops are compared with closing prices. I do not compare my stops with intraday noise. The closing price is always the most important price of the day and therefore the most meaningful price reference for our stops.

2. I do not use monetary stops, which is a stop where a trader decides to risk X amount of money. The market does not care about how much money you have to risk. All my stops are based on logical price points or trends. If I perceive a market is going higher and I am long, the market obviously should not be breaking down to new lows on the close. If it is behaving this way, then it is not going higher, and in fact is going lower. And in that case, I either want to be out or short, certainly not long.

In Figure 5.5, the left Y-axis of the equity graph shows accumulative gains and losses updated on a daily basis. The middle line that fluctuates around the horizontal axis shows the daily dollar fluctuation of the market. This is what I refer to as the *heartbeat* of the market. We use this middle

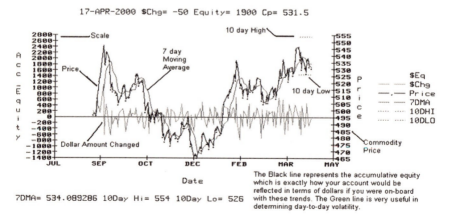

FIGURE 5.5 Equity graph showing daily fluctuation in dollars.

line (displayed in green on the computer graphs) to determine the risk level. This helps us determine how much money we can expect to gain or lose in a market per contract and on a daily basis.

The equity graphs also display a 7-day moving average and 10-day high/low channel. This channel represents the high and low of the market counting back 10 days from the previous close. We do not include the current day's high or low in the calculation, because if we did, we would never see penetration beyond these boundaries. The two things we look for in these boundaries are:

1. For swing traders, they represent potential swing tops and bottoms.

2. For position traders, penetration into and beyond these zones can represent breakouts, especially if other conditions are present (such as diverging RSI). This penetration can also be used as confirming indicators for our longer-term IMPA position trades. A market that is moving higher on a longer-term basis should be breaking out above its 10-day high, just as a market that is moving lower on a longer-term basis should be breaking out below its 10-day low.

While moving averages are lagging indicators, the shorter the time frame, the more responsive they will be to new prices. The 7-day moving average will normally respond to new prices faster than 10- or 18-day moving averages. There are advantages and disadvantages, however, to using the 7-day moving average versus 10- and 18-day moving averages. This can be advantageous for getting in or out of a market ahead of the crowd. The disadvantage is that the 7-day moving average also will have more false breakout signals since it is more sensitive to market fluctuations. At times, the 7-day will be the best moving average to follow and at other times it may not be. Also, some markets will respond better on occasion to the 7-day moving average than the 10-day and 18-day moving averages, while at other times it will not. It is up to the individual trader to become knowledgeable about how and when to apply this feature. Most of the time, I focus on the 18-day and 10-day moving averages. While these are widely followed, in this case, that is exactly what I want to be focusing on.

The method I use for calculating the 7-day moving average is slightly different from the standard calculation used for the 10-day and 18-day. The 7-day is calculated from the *average daily price* (High + Low/2). I also use the average daily price for the 50-day moving average plotted on my daily trend/swing graphs.

The 10- and 18-day moving averages are calculated from the closing prices of the market in keeping with general practice, since these indicators are also used for support and resistance and are widely followed. We want to view them the same way that everyone else does because the market will often stop rising (meeting resistance) right at the 18-day moving average or stop falling (finding support) at that point. This is a self-fulfilling prophecy at work in the market, and it is one time that we want to know what everyone else knows. At other times, we want to know what everyone else does not know; this is the value of using proprietary and unique indicators such as those contained in the IMPA system.

Weekly Graph

We look for evidence of a new trend on our weekly charts (see example, Figure 5.6). We use these charts to detect, measure, and monitor the intermediate to longer-term trends. A four-week moving average and nine-week moving average are used on the weekly graphs. Each day, I update the weekly graphs right along with the daily graphs. You do not need to monitor all the weekly graphs each day, but they are useful, and having them available and up-to-date often comes in handy.

Commercial Open Interest Graph

The commercial open interest graph (Figure 5.7) illustrates and highlights the relationship between the commercials and open interest. This is not a

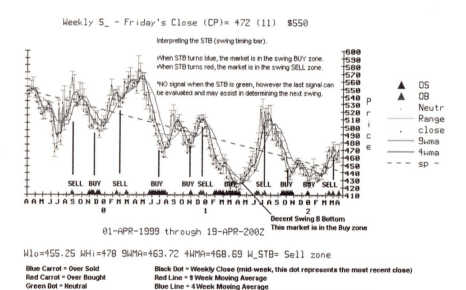

FIGURE 5.6 Weekly chart showing 9-week and 4-week moving averages.

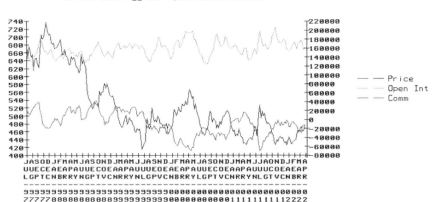

FIGURE 5.7 Commercial open interest graph showing the relationship of commercial position, open interest, and price.

graph that would be used daily or even weekly. By examining each market, I can visualize how the individual market is unique in relation to open interest and the commercials. As you become more seasoned in a particular market, you will be able to notice these relationships. In Figure 5.7, open interest is the line across the top. The line across the bottom is the commercial position, and the line that descends from the upper left to the far right is price.

STEP 6: ENTERING THE TRADE

At the sixth step of the IMPA trade setup, we are ready to explore how to enter a trade. For this to occur, the core criteria (discussed in Chapters 3 and 4) must be met:

- Trigger selection: Commercials holding an extreme one-sided position
- Public and/or funds holding an extreme (excessive) opposing position
- Proprietary RSI Indicator diverging in the direction of the IMPA selection
- Price structure showing signs and indications that a new trend is beginning

It is rarely in our best interest to buy or sell at the market. Timing is important, and this is what we focus on at this point. First I focus on identifying a logical stop, because without one I cannot determine the proper risk. I only enter the market when the stop and thus the risk is clear.

Once a trend is established, I can go with the market. In addition, I often look to enter at the point where it appears that the old trend is ending and the new trend is beginning. Since I never know for certain exactly when or where this transition will occur, I must always use a protective stop when entering. Although I have discussed stops, it bears repeating here: Unless I have a logical stop, I do not have an entry point. Once a logical stop is provided, I have a valid entry point with a valid risk. This is much better than simply pulling a monetary risk out of the air, so to speak. However, if the monetary risk provided by the logical stop is not acceptable (exceeding the 10 percent maximum rule). I will not adjust the monetary stop to lower the risk; instead, I will simply skip the trade or wait. Patience is key at this point.

Now, assume that the system is indicating a rising market. Therefore, we would buy on strength. An acceptable entry would be a move above the 18-day moving average for 2 days in a row. If the market has already proven itself (closing above a key area like the 18-day moving average for 2 consecutive days or more), and we missed the first leg up, there is no need to worry. We simply wait for the market to regress back to the same key area of support, such as the 18-day moving average or even the 10-day moving average, and enter there. It is common for prices to regress back to known neutral points during the early stages of a new trend.

The public, however, tends to chase markets up, buying the highs or selling the lows as a result of the emotional fear of missing that big move. To stay consistent and avoid emotional mistakes, professional traders follow plans and understand the importance of practicing patience as well as consistency. My technique for entry includes specific criteria, price patterns, and logical stops. The logical stops are the most important whether I am entering with the market (trend) or I am at a potential turning point. I may buy the market as it is moving to new highs or I may enter on a correction as the market regresses back to a neutral area, but in either case, I always must have a logical stop; otherwise I do not have an entry.

A sell strategy is the same except the orders are to sell. If we miss the first leg down, we simply and methodically wait for the market to regress back to a key area, such as the 18-day moving average.

If you are not ready or able to "pull the trigger" on a trade when the time is right, both bull and bear trends can easily get away. When this happens, wait for the regression back to a key area. Be careful not to chase markets. In addition, remember that markets tend to fall more quickly than they rise, which means a bear market can get away from you faster than a bull market. The exception is the commercial bull market, which tends to rise more quickly than noncommercial bull markets.

To recap, here are the key considerations when entering a trade:

Entry considerations: Understand the risk involved before you enter a trade. You do this by identifying the protective stop-loss areas based on the logical stop. The logical stop area may be around a pattern or a price. To precisely identify these areas, you must look more closely at the data, using charts and graphs. Stops based purely on individual monetary considerations are doomed to fail and are not recommended for position trades. Follow the 10 percent maximum rule (see section on Money Management, at the end of this chapter) on every entry consideration.

Measuring the risk: If you are not sure of the risk in a particular market, you can use equity graphs (discussed earlier in the chapter) to observe the day-to-day fluctuations in dollars per contract. This is what I teach new traders to use to understand what the largest loss or the largest profit in one day might be in any of the 44 markets studied on my web site. In addition, everyone has a threshold of what they can stand to make or lose in one day without it affecting their rationale. As an individual trader, you need to identify that threshold and stay within its boundaries, or you may end up becoming too emotional about gains, losses, and trading in general. Controlling gains is just as important as controlling and managing losses. In the beginning years, the gains a trader makes often leads to more trouble than losses.

The decision to enter the selection: Trigger analysis relies on the UCL/LCL statistical analysis to select the market(s) with the right conditions for a sustained move in one direction. The UCL/LCL graphs identify times when a significant imbalance exists between the two assumed commercial entities (producers and consumers). The imbalance in the futures market is either a reflection of supply and demand factors in the cash market or an early indication of a perceived change in the balance of supply and demand. We also use our IMPA, open interest and spread graphs to study and follow the intermarket relationships and other important factors that can enhance a selection or play an important role in the selection of certain trades such as spread and swings.

The decision to enter—timing: Each market and each setup condition will usually be a little different. Thus, we must approach each potential trade with somewhat of an open mind. Our schematic is simply history and what has occurred when certain conditions have existed in the past. The timing of an entry is done using daily price charts to identify logical stops, our technical data, equity graphs, and weekly graphs, along with other observations such as the number of days the market has closed up or down in a given number of past days and the day-of-week seasonal patterns. Trend analysis, trend reversal analysis, and pattern recognition analysis are done primarily using daily charts, weekly charts, and equity charts. Seasonal influences (discussed in depth in Chapter 7) can be studied on our seasonal price graphs. Day-of-week patterns can also be identified in the daily technicals and in the history of my daily activity reports, a unique automated report I devised that covers all markets and can be printed daily.

STEP 7: EXITING THE TRADE

Just as there were rules governing how and when to enter a trade, we have rules on how to manage and exit the trade.

The first is to *protect against loss* by using predetermined stops. Stops define the risk prior to entry. The stop must never be increased to allow for more risk. It can be adjusted to reduce risk, as well as adjusted back to the original stop if needed.

Second, *lock in a profit and reduce the risk of loss.* Use the 50 percent rule of reducing your position by half once you have made an initial profit objective. Profit objectives are determined based on the trader's skill at determining how far a market might run before it corrects or bounces. No one ever knows this for sure, however. Therefore, I recommend taking profits at different intervals, rarely do I recommend taking profits all at once.

Third, *manage your profit.* I use a wide variety of indicators to assist me in the analysis of a price trend and to determine the likely probability of a trend continuing or ending. Yet, I still leave money on the table. I have come to understand that money left on the table is the signature of a profitable trade. Expecting to enter at the bottom or top and exit at the top or bottom on every trade is simply unrealistic. I almost always get out of profitable trades early, and others do, too. The key, however, is to refrain from getting out of everything at once. Using trailing stops on multiple positions is the best method I know for capitalizing on big trends. If trading several positions, 50 percent profits can be taken more than once. For example, assume you are starting with eight positions. By taking off 50 percent, you will have four remaining positions. Then, take another 50 percent, leaving two. Finally, take another 50 percent, which leaves one position. This works very well in trending markets in which the IMPA has identified a significant turning point.

Once 50 percent profits are taken, the decision needs to be made on where to place the stop on the remaining 50 percent. I try to adjust the stop to breakeven or better on the first remaining 50 percent as quickly as possible to lock in the first 50 percent profit, while staying in the market with the remaining position. You must use careful judgment here. If the market has made a fairly substantial move and placing the stop to breakeven on the remaining 50 percent would be at an unreasonable level, you should tighten up the stop right away to lock in additional profits on the remaining 50 percent. This should be done on an ongoing basis as the trade continues to unfold and, perhaps, a new trend develops. The goal is to take as large a portion as possible out of the new trend with as many contracts as possible. However, having only one remaining contract is better than none. The 50 percent rule allows one to ride trends out further because markets always go farther than everyone believes they will. Resistance and support fails and markets make new highs or new lows. Over time, those using the 50 percent rule usually find that the bulk of their profits accumulate in the remaining 50 percent not in the initial 50 percent.

A few words of caution: You never want to raise or lower the stop by an amount that exceeds the original stop, which was determined *before* the position was entered. Generally, I do not raise or lower the stop on the remaining 50 percent to jeopardize the profits that were locked in from the first 50 percent. However, that option is open, and occasionally there is need for doing it. As long as the stop never exceeds (above or below) the original predetermined stop (not monetary, but technical), you are in compliance with the system.

New Stop Methodology

Our original position-management methodology used straight stops for both containing losses (an initial stop loss) and then managing the position, generally by placing the stop around the 18-day moving average to capture as much of the trend as possible. As discussed, use of straight stops intraday exposed the position to the risk of false stop-outs due to noise in the market. That noise includes excess price fluctuations and trading floor activity called *stop running*.

Both stop methods—initial and established—have gone through rigorous testing and improvement in recent years. Our current stop methods are variations of the original methodology. By testing different variations, the methods were modified to improve the performance of the IMPA position trading system. The result is improved performance on all our position and swing trading systems and strategies using these stop methods.

Our stop methods are essentially stand-alone systems, which means they can be applied to other trading systems, in addition to IMPA. Testing shows these new stop strategies improve the managing of our trades and therefore have a positive impact on the performance of our trading systems (increase our profits). These changes are also responsible for improvements in areas dealing with emotion and discipline, which are important but cannot be measured or back-tested as easily.

We have reduced the false intraday stop-outs caused by short-term spikes in price. These are frustrating to all traders. By decreasing their frequency, we have curtailed the frustration that often leads to error or poor performance because of compromised judgment. A significant improvement has been the reduction of false stop-outs from intraday spikes through the 18-day moving average. This kind of trading activity—which targets the 18-day moving average that is closely watched by traders—is often the result of stop running by floor traders. In the past, we have been stopped out on short-term (intraday) spikes through our stop. These stops may have been placed correctly, for example, around a contract high or low, key high or low, or above or below the 18-day moving average.

It may have seemed at the time that the floor traders knew the location of our stops; of course, they did not. Rather, prices can be pushed around during the day on a short-term basis and, as a result, our stops can get hit. Again, this doesn't necessarily mean that the stops were in the wrong place. They may have been perfectly placed on a technical basis, but by being active *intraday* they were exposed to short-term spikes up and down. These spikes also may be the result of noise that is not indicative of a larger, more meaningful movement—such as a large order executed during the quieter lunchtime trade, which has a bigger impact on the market than it otherwise would. It can cause prices to spike for a few minutes then return to their prespike level. If our stops are active all day, they will be exposed to the noise that can occur as mentioned (spikes and dips in price) as well as be exposed to the stop running of other traders, including floor traders.

If our stop is inside the daily price limit allowed by the exchange, then it is fair game on the floor and it can be hit on a short-term spike. To avoid this, you must get the stop away from this risk. We do this by using *stop close only* stops. These stops are based on closing prices rather than intraday prices. By the close, prices will likely have returned to fair value (as all participants are typically present for the close). The close is thus the most important price of the day, and it cannot be manipulated as easily as intraday prices can be.

Keep in mind that a stop close only order does not actually have to be placed. Some markets do not accept the traditional form of stop close only orders. In these markets, you can simply wait for the close and evaluate the closing price in relation to the stop. This is what I do. If the stop has been elected, then I would exit on the open of the next trading session (generally within the first 15 minutes of trading). When I refer to stop close only stops, I am generally referring to my method of waiting for the close and comparing the closing price to my stop. I then exit during the next session if my stop has been elected. I will occasionally still use the traditional form of stop close only orders in the markets that accept this type of order, but the majority of time I let the market close and compare the stop after the close.

By using stop close only stops, we not only avoid false stop-outs, but we also reduce the frequency of leaving additional money on the table. Leaving money on the table means getting out early and watching the market steam ahead without us.

Even though we made a profit, if the market keeps moving without us, our profit may be far less than it could have been. Face it—we traders all look at the money we "could have made" as a loss because we got out too early and weren't on board with a trade to profit from the larger move. This situation can be more emotionally devastating than simply having a loss. The distress and unnecessary stress that results can lead to poor judgment on subsequent positions. Therefore, the more we can reduce these vulnerabilities, the better we are likely to trade. The 50 percent rule obviously helps here as does using the closing price for the stop.

Trending Market Stop

Another type of stop to use while managing a trade is a trending market stop that moves with the market. This stop methodology is applied as the market is trending. A trending market stop is placed daily, following the 18-day moving average up or down. In other words, it is adjusted as we go with the trend. I also refer to this as the "established stop."

Confirmation of a trend is generally accepted (based on our methods) when the 10-day moving average crosses above or below the 18-day moving average with prices above or below both, and both moving averages are pointing in the direction of price (i.e., up in the case of a new upward trend and down in the case of a new downward trend). While this may seem straightforward and self-explanatory (and maybe even simple), the concept of the trending stop is important, nonetheless. I provide several examples of this in later chapters.

Money Management

Successful traders incorporate money management and risk control as part of their day-to-day business strategy. Too often, average traders tend to overlook money management. Without sound money management, even the best systems will fail. The amount of risk traders are exposed to must be predetermined for specific account sizes.

I advocate the "10 percent rule" for accounts ranging in size from $2,500 to $99,999 (see Risk per Trade, Table A, in the Appendix on p. 192). The percentage declines for larger accounts: 8 percent for $100,000, 7 percent for 200,000, 6 percent for 500,000 and 5 percent or less for $1,000,000— you should not risk 10 percent on a $1,000,000 account!

Using sound money management, you never want to risk more than 10 percent of your available risk capital (between $2,500 and $99,999) on any single trade. This is the maximum amount you ever want to risk. Ideally, you want your risk to be well below 10 percent. Once your account gets to a certain level, you should reduce this risk further, ranging between 8 percent and 5 percent (see Risk per Trade, Table B, in the Appendix on p. 192).

Risk management is vital to your long-term success. You must incorporate money management and risk control into your system. Every trade must have a predetermined stop-loss limit before you establish the trade. Stops are the most critical element of a successful trading system and must be strategically placed based on current and past market volatility and technical analysis.

Most unsuccessful traders use monetary stops that are based, instead, on what the trader is willing to risk. Remember, the market does not care what you are willing to risk.

Once the stop is determined, the monetary risk is established; the next step involves controlling this risk by using the 50 percent rule to capture profits on half of the position and then adjusting the stop to a breakeven or better level on the remaining 50 percent.

Cutting Losses, Letting a Profitable Trade Run— Using the 50 Percent Rule

As stated, we must always trade two or more contracts. This will help enforce one of the basic, yet extremely important, rules: Cut your losses and let your profitable trades run. However, sometimes emotions can cause traders to make the wrong decisions. They find themselves taking profitable trades off the table so they can bank the profit while holding onto losing positions in hopes that they will become profitable or at least will allow an exit at a better price. This approach is *wrong* and must be avoided as much as possible.

What I have found effective is trading an even number of contracts. When you initiate a trade using an even number of contracts, you are able to exit part of the position once you have made a nice profit and leave on 50 percent of the position so you can catch the few really big moves we get each year. These big moves pay for all the little losers that result from cutting losses short.

It is difficult to trade only a single contract at a time because you must keep your stop so far away from the market. This may cause profitable trades to turn into losing ones, which can be emotionally draining. If you follow the methodology of trading at least two contracts on each trade and taking a 50 percent profit at some juncture, you will reduce the number of trades that go from good to bad.

Your 50 percent profit objective can be a combination of a technical and a monetary objective. There is no strict rule here. In my position trades, I like to take profits on 50 percent of my position when I make enough to completely cover the initial margin. Sometimes I wait and take a little more; this just depends on the market and how well it is performing for my position.

The recent initial margin in soybean meal was $940. On a trade, I took a 50 percent profit when I had a $1,250 profit. After banking my 50 percent profit, I let the other half run using a breakeven stop or lower. At this point, I adjusted the stop on my remaining 50 percent to keep it where it needed to be in terms of market volatility and market activity while protecting some of the profit made on my initial 50 percent objective. Again there is no rule on when to take 50 percent profit. You can take the profit whenever you feel the need to do so. What is most important, however, is that you only take 50 percent while retaining your remaining 50 percent. Over time, I have found the bulk of my profits come from my remaining 50 percent. In a recent soybean trade, I took a 50 percent profit of $1,000 per contract while my remaining 50 percent went on to generate a $4,500 per contract profit.

Another important element of taking profits is paying yourself out of your trading account. When you make a good profit in your account, take a portion of it to pay yourself. Trading is a business, and as such, you must receive compensation for your work. This will also help prevent you from overtrading. The money in your trading account may not feel like "real money." By paying yourself, it becomes cash—real money—and it is from that trading account. The bottom line is to become a consistent trader. In whatever market you trade or system you use, consistency is paramount.

## CHAPTER 6

Plunger Patterns

As discussed, analysis of the weekly COT data is extremely valuable in identifying markets with specific, unique characteristics based on the positioning of the participants. The commercials are often called the "smart money," but they are only the so-called smart money at the major turning points. The day-to-day dominant market players and smart trading money tend to be the funds rather than the commercial hedgers. Commercial hedgers may be the most knowledgeable, but they are not the dominant force.

The commercial hedgers know certain things about the market that other traders, including the funds, do not know. The commercial hedgers are the most knowledgeable about supply and demand. That is why I call the commercial hedgers the *knowledgeable money* and the funds the *smart money*.

In previous chapters, I have also reviewed how I break the net-commercial category down into two entities that make up the net-commercial positions—I call these the commercial producers and commercial consumers. The producers are in the business of producing a particular commodity, whereas the consumers are in the business of consuming a particular commodity. Since these two entities are directly involved in the majority of the production and consumption, it stands to reason that they are the most knowledgeable about the supply and demand. We call this knowledge the *fundamentals*.

NET-COMMERCIAL AND NET-FUND POSITIONS

I use the net-commercial position along with my statistical reference points (UCL/LCL and EUCL/ELCL) as my core trigger selection indicators. When these reference points are penetrated, or when they are very close to being penetrated, it indicates that an unusual condition exists. We will only witness EUCL and ELCL penetration 0.27 percent of the time—it is a rare event. These unusual circumstances also correlate very strongly with the major turning points in the market; the unusual circumstances tend to lead the turns.

Further studies between historic price trends and size of the individual market participant positions reveal that once the size of the speculative (fund and/or large trader) market position has reached a certain threshold, the subsequent outcome (price direction) is much more predictable due to the inevitable unwinding of a large one-sided position. Once I identify a market that is exhibiting such a condition, I then focus on the price structure, price patterns, and price behavior to help identify the point in time that the unwinding is beginning to influence prices (meaning, it is beginning to act as the dominant influence in a sense). I often refer to the opposing fund position as the fuel for the trend. Sometimes this fuel burns evenly and consistently until the position is fully unwound and other times it burns more erratically, flickering on and off as if someone is purposely turning off the ignition and turning it back on. The result is a choppy directionless market.

The net-fund position can also be broken down further into its individual components of long and short positions just as the net-commercial position is broken down into commercial *consumer* longs and commercial *producer* shorts. When I break the net-fund position down, I simply break it into longs, shorts, and spreads. I have found that the more sophisticated funds tend to trade against the trends, and their positions are the most unusual since the net-fund position as a whole tends to be a trend-following position. Thus, there are times when it is enlightening to monitor the opposing fund position (which can be the long or short position, whichever is opposite of the current price trend).

In all cases, whether commercials or funds, the statistically unusually large positions tend to lead significant market turns. Once I identify a market that is exhibiting any of these unusual conditions, as defined by the size of the participant position and their orientation to the price trend, I then focus on the price structure. I begin employing traditional technical analysis along with pattern recognition analysis (including plunger patterns) to help identify the turn in the market so as to be positioned with a new trend.

I may see the net-commercial UCL/LCL penetration a week or several months in advance of the actual trend change. This always varies, which is

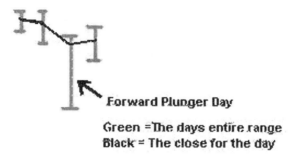

Forward Plunger Day

Green = The days entire range
Black = The close for the day

FIGURE 6.1 Examples of forward plunger patterns.

why it is necessary to combine various technical tools with the COT indicators. These tools include pattern recognition, seasonal studies, and traditional technical analysis. These tools, together with the COT indicators, enable me to both identify the upcoming move and to capitalize on it by capturing a portion of the new trend as it unfolds. I then enter and manage my position using my entry techniques, rules for managing risk and identifying the logical stops, and then the 50 percent rule and trailing stop methodology.

Let's start by discussing *plunger patterns.* Plungers are one of the tools I use with the IMPA system. They are end-of-day price patterns that can be used as springs to enter larger IMPA setups or simple swing trades.

There are two types of plunger:

1. *Forward plunger:* May occur at or near short-term lows (sign of capitulation), and occasionally at major lows (see Figure 6.1).

2. *Reverse plunger:* May occur at or near short-term highs (sign of a blow-off high), and occasionally at major highs (see Figure 6.2).

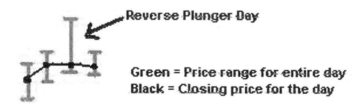

Reverse Plunger Day

Green = Price range for entire day
Black = Closing price for the day

FIGURE 6.2 Examples of reverse plunger patterns.

PLUNGER CRITERIA

The criteria for the daily plunger are that the market must meet or exceed a new 10-day high or 10-day low and then close in the opposite direction and in the top or bottom 30 percent of that day's range. The entire price range for that day must also be at least one-third of an average day's range for that market. This eliminates plungers with extremely small intraday ranges. The criteria for weekly plungers are essentially the same, except we evaluate the data on a weekly basis as opposed to a daily basis. Just as the close of each day is the most important price for a daily plunger pattern, the close on Friday is the most important price of the week for a weekly plunger. Daily plunger patterns, on average, are expected to produce a short-term market reaction of one to three days. This is what I define as the average yield of a daily plunger. The weekly plungers are a little trickier to evaluate, but overall their yield is essentially the same, except on a weekly basis instead of a daily basis. The best weekly plungers by far are the ones that are also embedded with daily plungers in the same direction.

A *forward plunger* occurs when the market meets or exceeds its 10-day low and then reverses intraday and closes in the upper 30 percent of the day's range. A market's full range is 0 to 100 percent, with the low of the day corresponding to 0 percent and the high of the day corresponding to 100 percent. (Thus, a market that finishes on its high finishes at 100 percent and a market that finishes on its low finishes at 0 percent.) A *reverse plunger* occurs when a market meets or exceeds its 10-day high and then reverses intraday and closes in the lower 30 percent of the day's range.

APPLYING THE THREE-DAY RULE TO PLUNGERS

The market must follow through in the direction of the plunger pattern (up with a forward plunger or down with a reverse plunger) within three days following its formation. In the case of a forward plunger, the market must exceed the plunger day high within three days following the plunger; otherwise, the plunger expires. In the case of a reverse plunger, the market must exceed the plunger day low within three days following the plunger formation, or the plunger expires.

During the three-day period following a plunger formation, the opposing plunger day high or low must not be exceeded on a closing basis. A forward plunger low must not be exceeded on a closing basis, just as a reverse plunger high must not be exceeded on a closing basis. If either occurs during the three-day period, the plunger is considered to have failed. It is possible for a secondary plunger to occur within three days of the initial plunger formation. In that case, the new lows and highs of the secondary plunger pattern take precedence over the prior plunger day high and low.

APPLYING THE HIGH/LOW RULE TO PLUNGERS

The high and low that are put in the day a plunger pattern is formed are very important. In the case of a forward plunger, the low on the formation day becomes substantial support or what I refer to as the logical stop area (see following section). If this low is exceeded on a closing basis, the plunger is no longer valid. In the case of a reverse plunger, the high struck on the day the reverse plunger forms becomes serious resistance, and therefore a logical stop area. If that high is exceeded on a closing basis, the plunger will no longer be valid.

Another important signal is the *failed plunger pattern.* Plunger patterns that immediately fail indicate a potential trade in the opposite direction. A forward plunger that immediately fails is often a good sell signal, and a reverse plunger that immediately fails is often a good buy signal.

TRADING WITH PLUNGER PATTERNS

As with any trading system, no pattern works 100 percent of the time. Sometimes plungers will occur, and the market will move opposite to what we anticipated. This can happen with all identifiable price patterns and is normal. If it happens during the three-day period that a plunger is active, an opposing signal is created.

One of the benefits of identifying plunger formations and using them as entry points is that they provide logical stop protection. If a forward plunger identifies a turning point, then the low of the plunger should not be penetrated. If the market moves higher following a forward plunger day, the low of that plunger is the logical area to place a protective sell stop as you enter a long (buy) position (see Figure 6.3).

With a reverse plunger, the high of the plunger should not be penetrated if the market is turning. The high of the plunger is the logical place for a protective buy stop as you enter a short (sell) position (see Figure 6.4).

You can take this stop placement a step further and use a stop close only type of protective stop. That means the market would need to close above or below the plunger day high/low to trigger the protective stop. The benefit of using this stop is that it allows you to avoid being stopped out on noise or other short-term fluctuations.

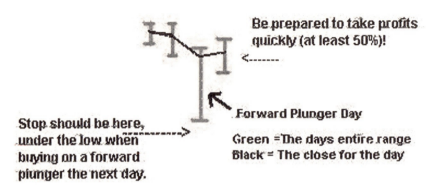

FIGURE 6.3 Stop placement on a forward plunger should be at the low of the plunger.

When a plunger pattern has been identified in a market, entry for the trade is easy to understand. As Figure 6.5 illustrates, a trader can enter a position as soon as the pattern is discovered, but must enter before a significant move has occurred. Additionally, the trade must be entered before the market turns back the other way, taking out the plunger high or low. While trading on plunger patterns, I avoid buying or selling gap-opens or sharp moves immediately following this pattern. Market orders, limit orders, and stop orders can be used for entry.

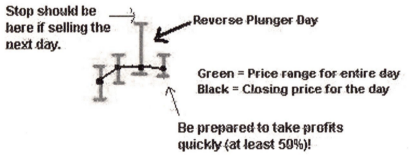

FIGURE 6.4 Stop placement on a reverse plunger should be at high of the plunger.

SPMAR2 01-FEB-2002 Open@ 1129, CP=1123.4 (-7) inside $-1750

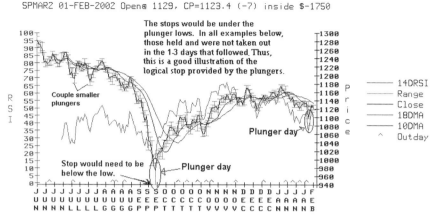

Tlo=1118.5 THi=1129.7 18MA=1134.75 10MA=1125.13 RSI=45.365019

FIGURE 6.5 Plunger patterns can act as "springs" to enter the market, buying after a forward plunger is formed and selling after a reverse plunger.

Trade Examples

Figures 6.6 through 6.9 show examples of recent plunger patterns as recorded on our proprietary price graphs. These examples contain my notes and observations and were extracted from my evening reports to clients. I left these notes on the graphs because this information may be useful to readers of this book.

In the aftermath of the September 11, 2001, tragedy, the stock market fell precipitously. Although other factors, including a weakening economy and corporate scandals in the headlines, contributed to the decline in the equity market, the events of September 11 and the days immediately following caused a sharp sell-off in stocks. The equity market would remain under pressure for months to come due mainly to economic factors, but Figure 6.6 shows how the immediate oversold conditions in S&P futures created a forward plunger that is also characteristic of a *washout bottom.*

Figure 6.7 shows a classic reverse plunger pattern (marked "X1") in wheat futures, signaling a top had been put in the market. This sell signal was also confirmed by two other technical indicators, as the 10-day and 18-day moving averages (which lag the market) turned decidedly lower as well.

Forward and reverse plungers can also be dramatic, highlighting extreme overbought or oversold conditions at the point of a blow-off top (with a reverse plunger) or at the point of capitulation (with a forward plunger). These patterns can occur just prior to a short-term change in the trend (or reversal) and sometimes longer-term as well. Consider the example in

The September 21st 2001 forward plunger in the S&P is also characteristic of a "washout bottom" in the stock market. Not all forward plungers are characteristic of "washout bottoms". This bottom occurred in conjunction with my traditional Q4 bias. We observed almost the same thing again in July 2002.

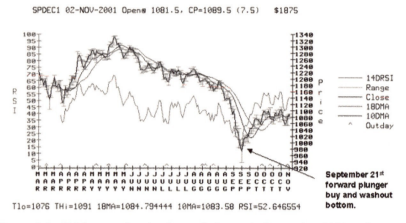

Figure 6.6 S&P futures showing forward plunger in September 2001, indicative of a washout bottom.

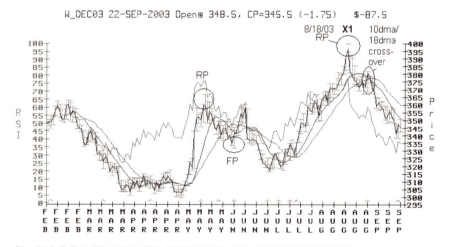

FIGURE 6.7 Reverse plunger patterns in wheat futures.

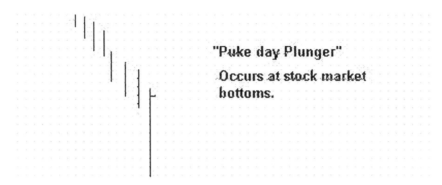

FIGURE 6.8 Washout or "puke-day plunger" shows dramatic bottom formed in the market.

Figure 6.8 of what is called a "puke-day plunger" in trader vernacular (also known as a "washout plunger"). These descriptive phrases tell exactly what is happening in the market: Traders are dumping positions to get out, regardless of price. Market activity not only reflects the current technical and fundamental factors, but also reflects the current emotional health of the market. Emotions such as euphoria and fear can be the cause

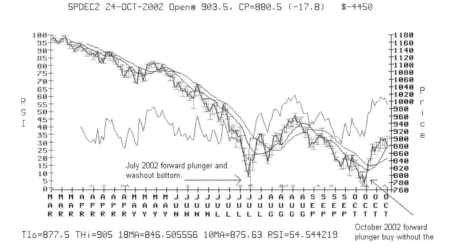

FIGURE 6.9 Two forward plungers in S&P futures in July and October 2002.

of the plungers. Fear can drive prices lower to the point of capitulation, which is where fear and greed meet!

Figure 6.9 shows two forward plungers in S&P futures, indicating buy setups. In Figure 6.9, notice the first forward plunger in July 2002 with the dramatic washout characteristics preceding the upward move that lasted through mid-August. The October 2002 forward plunger formed as the market retested the July lows. The plunger was less dramatic, lacking the same washout characteristics as the July forward plunger. That buy signal was also confirmed as the moving averages turned upward shortly thereafter.

Plunger Patterns and Stops

Plunger patterns can also provide an early entry point into an IMPA position trade. With a plunger pattern, you not only have an entry point, but you also have a stop that can provide a lower monetary risk on the initial entry. The reason is that the entry tends to be in close proximity to the stop, thus creating a lower monetary-risk entry point versus a later-stage entry, which would occur when the price moved above the moving averages or the moving averages crossed. These mature entry points tend to require wider stops versus the early entry points that the plunger patterns provide.

The mature entry points can be more reliable than the earlier plunger entries into IMPA-selected markets. The trade-off is lower monetary risk for less reliability. When the trade does work out, and if it is an IMPA selection, the profits from the successful trades will likely pay for the smaller losses on previous failed attempts to enter a market early on a plunger pattern.

Price Patterns

We pay attention to several classic price pattern formations when looking at price graphs. The following three patterns are helpful interpretative signals to gauge the setup of a trend, as well as stop placement:

1. *The "W" bottom:* The "W" forms as the market puts in a bottom, trades higher, retests the low area, and then trades higher a second time. (See Figure 6.10.) This is a common characteristic in the soft commodities (such as sugar and cotton), as well as energy, grains, and stock indices.

2. *The "V" bottom:* This price formation occurs when a market trades lower and then reverses sharply. (See Figure 6.11.) This is a common characteristic in the livestock futures markets.

3. *The "M" top:* The third price formation is known as the "M" top, which is essentially the opposite of a "W" bottom. This pattern forms when

"W" Bottom Formation

Common characteristic of the softs, energy, grains and stock indices.

FIGURE 6.10 W formation.

the market puts in a high, then trades lower, retests the high, and then trades lower a second time. (See Figure 6.12.) The "M" top is common in many markets.

TRADE MANAGEMENT WITH STOPS

There are two basic environments in which to use a stop to manage position trades. The first is the initial phase and the second is the established phase of a trend.

The initial phase is the time that the market is potentially establishing a new trend. Volatility tends to be high as old positions (based on the old

V-bottom

Common price characteristic of the livestock market (Hogs Bellies & Cattle)

FIGURE 6.11 V formation.

"M" Top formation. Common in most markets.

FIGURE 6.12   M formation.

trend) are being unwound and new positions (in the direction of the emerging trend) are being established. Because of these conditions, we typically need to have a wider stop, compared with later (established) phases when the trend is already in place.

As far as determining the specific placement of the stop during the initial phase, if the new trend is emerging based on the IMPA criteria, I require the price to close above/below the 18-day moving average for two consecutive days. During this initial phase, the stops need to be above/below contract high/lows, or an "X" day high/low (which could be the 10-day, 20-day, 50-day, and so forth, depending on the market conditions). If the monetary risk based on this stop placement is too high, a trader can elect to wait for a possible pattern to form, such as a plunger. The plunger then provides a logical stop that is closer to the entry.

I stay with the initial stop until the new trend has been established. There are several ways to determine when that has occurred (e.g., when the 10-day moving average crosses above/below the 18-day moving average and both moving averages are pointing in the same direction). Once we are in an established environment, the purpose of the stop moves from loss containment to profit protection.

As the trade matures, and after a 50 percent profit has been taken, the position is managed using trailing stops. One way to accomplish this is to use the 2-day, 18-day moving average rule. In an uptrend, the stop would be placed below the 18-day moving average and would be activated if the market closed for two consecutive days below that level. In a downtrend, the reverse would occur.

Assume that the market closes above/below the 18-day moving average for two consecutive days and you are stopped out of your trade. Now you are observing the market to decide whether a new opposing trend is emerging, or if it is possible to get back into the market once the existing trend resumes. One way to confirm that the trend is ending is if the 10-day moving average crosses back above or below the 18-day moving average, with both pointing in the opposite direction of the old trend (after an uptrend, the two moving averages are now pointing downward). If that is the case, and both have crossed, it is confirmation that the trend is over.

If that does not occur, you could look to reenter the market on a pattern the same way you would during the initial phase, or you could reenter when the closing price moves back above the 18-day moving average for two consecutive days. The lows/highs of the correction would then provide the logical stop for the reentry, just as the contract high/low provides the logical stop for the initial entry when a new trend is believed to be beginning. As the trend reestablishes itself, you would switch to an established stop using the 18-day moving average as before, after taking 50 percent profits on the newly established position.

As the trend continues in an established environment, the trailing stop is moved up/down and under/above the 18-day moving average to protect profits and to allow profits to grow. You would exit when the market closes above/below the 18-day moving average for two consecutive days.

An example of this occurred in the 10-year notes. A forward plunger formation occurred in March 2005. At that time, the IMPA was already bullish. The forward plunger low coincided with the contract low. This combination provides a strong initial logical stop. As this market moved higher following the plunger and in the direction of the IMPA setup, we moved to using an established stop. We did this after the market moved above the 18-day moving average. Then, in early May, the market had a correction back below the 18-day moving average for two days in a row, and we were stopped out. The 10-day moving average, however, did not cross below the 18-day moving average, which would have signaled the end of the uptrend. Instead, within a few days the market closed back above the 18-day moving average for two days in a row, which enabled traders to get back in the market as the trend resumed. The market continued higher until June 3, when we had a reverse plunger, signaling the end of the uptrend. After that, the market closed down for six consecutive days.

IMPA SELECTION FADING SYSTEM

Another strategy that can be used as part of the IMPA methodology is a *fading system* that is based primarily on the most significant price indicator: the trend itself. This system also takes advantage of the behavior of the market participants, particularly during the late stages of a trend. This phase is often associated with what appears to be the stubborn persistence of the existing trend. A new IMPA selection may have been identified at this point, but the new trend has not fully emerged yet because all the criteria have not been met. The IMPA system is very clear, and all its requirements must be fully satisfied before a position can be established in the direction of the new trend (such as the rule concerning two consecutive closes above/below the 18-day moving average).

During this phase, the old trend is still being supported. This is when a "fade position" can be established, based on traditional technical analysis, and it may persist until all the IMPA trade selection criteria are met. If/when that happens, the position can and in most cases should be reversed.

The IMPA Selection Fading System takes advantage of an optimum time when the majority of systems are already in a mature trend. Typically, that means they are adding to or reestablishing positions in the old trend. For the want of better words, the trend is being kept alive by participation support. It will take a significant development to change the sentiment at this phase, but as always, something will eventually occur to satisfy this necessity. However, the time that this takes can vary substantially. We have seen and measured instances when an IMPA selection is active, yet the old trend persists with almost stubborn defiance for many months.

Unless something drastically changes, the trend can and likely will continue for a little longer after the initial IMPA selection and before *all* criteria are satisfied. Again, this occurs toward the end of a trend based on the level of participation by the three core IMPA components:

1. Commercials
2. Funds (noncommercials, speculators)
3. Smaller speculators

Based on the data and what we know about trends and cycles, we can look back on a trend as an entity that goes through different phases. These phases can be measured in the behavior of price and in the participation by the three main IMPA components.

The phases of a trend can be described as:

- The establishment of a new trend, which can be volatile.
- The beginning leg of a new trend. Systems help establish a trend.
- The mid-point saturation, when the trend is widely recognized and mature.
- Late-stage trend, when systems support the trend.
- The ending of the trend, which can also be volatile.

Of these phases, the second and the fourth—the beginning leg and the late-stage trend—often exhibit large moves in the direction of the trend.

The existing price trend is the most important indication of future direction. In simple terms, if the trend is up, then an uptrend is likely to continue until that trend ends. It is important to note that the ending of one trend and the beginning of a new one often occur with an IMPA selection in the direction of the new trend (not the old). The old trend will often exhibit additional strength as it nears its end. We see this in the short term (such as in the washout conditions described earlier). In addition, we see it over the longer term through acceleration. Because of this tendency, there is an opportunity to take positions in the direction of the mature trend before it ends.

A trend is likely mature (not always, but more likely than not) when the IMPA data show an extreme accumulation of fund and/or small speculator positions in the direction of the trend. These participants are generally trend followers and trend generators. When they are holding extreme (large, one-sided) positions and the commercials are holding the opposing position (also extreme), an IMPA selection is usually generated.

This is only *one component* of the IMPA setup to be completed. Before we can enter a position based on the IMPA setup, *all* criteria must be satisfied. Thus, there is an opportunity to establish a position *with the existing trend* when only the IMPA selection is identified, but before all the other criteria are satisfied. At this time, there should not be any significant RSI divergence, and the old trend must remain in place as measured by the closing price in comparison to the 18-day moving average (with the 2-day, 18-day moving average rule applying).

Position Management of Fade Trades

The IMPA Fade System takes trades in the direction of the prevailing/current price trend when the IMPA criteria for a new trend have not completed setting up. These positions can be reversed when the IMPA is fully set up (as discussed). As always, the price trend is the most important indication of short-term price direction. This strategy focuses on establishing positions with existing trends and fading the IMPA selection until the selection is fully set up (which means meeting all criteria). At that time, as always, we would then go with the IMPA setup.

## CHAPTER 7

Seasonal Influences

There are certain markets in which seasonal influences are crucial. An obvious example is soybeans, which are planted in the spring and harvested in the fall. In this market, seasonal influences—from a wet spring to a hot, dry summer—could potentially affect the price. Understanding these influences helps me filter IMPA trade setups.

To succeed at trading commodities, one must have some understanding of seasonal influences. That is precisely why I have developed in-depth seasonal studies, along with the analysis that supports my IMPA methodology. As I mentioned previously, technical indicators or COT data alone is not enough. Only when everything is packaged together and viewed by an experienced person does it work. Experience or a lack of experience is the reason two traders viewing the same market conditions and using the same strategies can have two different results: One has experience and the other does not.

SEASONAL BEHAVIOR OF THE COMMERCIALS

I use seasonal information and insights as supportive data to complement the IMPA system. This allows me to take the traditional approach of price seasonality and combine it with the positioning of the commercial participants, which tend to hedge on a seasonal basis. I have found that those markets with a high degree of seasonal behavior usually are the best markets for IMPA position trades. This is because the commercials are the driving force in seasonal price behavior.

The commercials will hedge consistently, year after year, based on the season. Commercial soybean producers will hedge by selling short during the times of year when supply is low and prices tend to be higher. Commercial consumers will adjust their hedging to exploit those times when supply is plentiful and prices, therefore, are the softest. Thus, the seasonal price patterns correlate strongly with the positions held by the commercials. The trading behavior of the commercials is crucial to understanding the seasonality of these markets. They are the big buyers and sellers, and their trading behavior drives the seasonal influences.

SEASONAL GRAPH

I apply the same discipline and statistical methods to seasonal analysis that I devote to my COT analysis. I have leveraged my understanding and experience with the individual market participant analysis (IMPA) and have applied it to seasonal price behavior. By doing so, I have discovered several interesting correlations.

As might be expected, I found a correlation between the net-commercial position and price seasonality. I use this correlation to confirm seasonal price behavior and have developed specific indicators and graphs to help exploit the relationship for trading purposes.

The behavior of the commercial participants is crucial because they are the most consistent in their trading activity. They are hedging their physical positions—getting into and out of the market—at specific times of the year. They are not driven by emotion.

One way to view this is with a seasonal graph. Figure 7.1 shows the seasonality in price structure and net commercial positions in soybean futures based on monthly averages, from January 1983 through May 2005. The numbers (1 to 12) at the bottom correspond to each month (1 = January, 2 = February, and so forth). The left (Y-1) axis represents the commercial position, either long (positive numbers) or short (negative numbers). The right (Y-2) axis represents price.

Admittedly, this graph requires some interpretation, but the insights that can be derived from it are important. The squares represent the net-commercial position for the individual months going back to 1983 (all the Januarys, all the Februarys, and so forth). The line with the diamonds shows the mean price for each month. Looking at the price line, we can see, based on the mean of each month over time, that typically the highs are in May and June (months 5 and 6) and the lows are in October (month 10).

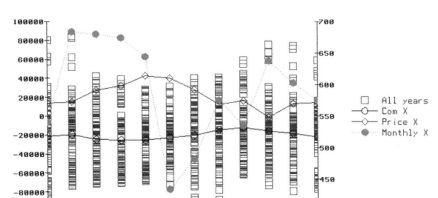

FIGURE 7.1 Seasonal graph in soybean futures.

Many traders only look at the seasonal trend of the average price for a commodity over time (usually several years). There are problems with this approach because of the skewing of price data from year to year based on changing market conditions from one year to the next. One year, the price for a particular commodity may be high compared with a previous year for reasons pertaining to the supply and demand for that particular year. A supply issue may have resulted in an unusually high price for the commodity during that particular year. The very next year, the supply issue may no longer exist and prices may be substantially less as a result. These two years now have very different prices. If the two prices are simply averaged together, a new price will result that may never have occurred in the market and is simply the result of averaging prices together. Thus, simply averaging prices together over a period of time to build a seasonal price structure has limits to its usefulness and accuracy. It can, however, provide some information.

What I have found to be a much better representation of seasonal price behavior is to measure the average net price change from month to month over a long period (several years). This method can identify specific months that tend to be more volatile than others, and it can also identify strong months versus weaker months. When this is correlated with the price structure and further correlated with the commercial positions, it can become a useful tool for tracking seasonal price behavior. My own seasonal price graphs contain this measure along with commercial data. I look at the average price for each month over several years as well as the average point gains and point losses for each month over many years. I plot this information on a graph along with the net-commercial positions for each month. The information is presented in a sequential month-to-month manner. In good seasonal markets, I find the average net-commercial position correlates in the usual leading fashion with seasonal price changes. If the price of a particular commodity tends to hit a seasonal high during June, we might see the net-commercial position averaging a large net-short position during May, ahead of the anticipated seasonal high.

The solid dots in the seasonal graph connected by a dotted line represent the average point gains and average point losses by month, as described. What is important to note about the solid dots is that they are separate points unique to each month. They are not connected or related to one another and should not be viewed as such. These points are a depiction of the seasonal average point gain or point loss for each month. In Figure 7.1, the month of June (month 6) shows the largest mean loss in points. This graph is of soybeans, and it is not unusual for June to be a volatile month in soybeans for specific reasons that repeat just about every June. That is because U.S. soybeans are planted at the same time every year and mature through various stages of development at or about the same time every year. This creates a seasonal pattern.

The line with the open circle (in the middle of the graph) shows the mean net commercial position for each month. The fluctuations from month to month are subtle, but over-time, certain patterns have emerged. In May (month 5) and June (month 6), the net-commercial position has a history of being closer to the LCL versus the months of September (month 9) and October (month 10). During these months, the net-commercial position has a history of gravitating toward the UCL. These subtle characteristics correspond to the seasonal price highs and lows in soybeans. The seasonal behavior is directly related to more active commercial hedging in the months corresponding to the planting and harvesting of crops. The seasonal price behavior in soybeans is a key factor driving my spring soybean options trade (buy) in February/March and the fall soybean options trade (buy) in August/September. I developed the spring and fall soybean trades using this data and my own observations over the years. Seasonal influences affect this market, which can be seen not only in price structure, but also in commercial activity.

The seasonal graph displays a visual connection between seasonal commercial hedging and seasonal price behavior. The net commercial positions are at the highest (net long) when prices are at the lowest, and the net commercial positions are at the lowest (net short) when prices are the highest, on a seasonal basis.

SEASONAL SOYBEAN OPTION TRADES

The seasonal price behavior in soybeans has provided me with many trading opportunities over the years. I have identified soybean options trades that will profit from the normal seasonal behavior in the market during spring and fall. These trades are based on seasonal influences, as well as other considerations such as when option prices are favorable (low), providing a low-risk trade, leveraging the seasonal behavior of the futures market. This particular trade is usually separate from my IMPA position trades.

The fall 2003 soybean options trade was particularly noteworthy because—for the first time in my records—it coincided with an IMPA buy in soybeans. This resulted in an explosive move upward. In this particular trade, for example, I sold options for $4,800 after having paid only $525 each for them.

This trade example also illustrates the power of combining one method with another (such as IMPA with a seasonal approach). Instead of conflicting with each other, the two systems result in a combined effort that creates a more potent overall strategy. IMPA does not necessarily compete with other systems and strategies. The IMPA criteria can be used in conjunction with other systems and strategies, resulting in a more significant outcome, as I experienced in August 2003 when the seasonal soybean trade coincided with an IMPA buy.

As Figure 7.2 shows, the IMPA buy selection occurred when the proprietary UCL (upper commercial limit) indicator was penetrated in August 2003. This coincided with my timing for the fall seasonal soybean options trade.

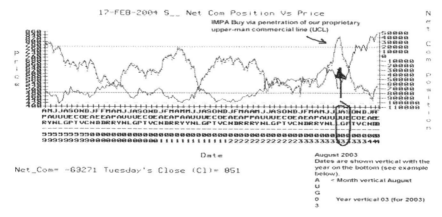

FIGURE 7.2 Soybean graph showing IMPA buy selection in August 2003.

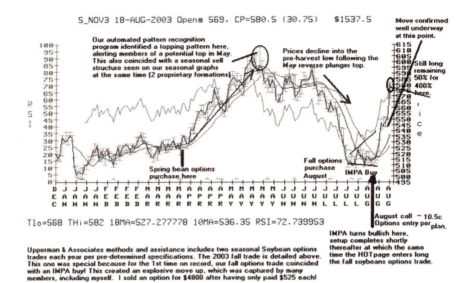

FIGURE 7.3 Spring soybean trade in March 2003.

Normally, the soybean options trade is determined by seasonal influences alone driven by commercial hedging activity contained inside the UCL and LCL. This was the basis of the spring soybean options trade that occurred in late March 2003 (see Figure 7.3).

As Figure 7.3 also shows, the spring options trade extended through mid-May 2003 when my automated pattern-recognition program identified a topping pattern. This signaled a potential top in the market, as indicated by a reverse plunger formation in May. This coincided with a seasonal sell structure seen on my seasonal graphs through two proprietary formations.

After the sell signal was generated in May, prices declined into the pre-harvest low. In late July and into early August, as I began studying the market for the fall soybean options trade, the IMPA buy setup began unfolding. In early August, the IMPA turned bullish, and the IMPA setup completed shortly thereafter. At the same time, the seasonal fall soybean options trade was gearing up. Putting the two together produced a powerful buy signal combination.

After the August 2003 buy signal, prices stayed above the key 18-day moving average for the entire time while the market trended higher, as illustrated in Figure 7.4. The 18-day moving average is the primary basis for most of my proprietary technical indicators, and I use it for trailing stops as well. Once the 18-day moving average was penetrated, I considered the

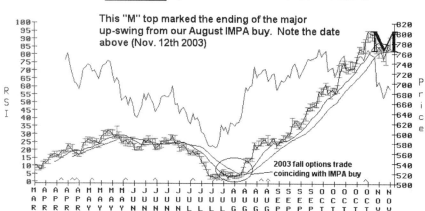

S_JAN04 12-NOV-2003 Open@ 769, CL=770 (-5.75) $-287.5

Tlo=768 THi=792 18MA=769.569444 10MA=775.125 RSI=58.635213

Notice how price stayed above the 18dma for the entire time the market was trending higher.

FIGURE 7.4   Prices stayed above the 18-day moving average throughout the entire uptrend from the August IMPA buy setup.

structure broken, although prices did eventually go a little higher. The next phase up proved to be much choppier, as prices moved back and forth through the 18-day moving average, eventually moving lower.

Finally, on November 12, 2003, an "M" top marked the end of the major upswing from the August IMPA buy.

Figure 7.5 gives a different view of the trade. This weekly graph shows the magnitude of the move from IMPA buy setup in August through the exit in November.

The lesson to take away from the fall 2003 soybean options trade is the power of combining systems, in this case a seasonal option trade with the IMPA buy setup. The two methodologies complemented each other and confirmed the potential for a significant trade.

PATIENCE AND INSTINCT

As these seasonal trade examples illustrate, trading requires patience. Sometimes I have to be patient for months, waiting for the right trade setup. As I tell both new and experienced traders, there is not always an opportunity to profit on a trade because markets can—and almost always do—move in

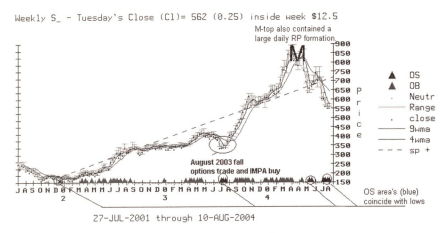

Weekly S_ - Tuesday's Close (Cl)= 562 (0.25) inside week $12.5

27-JUL-2001 through 10-AUG-2004

Wlo=560.5 WHi=575 9WMA=645.03 4WMA=576.06 W_STB= Buy zone

FIGURE 7.5 Weekly graph shows magnitude of move.

a random fashion. Therefore, traders must wait and be patient, knowing what to look for and having a predetermined plan ready to go.

Inexperienced traders tend to focus on trying to pick bottoms, buying and then exiting on emotion. While observing this activity, it is possible to note changes in the market—including the overall crowd opinion and attitude (which is easily monitored through Internet chat rooms and public message boards). As a rule of thumb, I have found that when the majority of inexperienced traders have finally become discouraged trying to pick a bottom, the market is probably closer to the bottom. This is based on simple observation and the understanding that comes from being an experienced position trader and from having experienced the emotional turbulence that all new traders endure.

When you have seen certain things occurring time and time again, you know what it means. This is where instinct in trading comes into play. Anyone with a little programming knowledge and a basic understanding of statistics can plug some parameters into a computer and trade off the probabilities. But that seldom produces the large profits everyone is looking for, particularly the smaller traders. In fact, it often produces mediocre or poor results, depending on the market. The key is to combine the value and insight of mathematics with solid instinct. This enables a professional trader to trade a larger position when instinct dictates it, as well as smaller positions when instinct dictates more caution over increasing risk.

Instinct is developed through the experience of observing a market. You know what they say are the three most important things in real estate:

location, location, location. Extending that maxim to trading, the three most important things are observation, observation, observation. This is what builds market knowledge and instinct over time. And with instinct comes the insight of knowing when to take a trade that your system has generated and, more importantly, how many contracts to trade. Call it discretion if you like; that is what it is. People like me are really *discretionary traders* as opposed to purely system traders. Unless you accept, without question, *every* trade a system produces, you are taking a discretionary approach.

What separates beginning traders from experts is experience. Through observation, we gain knowledge about the market and how it behaves. Over time, this knowledge shapes a trader's instinct, and eventually instinct becomes just as important as mechanical indicators. A successful trader must learn to adapt to all sorts of changing conditions and be able to recognize an authentic opportunity through all the variables (including variables outside the mathematics that determine the probabilities). And then, even with the best instinct, the random nature of the markets means that we will not always achieve the desired results. That is where money management and loss control come into play.

Waiting for the Setup

As I studied the market prior to entering the spring 2005 soybean trade—which I usually enter during February or March—patience and instinct came into play. I liked that the market had been wearing down the "bottom-pickers" for several months as the price continued to decline and then went nowhere on the upside. (This wears on the psyche of inexperienced traders who try to pick bottoms.) This is one of the things we often see ahead of a spring turn in soybeans. In addition, I am focusing on the premium and the implied volatility of the soybean options (see soybean options trade specifications, later in this chapter).

The weakness in early 2005 had been expected following the record-size soybean crop in 2004. I expected that the weak trend was likely to subside in the near future as the spring planting period neared. Even though it still was not time to plant, producers were already deciding what to plant (e.g., corn or soybeans). In addition, they would be thinking about such things as the weather, which had been a bit unusual in recent months and even extreme at times in certain locations throughout the growing regions. If this continued into the spring, it could possibly cause planting delays. Even if that did not happen, I knew that the fear of upcoming weather problems—as well as high costs for fertilizers and energy and other considerations—could play a role in halting the decline in price in the near term. This could spur many things, most notably short-covering by the funds. Furthermore, the size of the South American crop had been reduced because of weather problems. (During the winter months in the United States, the South American soybean crop is entering into the harvest period.)

At this time, the funds were extremely short—in fact, at a record level. I noted in my regular IMPA update posted on my web site that the net-fund position had just dipped to a new extreme short position. It is not unusual to see an extreme dip in the net-fund position right before an important low is struck. My instinct and experience were telling me that we were getting near that low.

The implied volatility in the July soybeans options contract had already come down to 23.5 from 28. At this point, I was looking at the July 560 calls, which had closed at 18 cents. I knew there could still be some room for these calls to come down in price a little further, but even at this level, we were getting close to our entry window (7.5 to 15 cents). I watched this closely into February, knowing that if prices did continue to fall, this might turn my attention to lower strike prices—such as the 540s or 520s. However, I did not anticipate targeting anything under 520 that year and would likely focus on the 540s and 560s.

The specifications for entering the spring option soybean trade are as follows:

- *Entry time frame:* Early February to end of March.
- *Contract:* July call option (basis July futures).
- *Strike:* Determined by adding 50 cents to the February break low. The February break usually occurs between early February and the end of March. The target strike for the July call option is 50 cents above the February break low.
- *Catalysts:* Changes in supply (planting) per the March 30 U.S. Department of Agriculture (USDA) prospective planting report stating less than ideal planting conditions and weather problems (e.g., too much rain or not enough rain). Unfavorable temperatures can also be a catalyst, but are usually a lesser issue than precipitation. Other catalysts could include the potential for an early frost in South America, as well as a smaller than expected crop, particularly if supplies are tight as measured by the carryover from the previous year's harvest.
- *Notes:* Once the market is close to a February break low (usually in February), the objective is to single out the strike price for July soybean calls that is within 50 cents of the low in the July soybean futures, and purchase that option at a price between 7.5 and 15 cents. The protective stop would be two thirds of the price (e.g., 0.66 times the entry price rounded off).

- *Exit strategy:* 50 percent rule applies, taking off half the position after achieving a desired profit. (Multiple 50 percent profits are the norm.) A trailing stop would apply on the remaining 50 percent. As a rule of thumb, in option purchases I look to at least double the initial investment. Once out with profits, or if stopped out, I do not reenter or try to get back in.
- *Additional trading strategies during this period (spring to early summer):*
  - — *1:* July/November soybean spread. Enter spread via buying July and selling the November.
  - — *Rules:* Traders should only enter the spread if the July is trading higher than the November, thus making the spread positive. Furthermore, entry should take place under 30 cents on the spread (yet above zero) and generally between March and May.
  - — *Note:* If the spread is negative, the November (distant) will be priced higher than the July (front).

The specifications for entering the fall option soybean trade are as follows:

- *Entry time frame:* End of July to beginning of September.
- *Contract:* January call option (basis the January futures).
- *Strike:* Determined by adding 50 cents to the preharvest low. This key low tends to be struck toward the middle to end of July to the beginning of September. The target strike price for the January call option is 50 cents above the preharvest low.
- *Catalyst:* Final USDA crop reports in August and September show smaller than anticipated yields or less supply (bushels) at harvest (through new crop). Potential for an early frost. The potential for an early frost is more of a catalyst in the years that the crop was planted late (due to spring planting problems or poor weather conditions in the spring and early summer).
- *Notes:* Once the market is close to a preharvest low (usually in August), the objective is to single out the strike (January soybean call) that is within 50 cents of the low in the January bean contract and purchase that option at a price between 7.5 to 15 cents. The protective stop should be two-thirds of the price (e.g., .66 × the entry price rounded off).
- *Exit strategy:* 50 percent rule applies. (Multiple 50 percent profits are the norm.) Trailing stop method applies on remaining 50 percent. As a rule of thumb, in option purchases look to at least double the initial investment. Once out with profits or if stopped out, do not reenter or try to get back in.

Spring 2005 Soybean Trade

I also focus on the funds to see how much fuel there is in the market to propel a move. I view the fund position as fuel because, as speculators, the funds usually have to exit their positions. I also watch to see when the funds begin to liquidate, even if the trend has not changed as yet. It is a powerful sign that the market is nearing the end of a trend.

Notice in Figure 7.6, the funds began liquidating longs at point "X" before the price trend up had turned down.

During the spring 2005 soybean options trade, the July soybean calls increased in value almost 1,000 percent in just a few weeks. Traders who got in on the spring trade entered the market in early February and were out a few weeks later with sizable gains. As my daily and weekly reports showed at the time, even after the spring options trade, I remained bullish on soybeans based on the IMPA analysis.

Many years ago, I took a liking to the soybean market, and over the years I have become somewhat of an expert in this market. This has driven me to create additional trading strategies that focus entirely on soybeans.

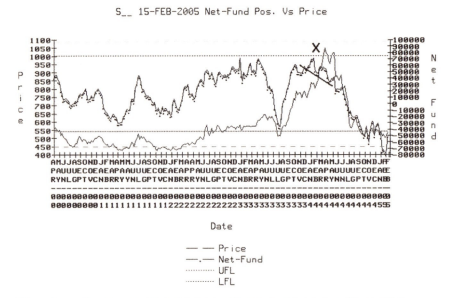

UFL = Upper Fund Limit (Over-bought). LFL=Lower Fund Limit (Over-sold).

FIGURE 7.6 Net fund activity in soybeans shows beginning of liquidation of positions.

As I mentioned previously, I recommend all individual traders selec
least one market to become an expert in. There are many thousands of
fluences that impact all markets, and it is nearly impossible in my opini·
to become an expert in all of them. I have discovered, however, that muc
can be learned about the general behavior of all markets by selecting on
market and learning everything about it.

at
in-
on
h
e

CHAPTER 8

Swing Trading and Other Strategies

There are three general or common approaches to commodity trading: position trading, swing trading, and short-term trading. In this chapter, I address my two basic methods for swing trading.

While I sometimes engage in swing trading, most of my time and attention are devoted to position trading using the IMPA position trading system or approach. As explained in Chapters 4 and 5, IMPA identifies specific market conditions including when the net-commercial position has reached or penetrates the upper commercial limit (UCL), which is bullish, or the lower commercial limit (LCL), which is bearish, and other official criteria (as outlined earlier). Because UCL/LCL penetration is a leading indicator, it can take months for an IMPA position trade to completely set up. Once the setup is complete, the new trend can continue for months.

I have provided unique tools and methods for swing trading on my web site since about 1999. A number of the tools and measures I have developed are derived from traditional data (open, high, low, close, open interest, and volume). However, I have devised unique approaches to using this information. For example, rather than focusing on support and resistance areas for trades, which is extremely popular today, I focus my attention on the behavior of price around popular patterns. As mentioned previously, often short-term price changes occur because everyone is looking at the same indicator or pattern. If everyone is getting a buy signal or sell signal at the same time, the market will have to absorb the collective response for a short while. The lack of a response says something, too. Longer-term, of course, the fundamentals always drive prices. But over the short-term the collective behavior of even the smallest participants can influence prices. This is why I combine my traditional technical measures with my own proprietary statistical analysis.

Swing trading seeks to capitalize on short-term trends in the market that may last two or three days or two or three weeks, compared with an IMPA position trade that might span several months. My swing-trading approach is a totally separate trading strategy from the IMPA position trade setups.

For swing trading, I have two main approaches:

1. *Swing Approach A:* This is my standard trend approach and also my favorite swing-trade approach. This method involves buying or selling with the trend and is the most reliable because it involves less predicting or forecasting. Swing Approach A follows the established trend, selling into preexisting downtrends and buying into preexisting uptrends.

2. *Swing Approach B:* This is my standard countertrend approach. It involves selling swing highs (tops) and identifying swing lows (bottoms) to buy. This method is less reliable than Swing Approach A because more forecasting and predicting are involved to call tops and bottoms—albeit relatively smaller ones, such as a weekly high or a weekly low, versus the more significant turning points identified by the IMPA criteria. Swing Approach B works best in channeling markets.

TOOLS FOR SWING TRADING

I use traditional technical indicators, moving averages, RSI, and so forth. I also use price patterns, including plungers, M tops, and W bottoms. In addition, my unique detrended analysis is used to determine high-probability oversold and overbought areas. I have also developed a computer program that recognizes various patterns as they form in the market. The program generates daily reports that alert me about markets exhibiting certain patterns. The automated plunger reports are updated on my web site and include optimal entry prices, logical stops, and calculated monetary risk.

Because price patterns are popular tools for trading, it is important to see them as they are forming and to take action on them ahead of the crowd. Ideally, I prefer to enter at a somewhat obvious juncture but before everyone else rushes into the market. Entering in front of the crowd not only gives me a better price, but also gets me into the market at the right moment. Then as I hold a position, I look for the price patterns that signal the time to exit (using the 50 percent rule), and I also look to exit ahead of the crowd. Entering ahead of the crowd is particularly important on short-sells, because markets often drop more quickly than they rise.

Success with swing trading—or any kind of trading for that matter—is typically determined by your ability to manage risk and exposure to risk effectively. The 10 percent rule is a guide for managing the amount of money risked per trade. In swing trading, as in position trading, I only use logical stops—*never* monetary stops. Stop placements are based on price patterns used for both trade entry and exit. I also use my 50 percent rule of taking off half a position after a certain profit has been realized—noting that I may also take multiple 50 percent profits.

In my swing trading, I use a set of unique tools, including my proprietary software. Developing and using my own charting software has made a world of difference in the reliability of my indicators. Two of the tools I have developed, which are displayed on my trend/swing trading graphs, use *slope polarity* and *detrended analysis*.

SLOPE POLARITY

Slope polarity looks at the prevailing trend in the market over the period of time represented on the graph (161 days on my graphs). Slope polarity is derived from a statistical formula, which measures the slope of a line. In this particular case, the line is derived from the trend over the 161-day period. This line is plotted on my charts. Essentially this line is a *linear moving mean*. If the market is trending higher, the mean will be trending higher, too. If it is trending lower, the mean will also be trending lower.

If there is no trend and the market is moving sideways, the market is flat and the slope polarity line will be displayed as a flat, horizontal line. If there is a downtrend, the slope polarity will angle downward. I define this as *negative* slope polarity. If the market is in an uptrend, the slope polarity line will slope upward, which I define as *positive* slope polarity. Figure 8.1 shows slope polarity in copper futures. The dashed line on the graph depicts the slope polarity, which is positive or angled upward.

The positive slope polarity means there is an upward bias in the market data over the 161-day sample period represented in the chart. Therefore, with a positive slope polarity and using Swing Approach A, I would look for opportunities to buy the market. Remember, Approach A seeks to trade with the established trend, buying in uptrends and selling in downtrends.

Notice the triangular shapes (carets) at the bottom of the graph. On our web site, these appear in color: blue for forward plungers (buy signals) and red for reverse plungers (sell signals). Since the market has an upward bias (as reflected by the positive slope polarity), using Approach A, I would ignore the reverse plungers and focus instead on the forward plungers, which are the buy signals. If I were using Approach B, however, I

HGN05 06-JUN-2005 [Trend/Swing graph] Cl=156.4 (0.65) $162.5

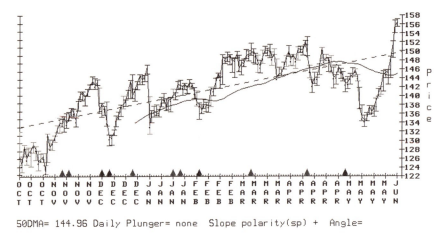

50DMA= 144.96 Daily Plunger= none Slope polarity(sp) + Angle=

FIGURE 8.1   Slope polarity depicted as dashed line on trend/swing graph.

would be doing just the opposite. Using the example of a market with a positive slope polarity, I would be looking to sell into the established trend by picking tops.

Another important tool to consider when using either Swing Approach A or B is the *detrended analysis*. This tool is a gauge for when the market is overbought or oversold, which is important when picking tops or bottoms in Approach B.

DETRENDED ANALYSIS

I have developed a unique form of detrended analysis and incorporated it into my proprietary software. I call this analysis detrended because I remove the trends from the price data (flattening out the slope polarity). This eliminates the skewing that the trend causes. Through detrended analysis, I can obtain a pure picture of the market that shows the overbought and oversold conditions, without the skewing caused by the trend. In Figure 8.2, the slope polarity line, represented by dashes, is flat because the trend has been removed from the price data.

The detrended analysis is derived from price structure and uses the same principles taught by Deming regarding the distribution of normalized data (see Chapter 2). The detrended analysis graphs include an upper and

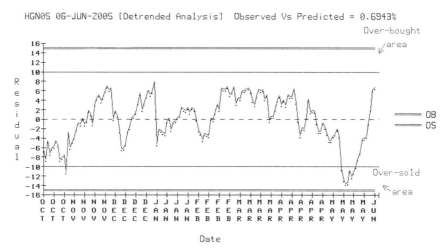

FIGURE 8.2 Detrended analysis graph.

lower control limit based on the location of the mean and a standard deviation measurement. On Figure 8.2, the extreme limits are represented by the double lines across the top and bottom of the graph. The top line delineates the overbought area, and the bottom line the oversold area.

When the detrended price data plotted on the graph touches or crosses into the upper or lower limits, the market is in an overbought or oversold condition. At these times, there are opportunities to swing trade. During these conditions, I would look for short-term price patterns to develop (such as a plunger pattern).

When using traditional oscillators, markets can enter into overbought or oversold conditions for long periods. Those conditions become skewed because of the influence of the prevailing trend, taking an overbought market even higher or an oversold market even lower. My detrended analysis is far less susceptible to this problem because of the way that I perform my analysis. The trending component is removed prior to the calculation, thus eliminating the skewing. This unique addition to my detrending analysis formula is what prevents the indicator from becoming overbought or oversold as often as the more traditional oscillators tend to become.

Across the top of Figure 8.2, note the "Observed versus Predicted = 0.6943%." This percentage rating (with 1.00 equaling 100 percent) is essentially a measure of how closely observed price changes are conforming to the linear trend-line prediction. This is also a way to measure how well the detrended analysis has been performing over the period that the chart represents (again, for my charts this is 161 days). The Observed versus Predicted rating of 69.43 percent represents an average performance (the higher the number, the better). No indicator is going to have a 100 percent rating. A measure in the 80 percent range or higher would be very good.

If the rating were in the 20 to 30 percent range or lower, it would show that the performance of the indicator was very low. The conditions of that market at that time may not be conducive to swing trading. There are times when some markets behave like this. In addition, some markets, such as orange juice futures or Fed funds, are thinly traded and may not react well to this indicator at certain times. Heavily traded markets with good liquidity are better suited to using the detrended analysis—and, thus, are better candidates for swing trading.

For entries into swing trades, I use price patterns, such as plungers, M tops, and W bottoms. One of the best reasons for using these patterns is that they provide a logical stop placement. For example, if I went long after a forward plunger or W bottom, I would place my stop at or just below the low of that price formation. Conversely, if I went short after a reverse plunger or M top, I would place my protective stop at or just above the high of that price formation. All my stops are based on closing prices only.

Now, let's look at how a swing trade setup might occur. Assume that there is a plunger formation in the market—a forward plunger that can be used as a buy signal. Then, turning to the detrended analysis, I might look to see where the market is compared with the overbought and oversold limits. If the market is in oversold territory, it would potentiate the forward plunger for making a swing trade. Using Swing Approach A, with a forward plunger and the market at or near oversold conditions, I would look to buy as the market moves higher after the forward plunger has formed.

For Swing Approach B, which is the countertrend approach, I would be trading opposite of the established trend. Assume the detrended analysis graph shows that the market is extremely overbought, but it has been trending higher. With Approach B, I would try to identify a top using a price pattern (such as an M or reverse plunger) and then sell against the trend. In a market that is extremely overbought, I know that when a reverse plunger forms, there is a good chance that the plunger marks the top of that move. This may not be the final top for the move, but it may result in a profitable swing trade. Keep in mind that these instances of extreme overbought/oversold conditions are rare. On the detrended analysis chart, the market enters into extreme overbought/oversold conditions roughly 0.27 percent of the time.

Now look at an example of Swing Approach A in action. Figure 8.3 shows a trend/swing graph of Kansas City Wheat futures from May 2003 through January 2004.

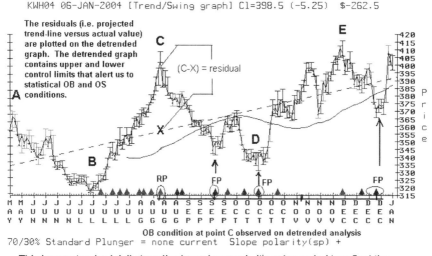

KWH04 06-JAN-2004 [Trend/Swing graph] Cl=398.5 (-5.25) $-262.5

FIGURE 8.3 My standard daily trend/swing price graph.

First, take note of the slope polarity, depicted by the dashes that angle upward on the chart. This shows that there is an uptrend in the market, or positive slope polarity. Therefore, with Swing Approach A, I would be looking to buy the market. This means I would look for forward plungers (on color charts displayed in blue) and ignore the reverse plungers (displayed in red). In Figure 8.3, the forward plungers (marked with the upward pointing arrows) align with the lows in the market. These plungers represent buying opportunities when trading with an uptrend, using Approach A. In addition, these forward plungers also correspond with the oversold conditions shown in Figure 8.3 and also in Figure 8.4.

The areas marked A, C, and E on Figure 8.3 represent overbought areas, which are clearly identified by the overbought lines in Figure 8.4. Conversely, B and D show the areas that are oversold. This is based on the detrended analysis of the same price data (again, see Figure 8.4). On the detrended analysis chart, the level of penetration at Point C is well beyond the extreme overbought limits, which is the top double line. The times that the data exceed this area are very rare.

Using Swing Approach A, I would be trading with the existing trend. Since the slope polarity line is positive, I know this market has an upward

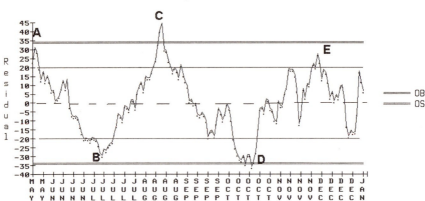

KWH04 06-JAN-2004 [Detrended Analysis]   Observed Vs Predicted = 0.6994%

The residual values plotted on this graph originate from the associated daily trend/swing price graph. The upper and lower double lines on this graph represent 3 standard deviations of market deviation from the projected trend-line contained on the daily trend/swing price graph. When the market meets or exceeds these reference points the statistical probability favors a regression back towards the center-line. Often however markets will over-shoot when they turn.

FIGURE 8.4   Detrended analysis showing overbought and oversold areas.

bias. Therefore, I would be looking for opportunities to buy the market. At Point D, the market is in an oversold condition. During this condition, a forward plunger formation occurred (see circled plunger at Point D on Figure 8.3). At that time, the forward plunger would have provided me with a logical stop, enabling me to enter the market long on the forward plunger formation during the oversold condition. Subsequent to this formation, the market began turning up and moving higher out of the oversold condition.

For Swing Approach B, using this example, I might look for opportunities to sell—even though the slope polarity is positive and the market has an upward bias. That is because Approach B is a countertrend approach. An example of this type of trade might occur at Point C (see Figure 8.3). We know from the history of the detrended analysis that a market in this condition will at some point very likely snap back, gravitating toward its linear moving mean (trend line). Traditional oscillators, however, may identify these conditions early, and the conditions can continue for some time.

My detrended analysis uses a unique approach and a unique formula that are more efficient at identifying the turning points when the market is overbought or oversold. While in an overbought condition, I would look to sell the market short, but I would need a pattern that would enable me to contain the risk with a logical stop. One such pattern is the reverse plunger. The reverse plunger provides the logical stop for entry into an overbought market.

I would not enter a market only because it is overbought or oversold. Rather, once I was alerted to that condition, I would be patient and wait for a pattern to form. One of the patterns I would look for in these conditions would be a plunger. The overbought or oversold condition is just a precursor for a potential trade. Additional criteria are needed, which would be pattern formations in the appropriate direction to provide an entry with a logical stop.

Once you have determined where to place your stop, you can see how much capital would be at risk on that particular trade. If the amount of capital you would risk exceeds the 10 percent rule, then *don't take that trade.* You cannot simply move your stop to lower the amount of capital at risk because you are very likely to be stopped out on that trade due to normal price fluctuations in the market. When that happens, you will lose the capital you have risked and you won't accomplish anything. In addition, since your stop was in the wrong place, the market is likely to move back in the direction that you thought it would. But since you have been stopped out, you won't profit from that trade—and that is a big emotional drain.

I know because I used to make the same mistakes. The lesson I learned is the importance of identifying a logical stop. Whether using a pattern or an indicator, the logical stop defines the entry. Logical stops contain the risk. Once the stop placement is identified, I can see whether the trade meets or exceeds the 10 percent rule. The one thing I have learned never to do is arbitrarily adjust the logical stop to reduce the monetary risk, because that is just asking to be stopped out. While some traders look to identify a place to enter the market first, my priority is identifying the logical stop. Once I know where the stop needs to be, then I look to enter the market.

COPPER SWING TRADE

From my trading archives, let's look at a swing trade setup in copper during May and June 2004. I had been watching copper closely during that time, given the formation of some important plunger patterns. First, note that the slope polarity for the time span shown in Figure 8.5 is positive. That means the market had an upward bias. Following Swing Approach A, which is my trend-following approach, I would be looking to buy the market.

There was a forward plunger on a major swing low in mid-May. Going long here would have provided a nice swing trade buy opportunity as the market moved steadily higher through early June. Then a reverse plunger marked the end of that advance.

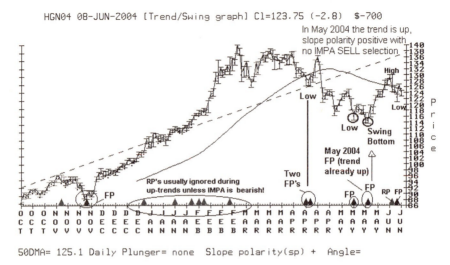

FIGURE 8.5 Trend/swing graph in copper futures, showing slope polarity and plunger patterns.

Following the reverse plunger in late May, a small forward plunger was formed on a minor swing low. While there was some followthrough after that, it was not much. However, the forward plunger had not failed yet, either. In addition, the reverse plunger that occurred the week before was more significant than the recent forward plunger. They both occurred on swings, but the reverse plunger was on a larger swing. That signaled to me there could be a bigger trend change coming in copper.

Also, after the reverse plunger, the market corrected right back to the 18-day moving average. This is where support came into play because the 18-day moving average is commonly used in standard technical analysis and many traders focus on this area. The forward plunger off this area, while important, was not as significant as the reverse plunger marking the turning point at the recent high.

It is important to understand from this example how to interpret opposing plungers (those that are against the slope polarity). Generally, when you are trading with the trend, you want to ignore opposing plungers. That is not, however, a hard and fast rule. The markets do not adhere to any single formation 100 percent of the time. Traders have to be flexible, using instinct, common sense, and experience along with technical tools such as price patterns and formations.

In addition, a more significant *previous* plunger may dictate the direction on a longer-term basis, while a more recent (but less significant) plunger dictates the direction over the extreme near term (1 to 3 days). We must always take into consideration any previous plungers that may still be active on a longer-term basis. This simply means that more recent plungers may result in short-term reactions in the market, while the market adheres to the trend-setting action of longer-term, more significant plungers. Both can be correct in their own window of time, but traders need to be observant of both patterns.

The core rule with plungers is the one- to three-day reaction. However, we also know that their lows or highs can become extremely important to the market on a much longer-term basis. Thus, the location of the plungers on minor or major swings is also an important factor in determining the strength and longevity of the plunger formation. That location may not be immediately understood at first. Only after more data have been collected and time has passed is it possible to point to a previous high or low and know with a high degree of confidence that this point was or was not a significant top, bottom, or turning point in the market. Tops and bottoms, obviously, are always seen in hindsight, not when they are occurring. That said, plungers can be a powerful, real-time clue to whether a particular reversal will go on to mark an important short-term or longer-term turning point in the market.

In the case of the copper market, the reverse plunger in late May proved to be more significant, as the market moved down sharply. On June 9, 2004, copper futures lost a hefty 7.30 points, which equated to a move down of $1,825 per contract. In early June, I remained bearish on the copper market, with the bigger clue to the market direction being the reverse plunger on the major swing high. Going forward, copper prices collapsed in July 2004, and then a large forward plunger occurred, after which prices began rising again. The longer-term trend in copper was upward (as captured by the positive slope polarity), and the uptrend resumed in July following the forward plunger.

NATURAL GAS SWING TRADE

In late May/early June 2005, I saw a good opportunity for a Swing Approach B countertrend swing trade in natural gas. As Figure 8.6 shows, the slope polarity was negative, indicating that the market had a downward bias. However, I saw a "W" (double bottom) taking shape on my weekly price graph. There was no doubt in my mind that this would bring some buyers into the market. Therefore, I saw this as a good setup for a countertrend swing-trade buy.

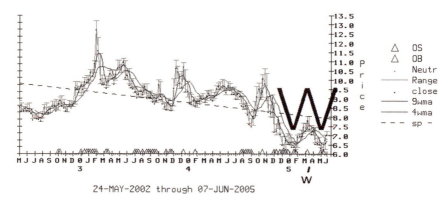

FIGURE 8.6 "W" pattern forming in natural gas shows opportunity for countertrend trade.

In addition, my detrended analysis (Figure 8.7) showed that natural gas was approaching the oversold area. This was further confirmation of the W pattern that was forming. To me, this was a clear example of a Swing Approach B trade setting up.

After the W formation, the market moved higher, crossing above the 18-day moving average. Three weeks later, natural gas had moved higher

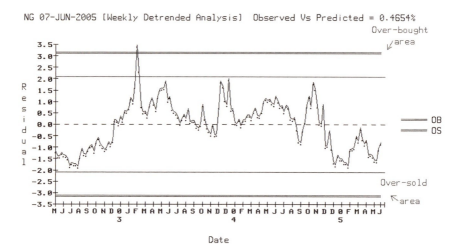

FIGURE 8.7 Detrended analysis in natural gas shows market approaching the oversold area.

by approximately $10,000 per contract, and by mid- to late June was continuing to move upward.

As the examples in this chapter illustrate, swing trades are short-term trades, generally lasting a few days to several weeks. With Swing Approach A, I look to trade with the established trend, as evidenced by the slope polarity. My trade entry is determined by a price formation, such as a plunger, which provides the logical stop. Further, through my detrended analysis, I examine the overbought/oversold conditions to confirm the price pattern.

With Swing Approach B, I am looking to make a countertrend trade against the established trend. My trade entry, again, is determined by a price formation, but this time I am looking at formations that would suggest at least a short-term top in a rising market or a short-term bottom in a declining one. I would use overbought/oversold conditions as a confirming indication that the market is likely to correct (to the downside) or bounce (to the upside), providing the opportunity for a countertrend trade. Once again, my logical stop is based on the price formation.

The long-term tops and bottoms are defined more reliably with the IMPA. But for short-term moves, these swing trade approaches can work well.

## CHAPTER 9

IMPA Trade Examples

The IMPA system for identifying potential trading opportunities is a unique approach that combines fundamental analysis, derived from the COT data, with traditional technical analysis, derived from price data. This combination of fundamental and technical information sheds light on the path ahead, providing valuable insight into market conditions that, experience tells us, often occur prior to significant changes in price.

By combining IMPA with traditional technical methods, my goal is to establish a position as often as possible on the right side of the market ahead of the main moves. Nothing works 100 percent of the time, but this method is the best I know of after more than a decade of testing and researching hundreds of systems and strategies.

This approach differs substantially from the majority of trading systems that rely entirely on indicators derived from price, volume, open interest, or some combination of them. This is where most new traders tend to get their insight; and some never get beyond this point because most books, software, and popular trading courses focus on these same indicators. They all work in a similar way and give similar signals.

I have concluded that successful trading is not necessarily the result of having the right indicator, but is more about using a trading approach that is unique both mechanically and instinctively. A separation from crowd thinking and behavior is essential in achieving an effective approach. This requires courage. The psychological need for comfort makes breaking away from crowd thinking and behavior difficult for the individual trader.

Many people fail in trading, not because they aren't smart enough or don't work hard enough, but because they are afraid to deviate from what is comfortable and accepted by the crowd. Most people are unaware of this tendency, and even if they realize it, they don't know how to overcome that fear.

In the old days, computers were expensive and software was difficult to come by. Today, access to powerful computer technology is widespread and cheap. Yet even now, with readily available computer power, the over-all majority of new individual commodity traders do not succeed. In fact, I believe there may be fewer succeeding today than in the past (although this may be partly because there are more people trying to trade these days) because of all the distractions of modern-day society. The primary reason, however, is that most new traders accept the same conclusions, the same explanations, and the same methods. Nothing has really changed in this respect although technology has made the markets significantly more accessible and much more connected: one market to another and around the world. Success in trading requires a bold step—a unique and often uncomfortable approach.

I experienced a *major* breakthrough several years ago after forcing myself (while short-term trading the Swiss franc and Deutsche mark) to do something that was very difficult: I forced myself to buy when I had *sell* signals and to sell when I had *buy* signals. The essential criterion was that the buy or sell that I was fading had to come with very strong convictions. I had to be absolutely certain that the market was going in a certain direction and then once I was assured of that in my mind, I had to place a trade in the opposite direction.

Let me tell you it was a difficult thing to do, and I don't know anyone else who has talked about doing this. But going through this process taught me a great deal about myself and my approach. It was also a humbling experience because I profited quite a bit of the time when I was fading my own signals. That was where the real insight came, when I saw how little I really knew about the markets and how random short-term fluctuations in price really are. I saw that there were times when I made money on a trade that was opposite to what I thought was "right." This revealing exercise helped me let go of some pride and ego and allowed me to focus on the main goal in trading: making a profit. In addition, I shifted my attention to other areas, such as managing the trade, managing the profits, managing the losses, and knowing—up front—how much was at risk before entering any position.

To succeed, you have to get to the point where you don't care if you profit from being right or wrong. Being right or wrong isn't the goal; the goal is to make money. I learned that I could make money when I was wrong. I learned to swallow my pride, and I came to realize what was more important: being right or making money. That is something all traders eventually have to decide, because we often must take positions that go against the common thinking or what the majority, including ourselves, think the market should do. We are bombarded with the same information, and it is easy to get sucked into thinking alike. A lot of the time, our reaction is subconscious. We don't recognize that we are using the same indicators that everyone else is and getting the same results. Eventually, all effective traders have to get past this blind spot.

From this exercise, I began to develop my own systems to achieve the goal of making a profit, not being right. To do this, I had to focus on being wrong and on knowing how I could manage that fallibility through loss control, profit management, and risk management.

The IMPA system that I developed can be used in conjunction with other trading systems and methodologies, including traditional technical indicators. The IMPA selection is based on the analysis of the net-commercial position. When this selection occurs, it puts the market on the radar screen because we know that the market conditions are potentially beginning to set up for a move in one direction. This is a leading indicator and other criteria need to be satisfied before a position can be taken. After the IMPA setup is complete, a trade then can be entered and a logical stop would already be determined using traditional technical indicators and patterns, or contract highs/lows. Using the contract highs and lows is logical because if the market is moving higher, it shouldn't be making new contract lows, and if it is moving lower, it shouldn't be making new contract highs.

With this understanding of the IMPA system, I want to recap some noteworthy position trades that illustrate these approaches and show the IMPA in action.

EQUITY TRADE

One of the most significant IMPA position trades that the system has ever identified was in the U.S. equity market in 1994. An IMPA buy selection occurred in 1994 and the upward trend that resulted basically remained in place until an IMPA sell was generated in early 2000 (see Figure 9.1). During this six-year period, the net-commercial position, at times, moved away from the upper commercial limit (UCL). However, a more in-depth look at the data suggested the overall conditions remained the same. To examine the data more closely, I look at the individual positions that make up the net-commercial and net-fund positions. In the financial markets, pension funds, endowments, and banking institutions make up some of the commercial interest. Their trading activity can be revealing.

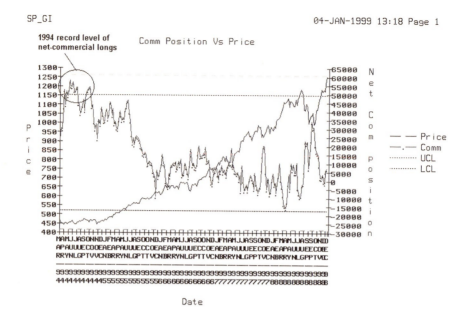

FIGURE 9.1 Net-commercial position in S&P futures in 1994 (upper line, far left) shows penetration of the UCL (upper commercial limit). In fact, the IMPA data at the time showed penetration all the way to the EUCL (extreme upper commercial limit), although it is not visible here due to the dynamic nature of the UCL/LCL and EUCL/ELCL lines (see explanation, later in this chapter).

As a market is trending higher, it is normal for the net-commercial position to move away from the UCL. This is what we expect. The things that I look for to tell me when an uptrend is likely to end and a new downtrend is emerging did not come into view until early 2000. There were times when I saw some small changes that indicated some sizable corrections, and they were accurate in that respect. Each time after the correction, however, the net-commercial position went right back up to the UCL. This told me that these were minor corrections; they were not the end of the big bull market.

Looking at the specifics of this trade, the IMPA position buy in U.S. equities was based on the penetration of the UCL—which in this case went all the way to the EUCL (extreme upper commercial limit) in S&P 500 futures. In fact, this was the deepest penetration of the EUCL I had ever seen in the S&P 500. What makes this even more outstanding is that it took place in the middle to end of 1994—a year in which the Federal Reserve had been raising short-term rates. According to many analysts, at that time the outlook for the stock market was dismal and yet, there it was: an EUCL penetration—the most dramatic I had ever seen—in the S&P 500. That told me that equities were likely to see a big upward move.

After the IMPA identified the buy selection in S&P futures, the other indices—the Nasdaq, the Russell 2000, and the Dow—followed shortly thereafter. By 1995, the equities market broke out to what were then all-time highs. The Dow Jones Industrial Average (DJIA) closed above 4000 in February 1995, and above 5000 in November 1995. In 1996, the DJIA topped 6000, and in 1997 it closed above 7000 and then 8000. In 1998, the Dow closed above 9000, and in 1999 closed above 10,000 and then 11,000 for the first time.

Although the IMPA buy selections were generated in the indices (S&P, Nasdaq, Russell, and Dow), I did not heavily buy stock index futures contracts. The reason is futures contracts are relatively short-term instruments. If you buy the front-month contract, by expiration, you must either exit that position or roll it into the next month.

Based on the extreme nature of the EUCL penetration, I was convinced this was going to be a long-term move. This encouraged me to focus my attention on individual stocks that I could buy and hold for a long time. In addition, stocks are the underlying physicals of the stock index futures contracts. Thus, while the IMPA buy setup was in place in the stock index futures, I knew I could buy the underlying commodity—in this case stock—and still participate in the move. This is a lot easier to do in stocks than in other commodities, such as soybeans, hogs, or crude oil. Buying stocks only requires that you have a brokerage account. If you want to buy soybeans or hogs, you need to have a farm!

By this time, I had already been trading technology stocks for a while. As outlined in Chapter 2, my background is in electronic engineering, and I had the privilege of working for some major technology companies. Given my knowledge in technology and my natural inclination toward this sector, I began buying technology stocks, options, and LEAPS (Long-Term Equity Anticipation Securities) to be long equities. Other traders who were following this system were also getting long equities, although many were buying stocks within other sectors as well. The whole market was rising, and although some individual stocks would rise more than others, it was a good time to be buying equities, given the strong IMPA buy signal. The IMPA system also proved helpful for managing individual retirement accounts (IRAs), Roth IRAs, and company 401(k) retirement plans.

By early 2000, I knew the market had already come a long, long way. Anyone who followed the market during this time knew that, and despite what some people might have wanted to believe, stocks could not keep going up at this pace forever. Alan Greenspan warned of "irrational exuberance" in the market. Investors such as George Soros and Warren Buffett were also cautionary about the market. Meanwhile, I was watching to see when an IMPA sell selection would be generated and the uptrend would likely come to an end.

In April 2000, the IMPA data changed profoundly. As Figure 9.2 shows, as the net-commercial position declined dramatically, the bullish bias turned to a sell, and I knew then that it was time to get out of equities.

The sell-off that followed in the market was evident in all the stock indices. On April 14, 2000, the Dow fell by 617 points, the Nasdaq Composite fell 355 points, and the S&P dropped 83 points. These were the largest one-day point losses ever in the indices. To illustrate what was happening in these other indices, Figure 9.3 shows the IMPA sell generated in the Nasdaq futures as the net-commercial position penetrated the lower commercial limit (LCL).

By following the IMPA system, I was able to participate in this long uptrend in equities and get out in 2000 before the big bear market. I had the IMPA system to thank for getting me into and out of equities at the right time.

Looking back at previous IMPA selections charts that display more recent data (such as Figure 9.4), it is important to understand why the line placement appears different. The reason is that the UCL and LCL lines are dynamic, as are the EUCL and ELCL. These lines are not fixed over time. As more data comes in (currently on a week-to-week basis), it will cause

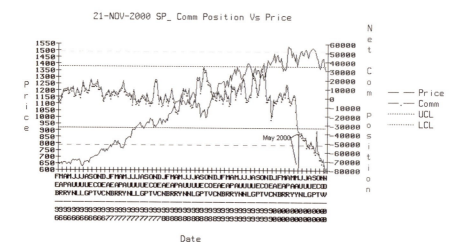

FIGURE 9.2 Net-commercial position in S&P futures declined dramatically in early 2000. A profound change in the market had ended the IMPA bullish bias and signaled an IMPA sell selection.

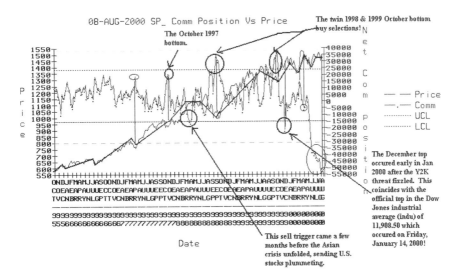

FIGURE 9.3 Net-commercial position in the Nasdaq futures shows the precipitous drop in early April 2000 below the LCL. This generated a major sell signal, and the top was put in the Nasdaq futures market.

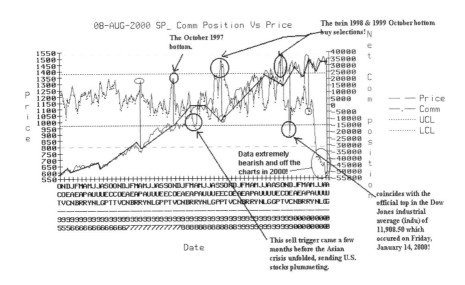

FIGURE 9.4 The net-commercial position in S&P futures, from 1995 through 2000, shows the overall bullish bias based on IMPA selection. The IMPA buy selection was basically in effect until April 2000.

the UCL/LCL and EUCL/ELCL lines to widen if it is outside the normal distribution. As those lines are redrawn, past selections will look different. (Some may not even appear to have been selections.)

If the UCL/LCL and EUCL/ELCL lines were static, they would be of little use in the current market conditions. The lines would not reflect the current data distribution. Only by analyzing the current data and comparing it to the past can we determine where the market is now in relation to its recent and long-term past.

The downside of viewing the market in real time is that it tends to minimize or distort the magnitude of previous conditions. Anyone who remembers "Black Monday" on October 19, 1987, can recall the trauma in the market when the DJIA fell 22.6 percent, its largest one-day decline ever. But if you look at a graph of the market from early 1987 until the present, Black Monday only looks like a little blip. The reason is that the market has made such dramatic moves since that time.

Another example is to consider open interest today versus what it was five years ago. As of 2005, open interest has exploded as a result of the globalization of the markets and the dramatic increase in the number of participants (particularly various investment funds) worldwide. With such a significant change in market dynamics, we have to view the market according to current conditions—not based on what it was like in the past. Thus, unless indicators are readjusted to compensate for new, changing market conditions, we would constantly have false signals due to the indicators being out of sync with current market conditions. This is why the UCL and LCL indicators must also be readjusted as markets continue to evolve.

IMPA BUYS IN THE RUSSELL, 2003 TO 2004

After the 2000 top, there have been subsequent IMPA buy selections in U.S. equities, particularly in the Russell 2000 during 2003 and 2004. Between March and June 2003, the IMPA became bullish in the Russell 2000, as well as in the Nasdaq, S&P 500, and the Dow.

Figure 9.5 shows the net-commercial position in the Russell 2000 had reached the UCL line in June 2003. This was a sudden shift from February 2003, when the net-commercial position in the Russell was at the LCL. Sudden sharp changes in the IMPA data often lead to significant moves in the market, just as penetration through the UCL or LCL areas also often leads to moves in the market. This significant shift in the data, along with the formation of subsequent price patterns, turned me bullish the Russell in mid-2003. I remained bullish until late 2004.

Figure 9.6 shows the net-commercial position in S&P 500 futures reaching the UCL in early to mid-2003. The S&P 500 is a broader index of

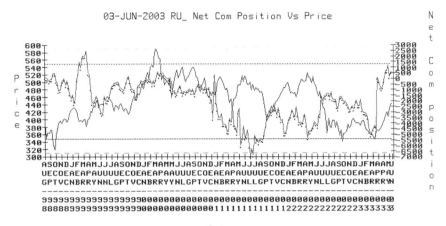

FIGURE 9.5 Net-commercial position in the Russell 2000 shows penetration of the UCL.

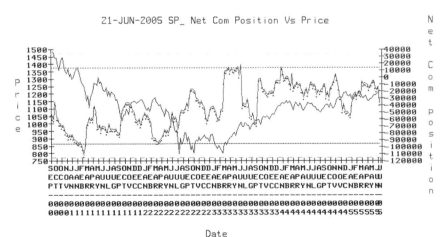

FIGURE 9.6 Net-commercial position in S&P 500 futures reaches UCL level in early to mid-2003.

large U.S. corporations versus the Russell 2000, which is representative of small-cap companies. In early to mid-2003, I felt the stock market overall was going to move higher because the IMPA was bullish in all the major stock indices, and I also observed that bullish price patterns were beginning to develop.

Later, in 2004, I noted that the IMPA data showed the net-commercial position had pulled back from the UCL in the Nasdaq and the Dow, and to a lesser degree in the S&P 500. While the Russell also went through a period in 2004 when it pulled away from the UCL area, by August of that year, the net-commercial position had pushed back through the UCL, reaching an all-time high (see Figure 9.7).

The Russell 2000 index subsequently moved to an all-time high as well, and was the only stock index to do so following the 2000 top (see Figure 9.8).

The August 2004 IMPA buy selection in the Russell was confirmed by price patterns in the market, including a W formation, a forward plunger, and other bullish indications. My detrended analysis also showed that the Russell was in an oversold condition at this time (see Figure 9.9). The W price formation (circled) can be seen clearly on Figure 9.9.

The August 2004 IMPA buy in the Russell 2000 was followed by a move of $50,000-plus per contract in just a few months (see Figure 9.10).

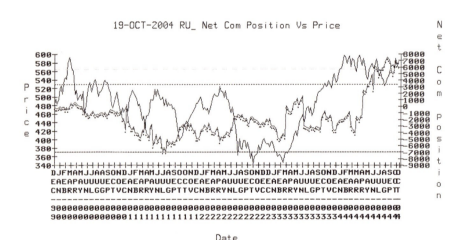

Net_Com= 6829 Tuesday's Close (C1)= 566

FIGURE 9.7   Net-commercial position in August 2004 shows record level of EUCL penetration.

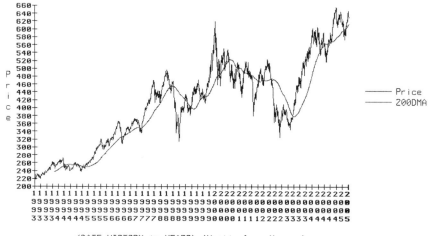

FIGURE 9.8 Price graph of Russell 2000 shows the index reaching an all-time high in late 2004.

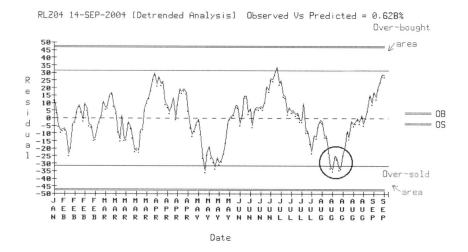

FIGURE 9.9 Detrended analysis of the Russell 2000 shows the market in the oversold area.

RLH05 14-DEC-2004 [Trend/Swing graph] Cl=644.9 (3.65) $1825

The buy of the year!
(2004)

FIGURE 9.10 August 2004 IMPA buy in the Russell preceded $50,000-plus move.

By the end of 2004, the IMPA data in the Russell and the other stock indices began to change. In the Russell, the net-commercial position suddenly shifted away from the UCL in a manner that prompted me to become much more cautious about holding long positions in the market. In fact, I began liquidating some of my stock positions shortly after this time, prior to 2005. As of this writing, the net-commercial position in the Russell remains in close proximity to the UCL. However, the net-commercial positions in the S&P 500, Dow, and Nasdaq have moved away from the UCL, and, in fact, the Dow is close proximity to the LCL. This represents a mixed picture.

IMPA GOLD BUY

As traders study a market for a long period, they begin to notice certain patterns and characteristics. As mentioned, one of the most critical things in trading is "observation, observation, observation." In the gold market in

September 1999, I observed a record level of net-commercial longs. This was significant to me. Remember, although the commercials (the producers and the consumers) are hedgers, they are the most knowledgeable participants. They are the ones who know the fundamentals—supply and demand—the best.

The record level of net-commercial longs told me that there was an imbalance in the gold market. The commercial consumers wanted more gold than the producers were willing or able to produce at the current price. The way to correct that situation—for supply and demand to come back into balance—is to have prices go higher.

While the commercial activity triggered an IMPA buy selection in September 1999, I knew that the funds would be the ones to cause the price to go higher with their buying. As stated, the funds are the dominant market participants. They are in the market day-to-day, and their positions are the fuel for the market. As pure speculators, the funds are going to take advantage of the trend. When they are buying or selling with the trend, this provides the momentum to sustain the trend. When the trend is changing, the actions of the funds—as they unwind existing positions and get into new positions—propels the market in the direction of the new trend.

Looking at the activity in gold at this time, I knew that when the uptrend started, the funds would exit short positions and begin to buy, and this activity would push the market higher. As prices rose, the hedge buying by the commercial consumers was going to stop, because they want to hedge at attractive prices. In addition, I knew that the funds were coming into this net-short. Therefore, they had to unwind their short positions by buying, and then they would be buying more to establish long positions. This meant plenty of fuel was available to power an uptrend.

Gold prices at this time were around $260 per once. That was the low, and we never returned to that level. The IMPA buy selection that I saw was the start of an uptrend that would take gold all the way to $440 an ounce.

Figure 9.11 shows the commercial, fund, and small trader positions in gold, along with price (to see a color version of chart, go to www.upperman.com, and click on "View Book Graphs"). Notice the line at the top in late 1998 and 1999. This is the net-commercial position. The line at the bottom of the graph at this time is price. Notice that when the net commercial position is at its high, the price tends to be at its low. This makes sense because commercial consumers want to hedge at attractive prices. Also notice that when the net-commercial position is at its low, this tends to correspond with higher prices. That makes sense as well because the commercial producers want to hedge at higher prices.

I am watching the gold market again for a potential IMPA sell. I have not identified a sell as yet, but the gold market is on my radar screen because

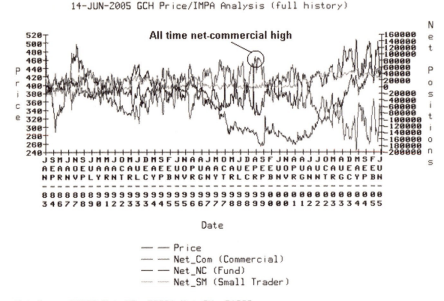

Net_Com= -88090 Net_NC= 56861 Net_SM= 31229

FIGURE 9.11   IMPA analysis in gold, showing commercial, fund, and small trader positions.

the net-commercial position has been moving lower and may reach the LCL line soon.

As these examples show, it takes time and experience to interpret what is happening in a particular market. Sometimes, it is just a matter of observation and seeing how the lines change and being able to detect unusual circumstances. What I have observed in gold as of this writing is the net-commercial position fluctuating between the UCL and the LCL as the commercial participants take advantage of price spikes in the market for their hedging activity. Overall, it does not appear that the commercial participants have changed their thinking.

I continue to monitor the net-commercial position in gold, knowing that at some point the commercial producers—who know the fundamentals firsthand—may change their thinking. As soon as they believe there is no more upside in gold, at least for the foreseeable future, they may collectively decide to increase their short-selling (hedging) to lock in current prices. When they do, I will watch the IMPA data for indications of this activity, which could signal the start of a trend change.

LEAN HOG TRADE

In lean hog futures, I had an IMPA buy selection on December 16, 2003. That meant I was on alert for a possible position trade to unfold in hogs, but as of this point I only had the selection (see Figure 9.12).

After the IMPA buy selection, twin forward plunger formations on December 19 and December 26, 2003, provided an early entry into the market (see Figure 9.13). The logical place for a stop was the low of those forward plunger formations. Keep in mind that although the IMPA criteria had not been fully satisfied as yet, these plunger patterns provided a lower-risk entry point.

Based on this data, I recognized that a buying opportunity was beginning to unfold in hogs, which was later confirmed with the crossing of the moving averages. Hog prices moved above the 18-day moving average, followed by the 10-day moving average crossing above the 18-day moving average. One of the important technical formations that I observed in hogs during this time was that after prices closed above the 18-day moving average for two consecutive days, the market did not close below the contract lows when the prices pulled back. Instead, prices began moving

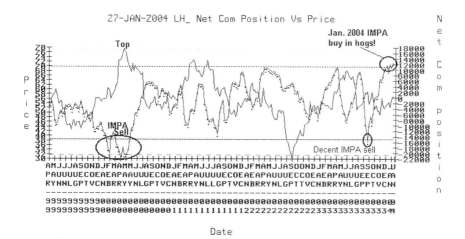

Net_Com= 12655 Tuesday's Close (Cl)= 57

FIGURE 9.12　Five-year history of lean hog futures shows the December 2003 IMPA buy selection, in context with previous moves including a five-year price high in early 2000.

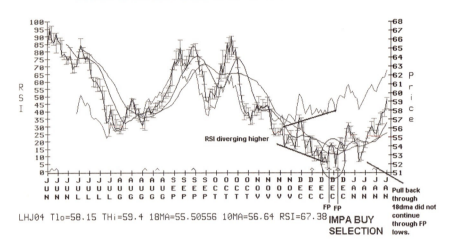

FIGURE 9.13 Lean hog futures chart shows twin plunger formations in December 2003, which coincided with the IMPA buy selection.

higher again. This provided a new or follow-up entry point with a logical stop now being under the most recent lows from the move below the 18-day moving average.

As the trend continued to unfold, using my IMPA position management methodology, traders could take 50 percent profits and continued to manage their remaining positions using trailing stops under the 18-day moving average.

British Pound IMPA Sell Trade

The next trade is an IMPA sell selection in British pound futures from July 2003. As with all IMPA position trades, it started with an IMPA trigger selection—in this case a sell selection. That is what first attracted me to this market. As Figure 9.14 shows, this market had been trending higher since early April. The IMPA sell selection, however, alerted me to a possible trend reversal and a move to the downside. At that point, I began to look for technical price patterns while waiting for the rest of the IMPA criteria to be satisfied. We often see plungers at the end of moves and the beginning of new moves. In Figure 9.14, you can see the reverse plunger that occurred near the top of the market. If the market was going to go lower, I knew it would not close above that plunger high. If it did close above that plunger high, then I would know that the market was going higher—not lower—and that the uptrend was resuming, not reversing.

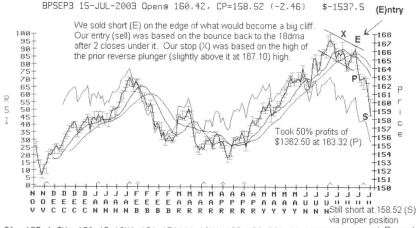

BPSEP3 15-JUL-2003 Open@ 160.42, CP=158.52 (-2.46) $-1537.5 (E)ntry

We sold short (E) on the edge of what would become a big cliff. Our entry (sell) was based on the bounce back to the 18dma after 2 closes under it. Our stop (X) was based on the high of the prior reverse plunger (slightly above it at 167.10) high.

Took 50% profits of $1362.50 at 163.32 (P).

Still short at 158.52 (S) via proper position management. Reward equals profit of $4362.50 on remaining 50% at S.

Tlo=158.4 THi=160.42 18MA=164.154444 10MA=163.172 RSI=29.34586

FIGURE 9.14   IMPA sell selection in British pound futures.

When the market traded higher, but failed to take out the high of the reverse plunger pattern, it provided an excellent entry point into a short position (sell). The logical place for the stop was the high of the plunger.

In my web site commentary, I sold short at 165.50 on July 1, 2003, based on a bounce back to the 18-day moving average, after two closes under it. On July 8, I recommended taking a 50 percent profit on short positions by buying contracts at 163.32 to cover half the original position. I continued to manage the remaining 50 percent. As the market trended lower, I moved the stop (close only) to 164.20 to lock in further profits. Managing a position with the 50 percent rule enables traders to take incremental profits—or as I call it to "peel off" profits. Generally, after the first 50 percent profit is taken, a larger profit is often made on the remaining half of the position. However, a trend can end abruptly. Some major event could cause the market to move suddenly and unexpectedly in the opposite direction, which would take away profits. Managing a profit using the 50 percent rule, however, allows one to remove that risk as the trade unfolds.

TEN-YEAR NOTES

The next example is an IMPA buy selection in the 10-year notes in the spring of 2005. The IMPA buy selection was based on a record level of penetration through the UCL and the EUCL (see Figure 9.15).

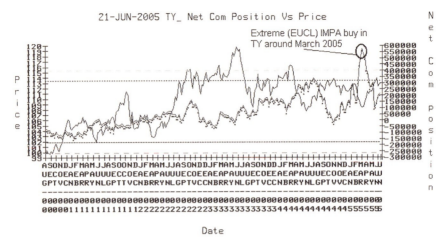

FIGURE 9.15 Net-commercial position in 10-year notes shows penetration of the UCL and EUCL levels.

The IMPA buy selection in mid-March also coincided with a forward plunger, which provided a logical stop for an early IMPA entry (see Figure 9.16). The market then moved above the 18-day moving average for a second day, making it an official, complete IMPA buy setup.

As stated, it is important to be able to take a position that is contrary to the prevailing opinion of the crowd. This is an excellent example of that because in early 2005 virtually everywhere I turned, economists and market commentators were overwhelmingly bearish this market. And yet, the IMPA data, through penetration of the UCL, led me to believe otherwise.

A long position in the 10-year notes from mid-March through May 2005 realized a profit of about $3,000 per contract, assuming an exit after the market closed under the 18-day moving average for two consecutive days (as shown on Figure 9.17). However, there was more left in this uptrend, and it resumed immediately after closing below the 18-day moving average for two consecutive days. As frustrating as this can be, it happens at times. As Figure 9.16 shows, the uptrend lasted until a reverse plunger was formed in early June.

The entire move from March through June equated to about $5,000 per contract. By exiting early, using the 18-day moving average 2-day rule, a trader would have captured a portion of that ($3,000), but left some money on the table. The lesson here is that you don't always get the whole move,

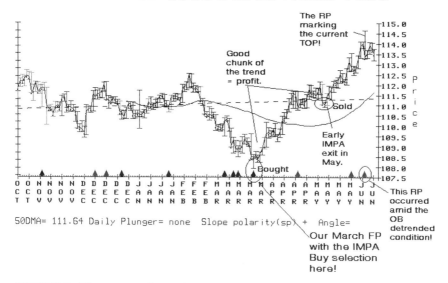

FIGURE 9.16 An IMPA buy selection in March 2005 in 10-year notes coincided with a forward plunger pattern.

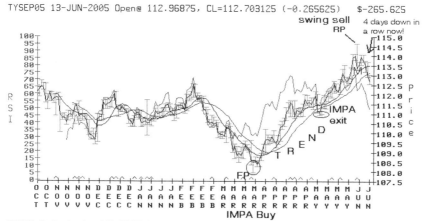

FIGURE 9.17 IMPA buy selection and uptrend in 10-year notes, from the forward plunger pattern through the IMPA exit and the reverse plunger at the top of the move.

and $3,000 per contract was certainly a decent profit. That brings to mind the old saying in trading: "Bulls and bears make money, but pigs get slaughtered." You can become too greedy in trading, trying to hold onto trades for too long and to squeeze out every last dime of a profit. If you get too piggish, you will get slaughtered, turning your profits into losses.

You must have rules that govern both entry and exit—such as the 18-day moving average 2-day rule—even if it gets you out before the move is over. You must be consistent in your trading, using a system such as IMPA to identify potential trading opportunities, and then using technical indicators and price patterns for your entry and logical stop placement.

By trading consistently, following the rules and methodology, and observing the market on a regular basis, a trader develops instincts over time. Combining instinct and experience along with a proven system can potentially increase a trader's chances for sustained success and profitability.

JUNE 2005 IMPA BUY IN HOGS

The final example is an IMPA buy selection in the Hog market during the summer of 2005. In this example, I illustrate the use of the commercial producer and commercial consumer graphs along with the net-commercial (trigger selection) graphs. Figure 9.18 shows the net-commercial UCL/LCL

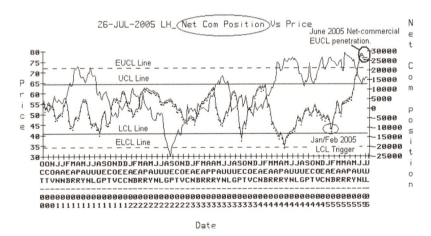

FIGURE 9.18   Net-commercial position at an extreme since June 2005 for hogs.

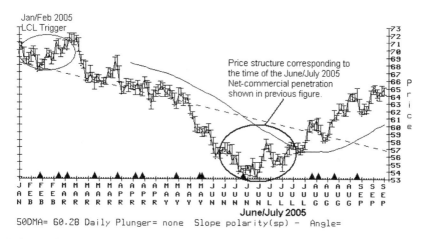

FIGURE 9.19   Price structure on a daily trend/swing.

graph for Hogs during July. The net-commercial position was at an extreme and had been since June 2005.

Figure 9.19 shows the price structure on a daily trend/swing graph. I have circled the date period that corresponds with the initial net-commercial UCL penetration during June/July 2005. Notice the price trend that has unfolded following the initial IMPA buy setup. The buy setup was completed after the market closed above the 18-day moving average for two consecutive days and the trend was confirmed up once the 10-day moving average crossed above the 18-day moving average. At the time of this writing (in September 2005), the trend is still up. If you would like to view the actual colored graphs you can do so at my web site at www.upperman.com or www,wizkid-trading.com.

Figure 9.20 shows the condition of the daily detrended analysis during the initial phases of the IMPA buy setup in hogs during June/July 2005. This graph also shows the trend higher that unfolded following the initial buy setup in hogs. The detrended analysis is not part of the core criteria but is something I look at. The market does not have to be penetrating the upper or lower areas for an IMPA buy or sell setup to succeed, but this certainly is something that can work in or favor.

Figure 9.21 is the commercial consumer graph for hogs. This study is constructed the same way the net-com study is constructed. Again, I am using statistical control limits (upper commercial and lower commercial limits) to identify extreme conditions. I have circled the extreme commercial consumer position during the June/July 2005 setup. Notice the position was exceeding its UCL. In addition, a corresponding price line is provided

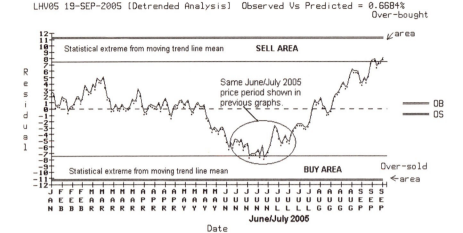

FIGURE 9.20   Daily detrended analysis during the initial phases of the IMPA buy setup in hogs during June/July 2005.

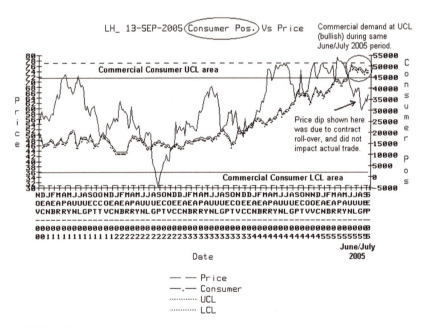

FIGURE 9.21   Commercial consumer position for hogs.

on this graph. The price line is created the same way for all the individual participant studies (except for the seasonal studies that is derived from monthly prices). The price lines contained in the individual participant graphs reflect Tuesday's closing prices only.

In addition, as of September 2005, I am not doing any backward adjusting on these graphs to remove the price gaps caused by contract rolls. Thus, some spikes and dips in the price line can be seen that are not seen in the actual price graphs. That's because these price graphs have been constructed to reflect the true price behavior of the market the way the trader would experience it. The participant studies, however, reflect Tuesday's closes only and actual prices. They are not back-adjusted to remove the gaps in price caused from contract to contract rollover. Back-adjusting of old prices to remove gaps is not necessary in these graphs because the indicator lines are derived from the COT data only and not from price. The price is provided for reference only. When I want to examine price structure closely, I use our specific price graphs (such as the daily or weekly price graph or the daily trend/swing graph, and so forth). In the future, I may decide to incorporate some backward adjusting in the participant studies as well to remove these false gaps. I have tried creating the graphs both ways and have noted that incorporating backward adjusting improves the price to net-commercial correlation. However, it does so while sacrificing true contract prices. I thought about this long and hard and finally decided it was more important that the price line on these graphs reflect actual contract prices from front month to front month in order to observe and record participant activity at true specific prices. However, there is still much to be considered here. Commercials, for example, often take advantage of cash-settled contracts and hold contracts longer than the funds or small speculators. Therefore, I am still considering doing backward adjusting here as well since a higher correlation coefficient reinforces the validity of the indicators and thus increases confidence as well.

Figure 9.22 is the commercial producer graph for hogs. I have highlighted the same June/July 2005 time period. Now I want to discuss something very powerful in my opinion (which I mentioned earlier in Chapter 5). One of the things I looked at and really liked regarding the 2005 June/July hog IMPA buy setup was the commercial consumer and commercial producer relationship. The commercial consumers were at their UCL as was shown in Figure 9.21. In Figure 9.22, you can see that the commercial producers were well off the commercial producer LCL area. In fact, the commercial producer position was up around the center of its distribution during the June/July 2005 period. I interpreted that to be bullish and an indication that the commercial producers, while *able* to move down to their LCL area and provide supply via shorting

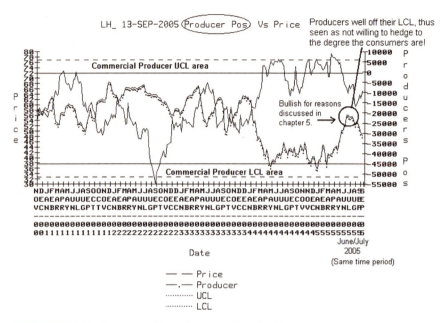

FIGURE 9.22   Commercial producer position for Hogs.

(selling), were simply unwilling to move back down to their LCL and sell at a statistically significant level, providing the liquidity the commercial consumers were demanding. Again this was at a time when the commercial consumer was clearly buying at a statistically significant level. That is precisely what I wanted to see. This is what really activated this setup for me and I mentioned this in my reports to members of my web site as well. It was the icing on the cake so to speak (and it turned out to be a sweet cake, too).

Figure 9.23 shows the net-fund position in hogs during the June/July 2005 period. The funds (large traders) represent the smart trading money. In Figure 9.23, you can see the degree of correlation between the net-fund position and the price trend. While the funds are the trend followers, they are not always right at the major turns. In fact, they are usually holding an opposing position at the turns. I often refer to this as the fuel for the next trend because it must first be liquidated before the funds can begin to establish a new position with a new trend. But this by no means indicates the funds aren't smart trading money. They are trend followers first and foremost and there are many of them. As a trend con-

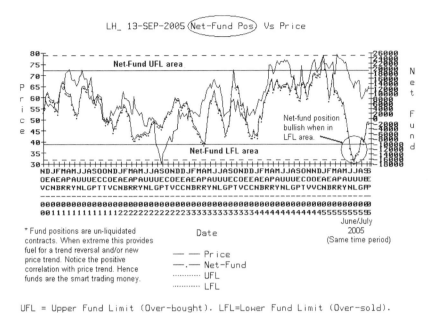

FIGURE 9.23 Net fund position in hogs during June/July 2005.

tinues to unfold, more and more funds enter into it and profits are often used to purchase more positions in the direction of the trend as well. This can continue for a good while. Although they may not appear to be the smart money at the major turns, they are the smart money the rest of the time. Traders need to keep in mind that most of the time the markets are not in the midst of a major reversal or turn: The markets are either in a trend or moving sideways. Occasionally, they go through a major reversal in front of a boom-or-bust period. The net of the large commercial positions tend to the smart money ahead of the major turning points. But the net-commercial position is almost always positioned early, too, which is also very important to understand.

Figure 9.24 is the standard daily price graph for hogs. I have circled the June/July 2003 period in this graph as well. This graph does incorporate backward adjusting of price. This is necessary in this case because without the backward adjusting of price the indicators would not work properly, and the reflected price structure would not be the same as what a trader is really experiencing.

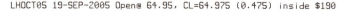

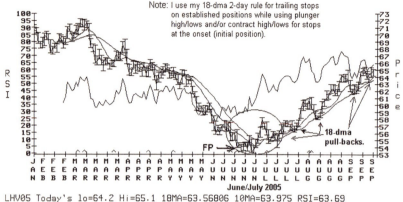

LHOCT05 19-SEP-2005 Open@ 64.95, CL=64.975 (0.475) inside $190

LHV05 Today's lo=64.2 Hi=65.1 18MA=63.56806 10MA=63.975 RSI=63.69
^ Red and Blue carrots along lower x-axis show outside days

The daily price graph is backward adjusted to remove the false gaps caused by contract roll-over. This adjustment is necessary to perserve and present the actual price structure in the way a trader would experience it. All my graphs that contain indicators derived from price are backward adjusted to address this.

FIGURE 9.24   Standard daily price position for hogs.

CONCLUSION

My trading strategies are derived from an in-depth analysis of the data in the weekly *Commitment of Traders* (COT) report and how that data relates to price behavior. I believe the COT is among the most underrated and least talked about data in the financial community. Over the years, I have found it to be extremely helpful and enlightening to monitor the COT activity across multiple markets to identify changing conditions and potential opportunities. As important as the COT is, it cannot be used alone.

My approach, as illustrated, begins with an analysis of the net-commercial positions (derived from COT) and includes in-depth studies of the individual commercial components—the producers and the consumers. I also follow the positions held by other participants, especially the funds—including the individual fund positions and the net fund position. Through this comprehensive approach, using proprietary technical indicators and patterns, I strive to identify potential trading opportunities before they occur, and then determine the appropriate and optimal entry and logical stop placement.

It is my hope that other traders will find ways to apply the COT data to their trading strategies. With an understanding of the COT data, combined with technical indicators, risk management, and the experience that comes from observing the markets over time, traders can improve their chances of achieving successful and profitable results.

Appendix

TABLE A.1 CFTC Reporting Levels

Current list of reporting levels in markets under Commodity Futures Trading Commission (CFTC) jurisdiction. (Current as of June 2005.)

Futures Market	Contracts
Agricultural	
Wheat	150
Corn	250
Oats	60
Soybeans	150
Soybean Oil	200
Soybean Meal	200
Cotton	100
Frozen Concentrated Orange Juice	50
Milk, Class III	50
Rough Rice	50
Live Cattle	100
Feeder Cattle	50
Lean Hogs	100
Sugar No. 11	500
Sugar No. 14	100
Cocoa	100
Coffee	50

(continues)

TABLE A.1 *(Continued)*

Futures Market	Contracts
Natural Resources	
Copper	100
Gold	200
Silver Bullion	150
Platinum	50
No. 2 Heating Oil	250
Crude Oil, Sweet	350
Unleaded Gasoline	150
Natural Gas	200
Crude Oil, Sweet--No. 2 Heating Oil Crack Spread	250
Crude Oil, Sweet--Unleaded Gasoline Crack Spread	150
Unleaded Gasoline--No. 2 Heating Oil Spread Swap	150
Financial	
3-month (13-Week) U.S. Treasury Bills	150
30-Year U.S. Treasury Bonds	1,500
10-Year U.S. Treasury Notes	2,000
5-Year U.S. Treasury Notes	2,000
2-Year U.S. Treasury Notes	1,000
10-Year German Federal Government Debt	1,000
5-Year German Federal Government Debt	800
2-Year German Federal Government Debt	500
3-Month Eurodollar Time Deposit Rates	3,000
30-Day Fed Funds	600
1-month LIBOR Rates	600
3-month Euroyen	100
Major-Foreign Currencies	400
Other Foreign Currencies	100
U.S. Dollar Index	50
Goldman Sachs Commodity Index	100
Broad-Based Security Indexes	
S&P 500 Stock Price Index	1,000
Municipal Bond Index	300
Other Broad-Based Securities Indexes	200
Security Futures Products	
Individual Equity Security	1,000
Narrow-Based Security Index	200
Other Products	
TRAKRS	50,000
HedgeStreet Products	125,000
All Other Commodities	25

Source: Commodity Futures Trading Commission (www.cftc.gov).

BACK-TESTING RESULTS—38 MARKETS

Results of 1998 back-testing studies in 38 markets (see Chapter 3). Results of the individual markets are shown in the following tables:

```
SP   10R x 7C                                    19-OCT-1998 11:20 Page 1

     Historic single contract trades from 21-SEP-1993 to 28-JUL-1998

0    1 MKT  2 B/S  3 Idate      4 Price  5 Odate      6 Price  7 W/L
----------------------------------------------------------------------
  1    SP    BUY   21-SEP-1993   453.40  04-NOV-1993   458.40    2500
  2    SP    BUY   01-MAR-1994   463.90  25-MAR-1994   459.95   -2625
  3    SP    BUY   19-APR-1994   443.10  21-JUN-1994   452.50    3775
  4    SP    BUY   05-JUL-1994   447.05  20-SEP-1994   463.95    7350
  5    SP    BUY   27-SEP-1994   463.95  04-OCT-1994   455.05   -4450
  6    SP    BUY   11-OCT-1994   467.40  21-NOV-1994   457.60   -4900
  7    SP    BUY   20-DEC-1994   460.45  20-DEC-1995   613.05   76300
  8    SP    SELL  28-OCT-1997   924.50  03-NOV-1997   945.70   -5300
  9    SP    SELL  26-MAY-1998  1094.00  05-JUN-1998  1117.40   -5850
 10    SP    SELL  28-JUL-1998  1135.50  13-OCT-1998  1003.00   33125

# Wins= 5 # Loses= 5 Largest Win= $76300 Largest Loss= $-5850 Ahead= $99925
```

```
NK   32R x 7C                                    19-OCT-1998 1:10 Page 1

     Historic single contract trades from 02-MAR-1993 to 11-AUG-1998

0     1 MKT  2 B/S  3 Idate      4 Price  5 Odate      6 Price  7 W/L
---------------------------------------------------------------------------
1     NK     BUY    02-MAR-1993    16880  18-MAY-1993    20165    16175
2     NK     BUY    06-JUL-1993    19870  23-JUL-1993    19730     -700
3     NK     BUY    27-JUL-1993    20000  16-SEP-1993    20505     -775
4     NK     BUY    12-OCT-1993    20215  26-OCT-1993    20000    -1075
5     NK     BUY    04-JAN-1994    17325  14-FEB-1994    18890     7825
6     NK     BUY    01-MAR-1994    20060  23-MAR-1994    19895    -1075
7     NK     SELL   21-JUN-1994    20475  30-JUN-1994    20750    -1375
8     NK     BUY    04-OCT-1994    19575  09-NOV-1994    19520     -275
9     NK     BUY    29-NOV-1994    18915  17-JAN-1995    19290     1275
10    NK     BUY    31-JAN-1995    18740  08-FEB-1995    18345    -1975
11    NK     BUY    28-MAR-1995    16790  31-MAR-1995    15955    -4175
12    NK     BUY    11-APR-1995    16385  12-MAY-1995    16395       50
13    NK     SELL   13-JUN-1995    14635  15-JUN-1995    15080    -2225
14    NK     SELL   27-JUN-1995    14685  05-JUL-1995    14910    -1125
15    NK     SELL   05-SEP-1995    17895  08-SEP-1995    18230    -1675
16    NK     SELL   19-SEP-1995    18795  27-SEP-1995    18235     2800
17    NK     SELL   17-OCT-1995    17880  20-OCT-1995    18110    -1150
18    NK     SELL   14-NOV-1995    17870  16-NOV-1995    18050     -900
19    NK     SELL   19-DEC-1995    19500  21-DEC-1995    19820    -1600
20    NK     SELL   20-FEB-1996    20655  01-MAR-1996    20160     2475
21    NK     SELL   07-MAY-1996    21460  15-MAY-1996    22190    -3650
22    NK     SELL   04-JUN-1996    22020  12-JUN-1996    22150     -650
23    NK     SELL   02-JUL-1996    22435  18-JUL-1996    21725     3550
24    NK     SELL   27-AUG-1996    20945  13-SEP-1996    21030     -275
25    NK     SELL   03-SEP-1996    20260  05-SEP-1996    20350     -450
26    NK     SELL   27-MAY-1997    19895  02-JUN-1997    20410    -2575
27    NK     SELL   01-JUL-1997    20285  14-JUL-1997    20325     -200
28    NK     SELL   30-SEP-1997    17630  14-OCT-1997    17445      925
29    NK     SELL   17-MAR-1998    17090  20-MAR-1998    16925      825
30    NK     SELL   31-MAR-1998    15985  07-APR-1998    16020     -175
31    NK     SELL   21-JUL-1998    16355  08-SEP-1998    14915     6875
32    NK     SELL   11-AUG-1998    15165  19-AUG-1998    15355     -950

# Wins= 10 # Loses= 22 Largest Win= $16175 Largest Loss= $-4175 Ahead= $13750
```

```
ED  6R × 7C                                    19-OCT-1998 1:09 Page 1

   Historic single contract trades from 04-JAN-1993 to 24-FEB-1998

0    1 MKT  2 B/S  3 Idate      4 Price  5 Odate      6 Price  7 W/L

---------------------------------------------------------------------
1    ED     BUY    04-JAN-1993  96.440   23-FEB-1993  96.680    600
2    ED     SELL   12-DEC-1995  94.570   15-DEC-1995  94.610   -100
3    ED     SELL   20-FEB-1996  94.670   23-FEB-1996  94.950   -250
4    ED     SELL   27-JAN-1998  94.385   29-JAN-1998  94.415    -75
5    ED     SELL   10-FEB-1998  94.380   12-FEB-1998  94.380      0
6    ED     SELL   24-FEB-1998  94.330   05-MAR-1998  94.340    -25

# Wins= 2 # Loses= 4 Largest Win= $600 Largest Loss= $-250 Ahead= $150
```

```
US   15R x 7C                               19-OCT-1998 1:10 Page 1

     Historic single contract trades from 04-JAN-1994 to 14-JUL-1998

0    1 MKT  2 B/S  3 Idate    4 Price  5 Odate    6 Price  7 W/L

-----------------------------------------------------------------------
 1    US    BUY   04-JAN-1994  114.219  04-FEB-1994  114.875    656.25
 2    US    BUY   27-SEP-1994   98.719  29-SEP-1994   98.688    -31.25
 3    US    BUY   24-JAN-1995   99.094  18-JUL-1995  112.688  14531.25
 4    US    SELL  21-NOV-1995  117.344  24-NOV-1995  117.594   -531.25
 5    US    SELL  19-DEC-1995  119.344  22-DEC-1995  120.031   -687.50
 6    US    SELL  20-FEB-1996  116.125  01-MAR-1996  115.531    125.00
 7    US    SELL  17-DEC-1996  112.531  20-DEC-1996  113.313   -781.25
 8    US    SELL  05-AUG-1997  114.594  28-AUG-1997  113.281    937.50
 9    US    SELL  26-AUG-1997  112.219  28-AUG-1997  113.281  -1062.50
10    US    SELL  09-DEC-1997  118.063  11-DEC-1997  119.406  -1343.75
11    US    SELL  30-DEC-1997  119.875  02-JAN-1998  121.469  -1593.75
12    US    SELL  20-JAN-1998  122.031  29-JAN-1998  121.875    156.25
13    US    SELL  24-FEB-1998  119.875  09-MAR-1998  119.906    -31.25
14    US    SELL  21-APR-1998  120.188  04-MAY-1998  120.344   -156.25
15    US    SELL  14-JUL-1998  122.438  21-JUL-1998  123.125   -687.50

# Wins= 5 # Loses= 10 Largest Win= $14531.25 Largest Loss= $-1593.75 Ahead= $950
```

TY 22R x 7C   19-OCT-1998 1:10 Page 1

   Historic single contract trades from 06-APR-1993 to 14-JUL-1998

0	1 MKT	2 B/S	3 Idate	4 Price	5 Odate	6 Price	7 W/L
1	TY	BUY	06-APR-1993	111.375	03-NOV-1993	113.938	125.00
2	TY	BUY	09-NOV-1993	113.875	11-NOV-1993	113.281	-593.75
3	TY	BUY	16-NOV-1993	114.313	08-FEB-1994	112.156	-1250.00
4	TY	BUY	15-FEB-1994	112.563	18-FEB-1994	111.406	-1156.25
5	TY	BUY	08-MAR-1994	108.906	10-MAR-1994	108.313	-593.75
6	TY	BUY	15-MAR-1994	108.438	29-MAR-1994	106.844	-1593.75
7	TY	BUY	31-MAY-1994	103.813	28-JUN-1994	103.594	-218.75
8	TY	BUY	12-JUL-1994	102.719	16-SEP-1994	101.938	250.00
9	TY	BUY	27-SEP-1994	101.469	05-OCT-1994	100.594	-875.00
10	TY	BUY	11-OCT-1994	101.531	04-NOV-1994	99.219	-2312.50
11	TY	BUY	08-NOV-1994	99.469	19-JUL-1995	108.656	10937.50
12	TY	BUY	01-AUG-1995	108.500	20-FEB-1996	112.344	4250.00
13	TY	BUY	05-MAR-1996	111.625	08-MAR-1996	108.531	-3093.75
14	TY	SELL	27-AUG-1996	106.688	09-SEP-1996	106.000	687.50
15	TY	SELL	17-DEC-1996	109.250	20-DEC-1996	109.656	-406.25
16	TY	BUY	07-JAN-1997	108.281	04-MAR-1997	107.375	-312.50
17	TY	BUY	18-MAR-1997	106.625	27-MAR-1997	105.563	-1062.50
18	TY	BUY	01-APR-1997	105.688	09-OCT-1998	118.594	13843.75
19	TY	SELL	30-DEC-1997	111.844	02-JAN-1998	112.750	-906.25
20	TY	SELL	20-JAN-1998	113.469	29-JAN-1998	113.469	0.00
21	TY	SELL	24-FEB-1998	112.344	09-MAR-1998	112.313	31.25
22	TY	SELL	14-JUL-1998	113.625	21-JUL-1998	113.844	-218.75

Wins= 8 # Loses= 14 Largest Win= $13843.75 Largest Loss= $-3093.75 Ahead= $155

```
TB   2R × 7C                                19-OCT-1998 1:10 Page 1

   Historic single contract trades from 25-MAY-1993 to 21-AUG-1998

0    1 MKT  2 B/S  3 Idate      4 Price  5 Odate      6 Price  7 W/L

-----------------------------------------------------------------------
1    TB     BUY    25-MAY-1993   96.85   01-AUG-1993   97.00    375
2    TB     BUY    21-AUG-1998   95.26   13-OCT-1998   96.12   2150

# Wins= 2 # Loses= 0 Largest Win= $2150 Largest Loss= $375 Ahead= $2525
```

```
BP  31R x 7C                          19-OCT-1998 1:09 Page 1

    Historic single contract trades from 23-FEB-1993 to 29-SEP-1998
```

0	1 MKT	2 B/S	3 Idate	4 Price	5 Odate	6 Price	7 W/L
1	BP	BUY	23-FEB-1993	145.38	10-MAY-1993	152.72	5212.5
2	BP	SELL	22-JUN-1993	146.84	28-JUN-1993	148.66	-1137.5
3	BP	BUY	17-AUG-1993	148.52	23-SEP-1993	149.72	1387.5
4	BP	BUY	09-NOV-1993	146.50	29-DEC-1993	146.86	637.5
5	BP	SELL	08-FEB-1994	146.46	14-FEB-1994	148.46	-1250.0
6	BP	BUY	01-MAR-1994	148.88	06-APR-1994	146.48	325.0
7	BP	BUY	12-APR-1994	147.26	21-JUL-1994	152.02	3125.0
8	BP	SELL	15-NOV-1994	157.46	23-NOV-1994	156.92	337.5
9	BP	BUY	29-NOV-1994	156.22	21-DEC-1994	154.16	-1275.0
10	BP	BUY	27-DEC-1994	154.52	06-FEB-1995	155.86	837.5
11	BP	BUY	29-AUG-1995	154.28	13-NOV-1995	154.96	612.5
12	BP	BUY	21-NOV-1995	155.72	28-NOV-1995	154.32	-875.0
13	BP	BUY	05-DEC-1995	154.30	17-JAN-1996	151.94	-1312.5
14	BP	BUY	30-JAN-1996	150.42	01-MAY-1996	149.02	-712.5
15	BP	SELL	16-JUL-1996	155.94	25-JUL-1996	155.78	100.0
16	BP	SELL	06-AUG-1996	153.68	08-AUG-1996	154.92	-775.0
17	BP	SELL	10-SEP-1996	155.46	16-SEP-1996	155.70	-150.0
18	BP	SELL	03-DEC-1996	164.28	09-DEC-1996	164.46	-325.0
19	BP	SELL	31-DEC-1996	171.24	02-JAN-1997	169.02	1387.5
20	BP	SELL	14-JAN-1997	166.86	04-FEB-1997	162.06	3000.0
21	BP	BUY	18-MAR-1997	158.68	28-JUL-1997	162.78	2775.0
22	BP	SELL	15-JUL-1997	167.46	21-JUL-1997	167.54	-50.0
23	BP	SELL	29-JUL-1997	162.52	26-AUG-1997	160.88	1025.0
24	BP	BUY	19-AUG-1997	160.34	04-DEC-1997	166.58	4275.0
25	BP	BUY	26-AUG-1997	160.88	25-NOV-1997	167.38	4062.5
26	BP	SELL	25-NOV-1997	167.38	11-DEC-1997	164.96	1087.5
27	BP	SELL	21-APR-1998	167.06	27-APR-1998	167.02	25.0
28	BP	BUY	19-MAY-1998	162.00	06-JUL-1998	162.96	1087.5
29	BP	BUY	16-JUN-1998	164.40	23-JUN-1998	166.08	1050.0
30	BP	BUY	18-AUG-1998	161.34	13-OCT-1998	169.98	5887.5
31	BP	BUY	29-SEP-1998	170.26	02-OCT-1998	169.18	-675.0

```
# Wins= 20 # Loses= 11 Largest Win= $5887.5 Largest Loss= $-1312.5 Ahead= $29700
```

```
CD   23R × 7C                              19-OCT-1998 1:09 Page 1

    Historic single contract trades from 04-MAY-1993 to 08-SEP-1998

0      1 MKT  2 B/S  3 Idate      4 Price  5 Odate      6 Price  7 W/L

--------------------------------------------------------------------
   1   CD     BUY    04-MAY-1993    78.47  11-AUG-1993    76.58   -1560
   2   CD     BUY    24-AUG-1993    75.84  22-NOV-1993    75.15     690
   3   CD     SELL   11-OCT-1994    74.40  25-OCT-1994    74.14     260
   4   CD     SELL   15-NOV-1994    73.30  31-JAN-1995    70.87    2430
   5   CD     BUY    22-NOV-1994    72.78  29-DEC-1994    70.95   -1810
   6   CD     BUY    03-JAN-1995    71.09  12-JAN-1995    70.32    -770
   7   CD     BUY    17-JAN-1995    70.36  14-SEP-1995    72.69    3030
   8   CD     BUY    31-JAN-1995    70.87  16-MAY-1995    73.58    2710
   9   CD     SELL   16-MAY-1995    73.58  08-JUN-1995    72.62     760
  10   CD     SELL   12-SEP-1995    74.07  19-SEP-1995    73.41     660
  11   CD     SELL   17-OCT-1995    74.67  31-OCT-1995    74.44     230
  12   CD     SELL   24-OCT-1995    73.01  27-OCT-1995    73.26    -250
  13   CD     SELL   07-MAY-1996    73.28  14-MAY-1996    73.09     190
  14   CD     SELL   19-NOV-1996    74.69  07-JAN-1997    74.02    1110
  15   CD     SELL   17-DEC-1996    73.72  23-DEC-1996    73.59     130
  16   CD     SELL   14-OCT-1997    72.59  04-NOV-1997    71.54    1050
  17   CD     BUY    04-NOV-1997    71.54  22-JAN-1998    69.00   -2820
  18   CD     BUY    10-FEB-1998    69.89  13-FEB-1998    69.35    -540
  19   CD     SELL   17-MAR-1998    70.69  25-MAR-1998    71.06    -370
  20   CD     SELL   31-MAR-1998    70.61  17-APR-1998    70.08     530
  21   CD     BUY    16-JUN-1998    68.16  24-JUL-1998    66.77   -1390
  22   CD     BUY    11-AUG-1998    65.74  21-AUG-1998    64.90    -840
  23   CD     BUY    08-SEP-1998    65.74  17-SEP-1998    65.37    -370

# Wins= 13 # Loses= 10 Largest Win= $3030 Largest Loss= $-2820 Ahead= $3060
```

DM 20R × 7C   19-OCT-1998 1:09 Page 1

Historic single contract trades from 16-FEB-1993 to 11-AUG-1998

0	1 MKT	2 B/S	3 Idate	4 Price	5 Odate	6 Price	7 W/L
1	DM	BUY	16-FEB-1993	61.00	05-MAR-1993	59.86	-1425.0
2	DM	BUY	09-MAR-1993	59.26	12-MAY-1993	61.72	3075.0
3	DM	BUY	25-MAY-1993	61.16	15-JUN-1993	60.07	-550.0
4	DM	BUY	13-JUL-1993	57.77	29-JUL-1993	57.14	-787.5
5	DM	BUY	03-AUG-1993	58.35	21-OCT-1993	59.70	2312.5
6	DM	BUY	09-NOV-1993	58.89	30-DEC-1993	57.29	-1500.0
7	DM	BUY	04-JAN-1994	57.30	06-JAN-1994	57.03	-337.5
8	DM	BUY	11-JAN-1994	57.15	13-JAN-1994	56.85	-375.0
9	DM	BUY	18-JAN-1994	57.03	05-APR-1994	58.05	1625.0
10	DM	SELL	15-NOV-1994	64.31	23-NOV-1994	64.39	-100.0
11	DM	BUY	06-DEC-1994	63.61	11-MAY-1995	69.88	7375.0
12	DM	BUY	16-APR-1996	66.48	19-APR-1996	66.38	-125.0
13	DM	BUY	07-MAY-1996	65.75	10-SEP-1996	66.60	112.5
14	DM	BUY	15-OCT-1996	65.16	27-NOV-1996	65.50	425.0
15	DM	BUY	12-AUG-1997	53.74	21-OCT-1997	56.04	2462.5
16	DM	BUY	20-JAN-1998	54.49	05-MAR-1998	54.45	-50.0
17	DM	BUY	10-MAR-1998	54.97	01-APR-1998	54.23	-925.0
18	DM	BUY	07-APR-1998	54.69	11-JUN-1998	55.56	725.0
19	DM	BUY	14-APR-1998	55.69	29-APR-1998	55.82	162.5
20	DM	SELL	11-AUG-1998	56.28	28-AUG-1998	56.96	-850.0

Wins= 9 # Loses= 11 Largest Win= $7375 Largest Loss= $-1500 Ahead= $11250

JY   30R × 7C   19-OCT-1998 1:09 Page 1

   Historic single contract trades from 23-MAR-1993 to 01-SEP-1998

0   1 MKT 2 B/S 3 Idate   4 Price 5 Odate   6 Price 7 W/L

1	JY	SELL	23-MAR-1993	86.07	26-MAR-1993	85.85	275.0
2	JY	BUY	21-SEP-1993	93.86	21-OCT-1993	92.37	-1862.5
3	JY	BUY	02-NOV-1993	92.89	29-DEC-1993	89.68	-412.5
4	JY	BUY	11-JAN-1994	88.98	10-MAY-1994	95.74	7962.5
5	JY	BUY	24-MAY-1994	95.63	28-JUL-1994	100.23	4962.5
6	JY	BUY	11-OCT-1994	100.27	15-NOV-1994	101.55	1600.0
7	JY	BUY	22-NOV-1994	101.87	02-DEC-1994	99.57	-2875.0
8	JY	BUY	06-DEC-1994	100.05	08-DEC-1994	100.47	-637.5
9	JY	BUY	13-DEC-1994	100.84	11-MAY-1995	117.29	19062.5
10	JY	BUY	07-NOV-1995	97.64	29-DEC-1995	97.73	-1575.0
11	JY	BUY	30-JAN-1996	93.87	21-MAR-1996	94.73	-375.0
12	JY	BUY	26-MAR-1996	94.91	09-APR-1996	93.22	-850.0
13	JY	BUY	16-APR-1996	93.19	15-MAY-1996	93.92	912.5
14	JY	BUY	11-JUN-1996	92.52	02-JUL-1996	91.54	-1225.0
15	JY	BUY	09-JUL-1996	91.56	12-JUL-1996	91.01	-687.5
16	JY	BUY	17-SEP-1996	91.85	02-OCT-1996	90.29	-525.0
17	JY	BUY	08-OCT-1996	90.56	25-OCT-1996	88.74	-2275.0
18	JY	BUY	05-NOV-1996	88.12	29-NOV-1996	88.02	-125.0
19	JY	BUY	14-JAN-1997	86.23	21-JAN-1997	85.38	-1062.5
20	JY	BUY	15-APR-1997	80.03	15-JUL-1997	87.32	7637.5
21	JY	BUY	07-OCT-1997	82.39	05-NOV-1997	81.71	-850.0
22	JY	BUY	16-DEC-1997	77.55	02-JAN-1998	76.24	-1637.5
23	JY	BUY	06-JAN-1998	75.49	08-JAN-1998	76.02	662.5
24	JY	BUY	13-JAN-1998	76.59	17-FEB-1998	79.24	3312.5
25	JY	BUY	27-JAN-1998	80.32	30-JAN-1998	79.15	-1462.5
26	JY	BUY	24-MAR-1998	77.63	01-APR-1998	75.64	-287.5
27	JY	BUY	07-APR-1998	75.70	30-APR-1998	75.67	-37.5
28	JY	BUY	16-JUN-1998	70.70	25-JUN-1998	71.06	450.0
29	JY	BUY	18-AUG-1998	69.22	25-SEP-1998	74.21	5000.0
30	JY	BUY	01-SEP-1998	73.53	09-SEP-1998	74.05	-587.5

Wins= 11 # Loses= 19 Largest Win= $19062.5 Largest Loss= $-2875 Ahead= $32487.

```
SF  33R x 7C                              19-OCT-1998 1:10 Page 1

    Historic single contract trades from 16-FEB-1993 to 28-JUL-1998

0    1 MKT  2 B/S  3 Idate     4 Price  5 Odate      6 Price  7 W/L
-----------------------------------------------------------------------
 1    SF    BUY   16-FEB-1993   66.20   05-MAR-1993   64.69  -1887.5
 2    SF    BUY   09-MAR-1993   64.55   12-MAY-1993   68.20   4562.5
 3    SF    SELL  11-MAY-1993   68.48   14-MAY-1993   68.91   -537.5
 4    SF    BUY   06-JUL-1993   65.89   09-JUL-1993   65.12   -962.5
 5    SF    BUY   13-JUL-1993   65.69   11-AUG-1993   65.11   -725.0
 6    SF    SELL  21-SEP-1993   69.88   28-SEP-1993   70.60   -900.0
 7    SF    SELL  19-OCT-1993   68.92   07-DEC-1993   68.50    525.0
 8    SF    BUY   09-NOV-1993   66.87   30-DEC-1993   67.30    712.5
 9    SF    SELL  08-FEB-1994   67.48   11-FEB-1994   67.45     37.5
10    SF    BUY   06-DEC-1994   75.36   07-FEB-1995   77.00   1600.0
11    SF    BUY   19-DEC-1995   87.22   16-JAN-1996   85.38  -2300.0
12    SF    BUY   06-FEB-1996   83.73   09-APR-1996   83.17  -1637.5
13    SF    BUY   07-MAY-1996   80.72   17-MAY-1996   79.53  -1487.5
14    SF    BUY   28-MAY-1996   78.71   06-SEP-1996   82.08   3487.5
15    SF    BUY   08-OCT-1996   80.57   15-OCT-1996   79.32  -1562.5
16    SF    BUY   22-OCT-1996   80.25   27-NOV-1996   77.51   -137.5
17    SF    BUY   10-DEC-1996   76.09   13-DEC-1996   76.22    162.5
18    SF    BUY   24-DEC-1996   74.84   26-DEC-1996   74.93    112.5
19    SF    BUY   31-DEC-1996   75.20   03-JAN-1997   74.16  -1300.0
20    SF    BUY   11-MAR-1997   68.62   08-APR-1997   68.41   -262.5
21    SF    SELL  03-JUN-1997   69.71   09-JUN-1997   70.33    162.5
22    SF    BUY   08-JUL-1997   68.79   16-JUL-1997   68.23   -150.0
23    SF    BUY   12-AUG-1997   65.77   17-OCT-1997   68.27   2250.0
24    SF    SELL  09-DEC-1997   69.54   11-DEC-1997   70.95  -1762.5
25    SF    BUY   20-JAN-1998   67.26   05-MAR-1998   66.99   -337.5
26    SF    BUY   17-MAR-1998   68.30   19-MAR-1998   67.44  -1075.0
27    SF    BUY   24-MAR-1998   67.79   01-APR-1998   65.79   -487.5
28    SF    BUY   07-APR-1998   66.15   11-JUN-1998   67.47    875.0
29    SF    BUY   21-APR-1998   68.00   24-APR-1998   67.48   -650.0
30    SF    BUY   16-JUN-1998   67.53   24-JUN-1998   66.84   -862.5
31    SF    BUY   07-JUL-1998   65.93   09-JUL-1998   65.28   -812.5
32    SF    BUY   14-JUL-1998   66.13   13-OCT-1998   76.11  11600.0
33    SF    BUY   28-JUL-1998   67.53   03-AUG-1998   66.87   -825.0

# Wins= 12 # Loses= 21 Largest Win= $11600 Largest Loss= $-2300 Ahead= $5425
```

```
DX   15R x 7C                              19-OCT-1998 1:10 Page 1

     Historic single contract trades from 12-OCT-1993 to 11-AUG-1998

0     1 MKT  2 B/S  3 Idate     4 Price  5 Odate      6 Price  7 W/L
     ------------------------------------------------------------------
 1    DX     SELL   12-OCT-1993   91.91  14-OCT-1993   93.06   -1150
 2    DX     SELL   07-DEC-1993   95.15  14-DEC-1993   96.62    -670
 3    DX     BUY    27-SEP-1994   87.58  19-OCT-1994   85.76    -220
 4    DX     SELL   06-FEB-1996   86.43  29-FEB-1996   86.32     110
 5    DX     SELL   20-FEB-1996   85.75  28-FEB-1996   85.97    -220
 6    DX     SELL   19-MAR-1996   86.19  21-MAR-1996   86.47    -280
 7    DX     SELL   07-MAY-1996   87.78  10-MAY-1996   87.92    -140
 8    DX     SELL   18-JUN-1996   87.20  21-JUN-1996   88.18    -980
 9    DX     SELL   24-SEP-1996   86.62  26-SEP-1996   87.63   -1010
10    DX     SELL   22-OCT-1996   87.45  01-NOV-1996   87.09     360
11    DX     SELL   24-DEC-1996   88.57  26-DEC-1996   88.48      90
12    DX     SELL   18-MAR-1997   94.70  20-MAR-1997   95.49    -790
13    DX     BUY    18-NOV-1997   96.07  23-JAN-1998   98.28    2440
14    DX     BUY    05-MAY-1998   98.49  28-AUG-1998   99.94    1670
15    DX     BUY    11-AUG-1998  101.55  20-AUG-1998  101.97     420

# Wins= 6 # Loses= 9 Largest Win= $2440 Largest Loss= $-1150 Ahead= $-370
```

```
AD  25R x 7C                                19-OCT-1998 1:10 Page 1

    Historic single contract trades from 28-DEC-1993 to 01-SEP-1998

0    1 MKT  2 B/S  3 Idate      4 Price  5 Odate      6 Price  7 W/L

--------------------------------------------------------------------------
 1    AD    SELL   28-DEC-1993   67.61   30-DEC-1993   67.42     190
 2    AD    SELL   01-MAR-1994   71.27   04-MAR-1994   71.54    -270
 3    AD    SELL   29-MAR-1994   70.22   01-APR-1994   70.47    -250
 4    AD    SELL   14-JUN-1994   72.99   17-JUN-1994   73.40    -410
 5    AD    SELL   02-AUG-1994   73.23   05-AUG-1994   74.27   -1040
 6    AD    SELL   03-JAN-1995   76.58   11-JAN-1995   76.65     -70
 7    AD    BUY    28-FEB-1995   73.88   22-MAR-1995   72.19     -50
 8    AD    SELL   17-OCT-1995   75.16   25-OCT-1995   74.72     440
 9    AD    SELL   21-MAY-1996   79.18   29-MAY-1996   79.78    -600
10    AD    SELL   03-DEC-1996   79.13   09-DEC-1996   80.24   -1270
11    AD    BUY    21-JAN-1997   77.79   23-JAN-1997   77.17    -620
12    AD    BUY    28-JAN-1997   76.85   30-JAN-1997   76.54    -310
13    AD    BUY    11-FEB-1997   75.71   03-APR-1997   77.65    2010
14    AD    BUY    10-JUN-1997   76.27   12-JUN-1997   75.21   -1060
15    AD    BUY    17-JUN-1997   75.16   16-JUL-1997   73.65      90
16    AD    BUY    22-JUL-1997   74.00   07-AUG-1997   73.02    -980
17    AD    BUY    12-AUG-1997   73.90   02-SEP-1997   72.62   -1280
18    AD    BUY    09-SEP-1997   72.96   11-SEP-1997   72.18    -780
19    AD    BUY    23-SEP-1997   72.11   21-OCT-1997   72.14      30
20    AD    BUY    13-JAN-1998   64.79   23-FEB-1998   66.72    1930
21    AD    BUY    27-JAN-1998   67.73   04-FEB-1998   68.10     370
22    AD    BUY    21-APR-1998   65.30   05-MAY-1998   64.05   -1250
23    AD    BUY    16-JUN-1998   59.43   27-JUL-1998   60.96    1530
24    AD    BUY    14-JUL-1998   62.42   22-JUL-1998   62.28    -140
25    AD    BUY    01-SEP-1998   58.27   09-OCT-1998   61.86    3530
```

Wins= 9 # Loses= 16 Largest Win= $3530 Largest Loss= $-1280 Ahead= $-260

Historic single contract trades from 08-JUN-1993 to 01-SEP-1998

0	1 MKT	2 B/S	3 Idate	4 Price	5 Odate	6 Price	7 W/L
1	GC	SELL	08-JUN-1993	375.6	23-JUN-1993	375.5	10
2	GC	SELL	10-AUG-1993	384.4	21-SEP-1993	365.0	1940
3	GC	SELL	07-SEP-1993	352.5	16-SEP-1993	354.7	-220
4	GC	SELL	11-JAN-1994	388.7	13-JAN-1994	390.6	-190
5	GC	SELL	29-MAR-1994	388.5	31-MAR-1994	394.3	-580
6	GC	SELL	02-AUG-1994	384.4	11-AUG-1994	384.0	40
7	GC	SELL	04-OCT-1994	395.7	15-NOV-1994	387.4	830
8	GC	BUY	13-DEC-1994	380.3	04-JAN-1995	375.3	-500
9	GC	BUY	10-JAN-1995	375.1	26-APR-1995	388.0	690
10	GC	SELL	13-FEB-1996	405.1	21-MAR-1996	398.7	640
11	GC	SELL	20-FEB-1996	401.1	28-FEB-1996	402.1	-100
12	GC	SELL	02-APR-1996	396.6	08-APR-1996	400.7	-410
13	GC	BUY	24-SEP-1996	385.7	27-NOV-1996	375.0	-180
14	GC	BUY	22-JUL-1997	329.4	06-AUG-1997	322.5	-690
15	GC	BUY	19-AUG-1997	326.5	16-OCT-1997	326.8	30
16	GC	BUY	16-DEC-1997	285.4	07-JAN-1998	284.7	240
17	GC	BUY	24-MAR-1998	301.8	01-APR-1998	301.9	10
18	GC	BUY	16-JUN-1998	290.0	27-JUL-1998	294.8	30
19	GC	BUY	18-AUG-1998	289.0	27-AUG-1998	280.1	-890
20	GC	BUY	01-SEP-1998	282.2	13-OCT-1998	298.5	1630

Wins= 11 # Loses= 9 Largest Win= $1940 Largest Loss= $-890 Ahead= $2330

```
SI   18R x 7C                                20-OCT-1998 9:19 Page 1

    Historic single contract trades from 01-JUN-1993 to 24-FEB-1998

0     1 MKT  2 B/S  3 Idate     4 Price  5 Odate      6 Price  7 W/L

------------------------------------------------------------------------
    1    SI     SELL   01-JUN-1993   440.5  23-JUN-1993   442.7     45
    2    SI     SELL   01-JUN-1993   440.5  17-JUN-1993   434.0    325
    3    SI     SELL   07-SEP-1993   430.0  16-SEP-1993   409.7   1015
    4    SI     SELL   04-JAN-1994   523.0  06-JAN-1994   513.7    465
    5    SI     SELL   25-JAN-1994   510.7  01-FEB-1994   529.0   -915
    6    SI     SELL   22-FEB-1994   525.2  28-FEB-1994   539.0   -690
    7    SI     SELL   08-MAR-1994   523.5  10-MAR-1994   542.2   -935
    8    SI     SELL   05-APR-1994   555.5  28-APR-1994   528.5   1565
    9    SI     SELL   31-MAY-1994   555.0  15-JUN-1994   552.2    140
   10    SI     SELL   21-JUN-1994   559.5  19-JUL-1994   534.5   1495
   11    SI     SELL   02-AUG-1994   520.5  19-AUG-1994   521.5    -50
   12    SI     SELL   16-AUG-1994   510.7  18-AUG-1994   516.2   -275
   13    SI     SELL   11-OCT-1994   553.0  19-OCT-1994   540.5    625
   14    SI     BUY    21-JAN-1997   471.5  21-MAR-1997   516.5   2000
   15    SI     BUY    29-JUL-1997   432.5  16-SEP-1997   461.5   1100
   16    SI     BUY    13-NOV-1997   513.5  18-FEB-1998   656.0   7125
   17    SI     SELL   17-FEB-1998   677.0  19-FEB-1998   682.0   -250
   18    SI     SELL   24-FEB-1998   636.5  27-FEB-1998   648.0   -575

# Wins= 11 # Loses= 7 Largest Win= $7125 Largest Loss= $-935 Ahead= $12210
```

168

```
PL   26R x 7C                                    19-OCT-1998 1:09 Page 1

    Historic single contract trades from 02-MAR-1993 to 06-OCT-1998

0      1 MKT  2 B/S  3 Idate     4 Price  5 Odate      6 Price  7 W/L
    -----------------------------------------------------------------------
    1     PL    SELL   02-MAR-1993   341.0  05-MAR-1993   343.5   -125
    2     PL    SELL   04-MAY-1993   377.3  07-MAY-1993   384.6   -365
    3     PL    SELL   01-JUN-1993   392.1  03-JUN-1993   392.6   -25
    4     PL    SELL   15-JUN-1993   380.7  18-JUN-1993   379.6    55
    5     PL    SELL   10-AUG-1993   395.9  30-SEP-1993   362.2   1790
    6     PL    SELL   07-SEP-1993   360.1  16-SEP-1993   360.3   -10
    7     PL    SELL   23-NOV-1993   374.1  01-DEC-1993   374.9   -40
    8     PL    SELL   11-JAN-1994   390.5  17-JAN-1994   396.5   -300
    9     PL    SELL   22-FEB-1994   397.1  28-FEB-1994   397.7   -30
   10     PL    SELL   12-APR-1994   400.8  22-APR-1994   391.1   485
   11     PL    SELL   31-MAY-1994   404.2  10-JUN-1994   403.0    60
   12     PL    SELL   05-JUL-1994   413.4  11-JUL-1994   409.3   205
   13     PL    SELL   02-AUG-1994   418.2  19-AUG-1994   417.0    60
   14     PL    SELL   02-AUG-1994   418.2  10-AUG-1994   415.1   155
   15     PL    SELL   13-SEP-1994   418.1  20-SEP-1994   420.7   -130
   16     PL    SELL   11-OCT-1994   419.6  18-OCT-1994   421.7   -105
   17     PL    SELL   01-NOV-1994   420.5  12-DEC-1994   409.7   540
   18     PL    SELL   27-FEB-1996   410.1  29-FEB-1996   414.2   -205
   19     PL    BUY    18-NOV-1997   392.8  21-NOV-1997   389.0   -190
   20     PL    BUY    02-DEC-1997   388.5  04-DEC-1997   381.0   -375
   21     PL    BUY    23-DEC-1997   351.7  17-FEB-1998   380.8   1455
   22     PL    BUY    13-JAN-1998   372.2  20-JAN-1998   374.5   115
   23     PL    BUY    01-SEP-1998   364.9  08-SEP-1998   361.2   -185
   24     PL    BUY    15-SEP-1998   368.6  17-SEP-1998   360.4   -410
   25     PL    BUY    29-SEP-1998   348.0  01-OCT-1998   353.4   270
   26     PL    BUY    06-OCT-1998   344.2  09-OCT-1998   345.5    65
```

Wins= 12 # Loses= 14 Largest Win= $1790 Largest Loss= $-410 Ahead= $2760

```
PA  33R x 7C                              19-OCT-1998 1:09 Page 1

    Historic single contract trades from 11-OCT-1994 to 06-OCT-1998
```

0	1 MKT	2 B/S	3 Idate	4 Price	5 Odate	6 Price	7 W/L
1	PA	SELL	11-OCT-1994	152.35	14-OCT-1994	153.40	-105
2	PA	BUY	14-MAR-1995	161.50	20-APR-1995	169.05	755
3	PA	BUY	13-JUN-1995	161.80	22-JUN-1995	159.00	-280
4	PA	BUY	27-JUN-1995	161.25	05-JUL-1995	158.70	-255
5	PA	BUY	25-JUL-1995	154.30	27-JUL-1995	155.00	70
6	PA	BUY	08-AUG-1995	153.00	10-AUG-1995	151.90	-110
7	PA	BUY	22-AUG-1995	152.30	25-AUG-1995	150.45	-185
8	PA	BUY	12-SEP-1995	149.55	20-SEP-1995	143.45	-610
9	PA	BUY	24-OCT-1995	136.40	26-OCT-1995	135.30	-110
10	PA	BUY	31-OCT-1995	139.40	02-NOV-1995	136.40	-300
11	PA	BUY	07-NOV-1995	135.95	16-NOV-1995	135.20	-75
12	PA	BUY	05-DEC-1995	135.50	15-DEC-1995	133.00	-250
13	PA	BUY	02-JAN-1996	133.25	09-JAN-1996	131.15	-210
14	PA	BUY	16-JAN-1996	132.85	24-JAN-1996	130.05	-280
15	PA	BUY	07-MAY-1996	137.00	17-MAY-1996	133.25	-375
16	PA	BUY	18-JUN-1996	130.50	08-JUL-1996	131.20	70
17	PA	BUY	27-AUG-1996	127.95	29-AUG-1996	127.50	-45
18	PA	BUY	01-OCT-1996	120.50	09-OCT-1996	118.50	-75
19	PA	BUY	22-OCT-1996	120.75	25-OCT-1996	118.25	-250
20	PA	BUY	12-NOV-1996	119.95	25-NOV-1996	117.60	-370
21	PA	BUY	10-DEC-1996	121.00	27-DEC-1996	118.75	-225
22	PA	SELL	18-MAR-1997	145.50	21-MAR-1997	154.30	-880
23	PA	SELL	08-JUL-1997	163.75	14-JUL-1997	152.45	1130
24	PA	BUY	30-DEC-1997	203.75	18-FEB-1998	229.90	2615
25	PA	BUY	13-JAN-1998	236.40	20-JAN-1998	230.85	-555
26	PA	BUY	03-MAR-1998	234.05	30-MAR-1998	253.75	1970
27	PA	BUY	10-MAR-1998	246.25	18-MAR-1998	258.10	1185
28	PA	BUY	14-APR-1998	287.05	27-MAY-1998	290.50	4445
29	PA	BUY	12-MAY-1998	332.85	20-MAY-1998	350.30	1745
30	PA	BUY	16-JUN-1998	268.90	29-JUL-1998	298.90	3000
31	PA	BUY	23-JUN-1998	301.85	26-JUN-1998	289.70	-1215
32	PA	BUY	01-SEP-1998	277.00	22-SEP-1998	278.75	175
33	PA	BUY	06-OCT-1998	282.60	12-OCT-1998	278.50	-410

```
# Wins= 11 # Loses= 22 Largest Win= $4445 Largest Loss= $-1215 Ahead= $9990
```

Historic single contract trades from 20-APR-1993 to 06-OCT-1998

0	1 MKT	2 B/S	3 Idate	4 Price	5 Odate	6 Price	7 W/L
1	CL	SELL	20-APR-1993	20.32	29-APR-1993	20.58	-260
2	CL	BUY	27-JUL-1993	18.42	04-AUG-1993	17.80	-620
3	CL	BUY	10-AUG-1993	17.52	01-SEP-1993	17.97	80
4	CL	SELL	29-MAR-1994	14.32	31-MAR-1994	14.79	-470
5	CL	SELL	26-APR-1994	16.91	28-APR-1994	16.57	340
6	CL	SELL	28-JUN-1994	19.27	01-JUL-1994	19.53	-260
7	CL	SELL	09-AUG-1994	19.30	07-SEP-1994	17.81	1420
8	CL	SELL	16-AUG-1994	17.82	29-AUG-1994	17.63	190
9	CL	SELL	11-OCT-1994	17.79	18-OCT-1994	17.35	440
10	CL	SELL	15-NOV-1994	17.61	21-NOV-1994	17.56	50
11	CL	SELL	07-FEB-1995	18.46	10-FEB-1995	18.46	0
12	CL	SELL	28-FEB-1995	18.49	03-MAR-1995	18.63	-140
13	CL	SELL	07-MAR-1995	18.63	20-MAR-1995	18.47	90
14	CL	SELL	02-MAY-1995	20.09	04-MAY-1995	20.29	-200
15	CL	SELL	09-MAY-1995	19.61	16-MAY-1995	19.92	-480
16	CL	SELL	09-MAY-1995	19.61	15-MAY-1995	19.73	-290
17	CL	SELL	20-JUN-1995	17.97	27-JUN-1995	17.77	200
18	CL	SELL	16-JAN-1996	17.69	18-JAN-1996	18.39	-700
19	CL	SELL	27-MAY-1997	20.79	17-JUN-1997	19.35	1800
20	CL	BUY	24-JUN-1997	19.03	14-JUL-1997	19.13	-60
21	CL	SELL	14-OCT-1997	20.80	17-OCT-1997	20.74	60
22	CL	BUY	27-JAN-1998	16.98	02-FEB-1998	17.05	70
23	CL	SELL	06-OCT-1998	15.50	12-OCT-1998	14.42	1260

Wins= 13 # Loses= 10 Largest Win= $1800 Largest Loss= $-700 Ahead= $2520

```
HO  22R x 7C                                    19-OCT-1998 1:09 Page 1

     Historic single contract trades from 31-AUG-1993 to 22-DEC-1997

0     1 MKT  2 B/S  3 Idate     4 Price  5 Odate     6 Price  7 W/L

-----------------------------------------------------------------------
  1    HO    SELL  31-AUG-1993  53.64   20-SEP-1993  54.37    126.0
  2    HO    SELL  07-SEP-1993  51.13   13-SEP-1993  52.42   -109.2
  3    HO    SELL  26-OCT-1993  52.89   11-NOV-1993  52.58    466.2
  4    HO    SELL  26-APR-1994  47.38   28-APR-1994  46.57    340.2
  5    HO    SELL  17-MAY-1994  47.49   19-MAY-1994  48.29   -336.0
  6    HO    SELL  24-MAY-1994  48.07   27-MAY-1994  48.56   -205.8
  7    HO    SELL  07-JUN-1994  46.47   10-JUN-1994  46.91   -184.8
  8    HO    SELL  28-JUN-1994  50.23   01-JUL-1994  50.78   -231.0
  9    HO    SELL  05-JUL-1994  50.32   12-JUL-1994  51.43    -88.2
 10    HO    SELL  09-AUG-1994  50.17   02-SEP-1994  49.72    558.6
 11    HO    SELL  13-SEP-1994  49.18   19-SEP-1994  49.40    -92.4
 12    HO    SELL  11-OCT-1994  49.74   20-OCT-1994  50.43   -289.8
 13    HO    SELL  15-NOV-1994  49.20   21-NOV-1994  49.14     25.2
 14    HO    SELL  02-MAY-1995  50.94   04-MAY-1995  51.27   -138.6
 15    HO    SELL  09-MAY-1995  49.14   18-MAY-1995  50.64   -550.2
 16    HO    BUY   27-JUN-1995  47.53   29-JUN-1995  47.26   -113.4
 17    HO    SELL  19-SEP-1995  51.90   24-OCT-1995  49.64   1192.8
 18    HO    SELL  16-JAN-1996  51.41   18-JAN-1996  52.86   -609.0
 19    HO    SELL  15-OCT-1996  72.73   18-OCT-1996  73.68   -399.0
 20    HO    SELL  05-NOV-1996  65.42   07-NOV-1996  66.89   -617.4
 21    HO    SELL  13-OCT-1997  59.46   18-DEC-1998  53.09   2675.4
 22    HO    SELL  22-DEC-1997  51.51   26-JAN-1998  47.57   1654.8

# Wins= 8 # Loses= 14 Largest Win= $2675.4 Largest Loss= $-617.4 Ahead= $3074.4
```

```
HU  28R x 7C                                        20-OCT-1998 9:00 Page 1

    Historic single contract trades from 09-FEB-1993 to 01-SEP-1998

0     1 MKT  2 B/S  3 Idate     4 Price  5 Odate      6 Price  7 W/L

------------------------------------------------------------------------
 1     HU    SELL   09-FEB-1993   55.13  19-FEB-1993   57.91    399.0
 2     HU    SELL   23-MAR-1993   58.11  25-MAR-1993   59.72   -676.2
 3     HU    SELL   11-MAY-1993   60.93  09-SEP-1993   48.85   5074.0
 4     HU    BUY    28-SEP-1993   49.75  21-OCT-1993   50.74    365.4
 5     HU    BUY    16-NOV-1993   47.37  18-NOV-1993   47.14    -96.6
 6     HU    SELL   08-FEB-1994   44.67  24-FEB-1994   46.36    306.6
 7     HU    SELL   15-FEB-1994   44.25  22-FEB-1994   45.26   -424.2
 8     HU    SELL   08-MAR-1994   43.89  11-MAR-1994   45.73   -411.6
 9     HU    SELL   29-MAR-1994   44.93  31-MAR-1994   47.43  -1050.0
10     HU    SELL   26-APR-1994   51.11  29-APR-1994   49.99    470.4
11     HU    SELL   03-MAY-1994   49.56  06-MAY-1994   50.10   -226.8
12     HU    SELL   07-JUN-1994   51.35  15-JUN-1994   54.20  -1188.6
13     HU    SELL   07-JUN-1994   51.35  14-JUN-1994   52.24   -365.4
14     HU    SELL   28-JUN-1994   54.32  30-JUN-1994   53.59    306.6
15     HU    SELL   16-AUG-1994   51.83  18-AUG-1994   52.67   -352.8
16     HU    SELL   28-FEB-1995   58.57  22-MAR-1995   57.56    554.4
17     HU    SELL   23-MAY-1995   63.01  25-MAY-1995   62.29    302.4
18     HU    SELL   14-NOV-1995   50.04  16-NOV-1995   51.07   -432.6
19     HU    SELL   05-MAR-1996   59.09  12-MAR-1996   60.19   -575.4
20     HU    SELL   30-APR-1996   69.48  03-MAY-1996   69.92   -184.8
21     HU    SELL   25-JUN-1996   57.42  27-JUN-1996   59.35   -810.6
22     HU    SELL   14-JAN-1997   67.68  23-JAN-1997   68.46   -327.6
23     HU    SELL   25-MAR-1997   66.09  21-APR-1997   62.11   1583.4
24     HU    SELL   01-APR-1997   62.67  08-APR-1997   61.17    630.0
25     HU    SELL   26-AUG-1997   58.91  28-AUG-1997   61.18   -953.4
26     HU    SELL   16-SEP-1997   56.90  22-SEP-1997   56.85     21.0
27     HU    SELL   14-OCT-1997   58.74  17-OCT-1997   58.71     12.6
28     HU    BUY    01-SEP-1998   41.73  01-OCT-1998   45.94   1768.2

# Wins= 13 # Loses= 15 Largest Win= $5074 Largest Loss= $-1188.6 Ahead= $3717.4
```

Historic single contract trades from 31-AUG-1993 to 15-SEP-1998

0	1 MKT	2 B/S	3 Idate	4 Price	5 Odate	6 Price	7 W/L
1	NG	SELL	31-AUG-1993	2.375	02-SEP-1993	2.406	-310
2	NG	SELL	07-SEP-1993	2.272	20-SEP-1993	2.297	720
3	NG	BUY	12-OCT-1993	2.151	14-OCT-1993	2.167	160
4	NG	BUY	26-OCT-1993	2.305	11-NOV-1993	2.297	-80
5	NG	SELL	15-FEB-1994	2.189	17-FEB-1994	2.240	-510
6	NG	SELL	26-APR-1994	2.103	06-MAY-1994	2.037	660
7	NG	BUY	16-AUG-1994	1.860	18-AUG-1994	1.823	-370
8	NG	BUY	13-SEP-1994	1.675	20-SEP-1994	1.818	-1050
9	NG	BUY	25-OCT-1994	1.947	02-NOV-1994	1.869	-780
10	NG	BUY	06-DEC-1994	1.691	14-DEC-1994	1.714	230
11	NG	SELL	11-APR-1995	1.623	17-APR-1995	1.733	-330
12	NG	SELL	30-MAY-1995	1.718	28-JUL-1995	1.523	2410
13	NG	SELL	05-SEP-1995	1.701	13-SEP-1995	1.720	-190
14	NG	SELL	19-SEP-1995	1.746	25-SEP-1995	1.764	-180
15	NG	SELL	10-OCT-1995	1.802	30-OCT-1995	1.850	560
16	NG	SELL	17-OCT-1995	1.804	20-OCT-1995	1.823	-190
17	NG	SELL	16-JAN-1996	1.960	18-JAN-1996	2.043	-830
18	NG	SELL	16-JUL-1996	2.745	19-AUG-1996	2.254	5570
19	NG	SELL	27-AUG-1996	1.882	06-SEP-1996	1.863	190
20	NG	SELL	21-JAN-1997	2.632	27-JAN-1997	2.615	170
21	NG	SELL	07-OCT-1997	2.877	10-OCT-1997	3.082	-2050
22	NG	SELL	23-DEC-1997	2.208	29-DEC-1997	2.280	-720
23	NG	SELL	21-APR-1998	2.613	01-JUN-1998	2.191	4670
24	NG	SELL	28-APR-1998	2.311	11-MAY-1998	2.215	960
25	NG	BUY	16-JUN-1998	2.021	10-JUL-1998	2.309	2880
26	NG	BUY	23-JUN-1998	2.438	25-JUN-1998	2.394	-440
27	NG	BUY	18-AUG-1998	2.007	25-AUG-1998	1.857	-1500
28	NG	BUY	08-SEP-1998	1.874	08-OCT-1998	2.254	1120
29	NG	BUY	15-SEP-1998	2.391	23-SEP-1998	2.374	-170

Wins= 13 # Loses= 16 Largest Win= $5570 Largest Loss= $-2050 Ahead= $10600

```
C_  21R × 7C                                   19-OCT-1998 1:09 Page 1

    Historic single contract trades from 27-APR-1993 to 06-OCT-1998

0      1 MKT  2 B/S  3 Idate      4 Price  5 Odate      6 Price  7 W/L

--------------------------------------------------------------------------
 1     C_     SELL   27-APR-1993  228.00   30-APR-1993  232.50   -225.0
 2     C_     SELL   27-JUL-1993  244.50   03-AUG-1993  241.25    162.5
 3     C_     SELL   17-AUG-1993  238.00   19-AUG-1993  237.75     12.5
 4     C_     SELL   31-AUG-1993  237.50   07-SEP-1993  233.00    225.0
 5     C_     SELL   05-OCT-1993  236.50   07-OCT-1993  241.50   -250.0
 6     C_     SELL   14-DEC-1993  293.50   17-DEC-1993  296.00   -125.0
 7     C_     SELL   18-JAN-1994  301.25   24-JAN-1994  300.50     37.5
 8     C_     BUY    04-OCT-1994  217.50   07-OCT-1994  214.25   -162.5
 9     C_     BUY    11-OCT-1994  213.75   23-NOV-1994  222.25   -100.0
10     C_     SELL   27-JUN-1995  268.25   30-JUN-1995  278.00   -487.5
11     C_     SELL   14-NOV-1995  321.75   17-NOV-1995  328.00   -312.5
12     C_     SELL   09-JAN-1996  366.75   16-JAN-1996  354.00    637.5
13     C_     SELL   28-MAY-1996  478.50   10-JUN-1996  471.00    375.0
14     C_     BUY    12-NOV-1996  268.00   03-DEC-1996  263.00   -250.0
15     C_     BUY    17-DEC-1996  265.50   02-JAN-1997  258.50     12.5
16     C_     BUY    07-JAN-1997  258.25   09-JAN-1997  258.25      0.0
17     C_     BUY    14-JAN-1997  270.75   04-APR-1997  294.25   1137.5
18     C_     BUY    05-MAY-1998  256.50   11-MAY-1998  247.75   -437.5
19     C_     BUY    23-JUN-1998  262.00   26-JUN-1998  258.75   -162.5
20     C_     BUY    29-SEP-1998  211.75   01-OCT-1998  204.75   -350.0
21     C_     BUY    06-OCT-1998  210.25   13-OCT-1998  228.00    887.5
```

Wins= 10 # Loses= 11 Largest Win= $1137.5 Largest Loss= $-487.5 Ahead= $625

S_   38R x 7C   19-OCT-1998 1:10 Page 1

Historic single contract trades from 20-APR-1993 to 07-OCT-1998

0	1 MKT	2 B/S	3 Idate	4 Price	5 Odate	6 Price	7 W/L
1	S_	SELL	20-APR-1993	590.50	23-APR-1993	594.25	-100.0
2	S_	SELL	01-JUN-1993	589.00	08-JUN-1993	590.25	-62.5
3	S_	SELL	15-JUN-1993	582.75	17-JUN-1993	601.25	-925.0
4	S_	SELL	27-JUL-1993	703.25	27-AUG-1993	673.00	1600.0
5	S_	SELL	10-AUG-1993	669.75	18-AUG-1993	657.25	625.0
6	S_	SELL	31-AUG-1993	663.50	23-SEP-1993	649.25	712.5
7	S_	SELL	07-SEP-1993	640.50	17-SEP-1993	636.00	225.0
8	S_	SELL	28-SEP-1993	631.50	11-OCT-1993	614.75	837.5
9	S_	SELL	30-NOV-1993	671.50	02-DEC-1993	681.00	-475.0
10	S_	SELL	30-NOV-1993	671.50	03-DEC-1993	679.00	-375.0
11	S_	SELL	11-JAN-1994	693.25	13-JAN-1994	719.50	-1312.5
12	S_	SELL	25-JAN-1994	698.50	23-FEB-1994	688.00	887.5
13	S_	SELL	22-FEB-1994	686.25	24-FEB-1994	689.25	-150.0
14	S_	SELL	05-APR-1994	654.00	13-APR-1994	659.75	-287.5
15	S_	SELL	24-MAY-1994	695.00	31-MAY-1994	701.00	-300.0
16	S_	SELL	07-JUN-1994	660.50	09-JUN-1994	672.75	-612.5
17	S_	BUY	13-SEP-1994	574.00	15-SEP-1994	557.50	-825.0
18	S_	BUY	18-OCT-1994	544.75	01-DEC-1994	556.75	37.5
19	S_	BUY	24-JAN-1995	553.50	01-FEB-1995	546.50	-50.0
20	S_	BUY	07-FEB-1995	548.50	30-MAR-1995	573.00	700.0
21	S_	SELL	09-JAN-1996	745.50	19-JAN-1996	745.25	-500.0
22	S_	SELL	05-MAR-1996	723.50	08-MAR-1996	722.50	50.0
23	S_	SELL	30-APR-1996	795.00	02-MAY-1996	809.50	-725.0
24	S_	SELL	14-MAY-1996	818.75	16-MAY-1996	828.75	-500.0
25	S_	SELL	21-MAY-1996	798.50	18-JUN-1996	791.00	375.0
26	S_	SELL	21-MAY-1996	798.50	24-MAY-1996	807.50	-450.0
27	S_	SELL	04-JUN-1996	769.75	07-JUN-1996	775.50	-287.5
28	S_	SELL	23-JUL-1996	764.50	08-AUG-1996	767.75	-162.5
29	S_	SELL	18-MAR-1997	831.00	20-MAR-1997	852.00	-1050.0
30	S_	SELL	15-APR-1997	836.00	17-APR-1997	838.50	-125.0
31	S_	BUY	26-AUG-1997	615.25	10-OCT-1997	719.00	5187.5
32	S_	BUY	07-OCT-1997	691.00	17-NOV-1997	726.00	1750.0
33	S_	BUY	24-MAR-1998	651.50	27-MAR-1998	646.25	-262.5
34	S_	BUY	14-APR-1998	630.25	19-MAY-1998	632.00	150.0
35	S_	BUY	21-APR-1998	650.75	27-APR-1998	648.00	-75.0
36	S_	BUY	16-JUN-1998	594.50	26-JUN-1998	613.75	962.5
37	S_	BUY	18-AUG-1998	538.50	20-AUG-1998	537.50	-50.0
38	S_	BUY	07-OCT-1998	543.25	13-OCT-1998	574.00	1537.5

Wins= 15 # Loses= 23 Largest Win= $5187.5 Largest Loss= $-1312.5 Ahead= $5975

```
SM  35R x 7C                                    19-OCT-1998 1:10 Page 1

    Historic single contract trades from 23-FEB-1993 to 06-OCT-1998

0      1 MKT  2 B/S  3 Idate    4 Price  5 Odate     6 Price  7 W/L

-----------------------------------------------------------------------
    1   SM    BUY    23-FEB-1993   178.1  05-MAR-1993   178.1      0
    2   SM    SELL   01-JUN-1993   186.6  07-JUN-1993   188.8   -220
    3   SM    SELL   27-JUL-1993   226.6  15-OCT-1993   192.2   3130
    4   SM    SELL   10-AUG-1993   213.7  12-AUG-1993   210.6    310
    5   SM    SELL   23-NOV-1993   205.6  03-DEC-1993   204.6    100
    6   SM    SELL   30-NOV-1993   203.1  27-DEC-1993   203.7    -30
    7   SM    SELL   14-DEC-1993   199.5  22-DEC-1993   201.1   -130
    8   SM    SELL   04-JAN-1994   201.0  06-JAN-1994   201.1    -10
    9   SM    SELL   11-JAN-1994   196.2  13-JAN-1994   200.6   -440
   10   SM    SELL   22-FEB-1994   195.9  24-FEB-1994   196.0    -10
   11   SM    SELL   07-JUN-1994   190.9  10-JUN-1994   197.2   -630
   12   SM    SELL   21-JUN-1994   194.7  28-JUN-1994   197.6   -270
   13   SM    BUY    20-DEC-1994   158.6  29-DEC-1994   160.4   -170
   14   SM    BUY    17-JAN-1995   160.2  30-JAN-1995   157.1   -310
   15   SM    BUY    21-FEB-1995   154.6  28-FEB-1995   157.7    -80
   16   SM    SELL   18-APR-1995   165.3  02-MAY-1995   168.8    180
   17   SM    SELL   30-MAY-1995   168.9  01-JUN-1995   173.3   -440
   18   SM    SELL   06-JUN-1995   173.4  08-JUN-1995   173.1     30
   19   SM    SELL   13-JUN-1995   171.2  15-JUN-1995   173.9   -270
   20   SM    SELL   27-JUN-1995   173.1  03-JUL-1995   176.5   -340
   21   SM    SELL   01-AUG-1995   181.2  21-AUG-1995   178.5    270
   22   SM    SELL   03-OCT-1995   192.9  06-OCT-1995   193.6    -70
   23   SM    SELL   14-NOV-1995   206.5  16-NOV-1995   209.6   -310
   24   SM    SELL   16-JAN-1996   235.8  18-JAN-1996   237.5   -170
   25   SM    SELL   05-MAR-1996   230.1  08-MAR-1996   230.9    -80
   26   SM    SELL   30-APR-1996   245.4  02-MAY-1996   249.3   -390
   27   SM    SELL   21-MAY-1996   245.5  28-MAY-1996   245.9    -40
   28   SM    SELL   08-APR-1997   282.8  10-APR-1997   284.0   -120
   29   SM    SELL   15-APR-1997   275.0  25-APR-1997   278.5   -560
   30   SM    SELL   01-JUL-1997   206.0  08-JUL-1997   213.9   -790
   31   SM    SELL   02-DEC-1997   222.5  08-DEC-1997   226.4   -390
   32   SM    BUY    10-MAR-1998   179.8  12-MAR-1998   177.4   -240
   33   SM    BUY    12-JUN-1998   154.7  23-JUN-1998   175.2   2050
   34   SM    BUY    22-SEP-1998   130.9  30-SEP-1998   129.8   -110
   35   SM    BUY    06-OCT-1998   130.2  13-OCT-1998   149.2   1900

 # Wins= 9 # Loses= 26 Largest Win= $3130 Largest Loss= $-790 Ahead= $1350
```

BO 21R × 7C   19-OCT-1998 1:10 Page 1

   Historic single contract trades from 08-FEB-1994 to 19-MAY-1998

0	1 MKT	2 B/S	3 Idate	4 Price	5 Odate	6 Price	7 W/L
1	BO	SELL	08-FEB-1994	27.83	10-FEB-1994	28.38	-330
2	BO	SELL	29-MAR-1994	28.78	13-APR-1994	27.70	648
3	BO	SELL	24-MAY-1994	29.23	17-JUN-1994	28.13	660
4	BO	SELL	07-JUN-1994	27.19	09-JUN-1994	27.62	-258
5	BO	SELL	10-JAN-1995	26.81	24-JAN-1995	26.47	204
6	BO	SELL	04-APR-1995	25.51	06-APR-1995	25.94	-258
7	BO	SELL	18-JUL-1995	27.82	21-JUL-1995	27.49	198
8	BO	SELL	05-SEP-1995	25.75	12-SEP-1995	26.12	-222
9	BO	BUY	12-DEC-1995	24.87	05-JAN-1996	24.79	-222
10	BO	BUY	23-JAN-1996	23.98	29-FEB-1996	24.18	-84
11	BO	SELL	14-MAY-1996	27.48	11-JUL-1996	26.26	960
12	BO	SELL	14-MAY-1996	27.48	17-MAY-1996	27.42	36
13	BO	SELL	09-JUL-1996	25.18	11-JUL-1996	26.26	-648
14	BO	SELL	18-MAR-1997	24.63	27-MAR-1997	24.42	126
15	BO	SELL	30-SEP-1997	23.87	03-OCT-1997	24.13	-156
16	BO	SELL	18-NOV-1997	25.96	26-DEC-1997	25.44	738
17	BO	SELL	30-DEC-1997	25.49	20-JAN-1998	25.65	-96
18	BO	SELL	06-JAN-1998	24.53	09-JAN-1998	24.86	-198
19	BO	SELL	03-MAR-1998	26.64	10-MAR-1998	27.06	-252
20	BO	SELL	31-MAR-1998	27.33	08-APR-1998	27.17	96
21	BO	SELL	19-MAY-1998	27.58	04-JUN-1998	25.92	996

Wins= 10 # Loses= 11 Largest Win= $996 Largest Loss= $-648 Ahead= $1938

```
W_  21R x 7C                               19-OCT-1998 1:10 Page 1

    Historic single contract trades from 16-MAR-1993 to 25-AUG-1998

0     1 MKT  2 B/S  3 Idate      4 Price  5 Odate     6 Price  7 W/L

----------------------------------------------------------------------
    1   W_    BUY   16-MAR-1993   332.25  05-MAY-1993  292.00    37.5
    2   W_    BUY   11-MAY-1993   293.50  13-MAY-1993  293.25   -12.5
    3   W_    BUY   18-MAY-1993   297.00  25-MAY-1993  288.75  -412.5
    4   W_    SELL  24-AUG-1993   316.00  31-AUG-1993  315.50    25.0
    5   W_    SELL  18-JAN-1994   375.75  24-JAN-1994  379.00  -162.5
    6   W_    SELL  21-JUN-1994   324.50  28-JUN-1994  328.75   137.5
    7   W_    SELL  18-OCT-1994   394.75  24-OCT-1994  404.00  -462.5
    8   W_    BUY   14-MAR-1995   344.75  31-MAR-1995  343.25   -75.0
    9   W_    SELL  16-MAY-1995   360.50  18-MAY-1995  359.75    37.5
   10   W_    SELL  03-JUL-1995   435.25  05-JUL-1995  427.00   412.5
   11   W_    SELL  11-JUL-1995   426.50  13-JUL-1995  432.25  -287.5
   12   W_    SELL  01-AUG-1995   462.25  21-AUG-1995  434.00  1412.5
   13   W_    SELL  10-OCT-1995   483.75  13-OCT-1995  485.75  -100.0
   14   W_    SELL  16-JAN-1996   480.00  22-JAN-1996  482.25  -112.5
   15   W_    SELL  20-FEB-1996   513.00  29-FEB-1996  501.50   -50.0
   16   W_    SELL  12-MAR-1996   483.00  20-MAR-1996  481.00   100.0
   17   W_    SELL  28-MAY-1996   546.00  10-JUN-1996  519.50  1325.0
   18   W_    SELL  09-SEP-1997   382.75  07-OCT-1997  365.75   850.0
   19   W_    SELL  30-SEP-1997   354.25  03-OCT-1997  357.75  -175.0
   20   W_    SELL  28-JUL-1998   256.00  07-AUG-1998  251.50   225.0
   21   W_    SELL  25-AUG-1998   264.50  04-SEP-1998  261.75   137.5

# Wins= 11 # Loses= 10 Largest Win= $1412.5 Largest Loss= $-462.5 Ahead= $2850
```

MW 20R × 7C   19-OCT-1998 1:10 Page 1

     Historic single contract trades from 29-JUN-1993 to 15-SEP-1998

0   1 MKT 2 B/S 3 Idate   4 Price 5 Odate   6 Price 7 W/L

----
     1   MW   BUY   29-JUN-1993 285.75 29-JUL-1993 313.75 1400.0
     2   MW   SELL   05-OCT-1993 321.00 07-OCT-1993 327.50 -325.0
     3   MW   SELL   04-JAN-1994 392.25 10-JAN-1994 398.00 -287.5
     4   MW   SELL   18-JAN-1994 383.00 02-FEB-1994 372.00   550.0
     5   MW   SELL   15-FEB-1994 377.25 04-APR-1994 337.50 1275.0
     6   MW   BUY   22-AUG-1995 451.25 02-NOV-1995 494.50 2162.5
     7   MW   BUY   18-JUN-1996 583.25 27-JUN-1996 517.50 -900.0
     8   MW   BUY   16-JUL-1996 501.50 18-JUL-1996 497.25 -212.5
     9   MW   BUY   13-AUG-1996 470.25 15-AUG-1996 461.50 -437.5
    10   MW   BUY   20-AUG-1996 465.00 29-AUG-1996 455.25 -237.5
    11   MW   SELL   01-APR-1997 409.50 07-APR-1997 411.50 -100.0
    12   MW   SELL   06-MAY-1997 420.00 09-MAY-1997 433.00 -650.0
    13   MW   BUY   08-JUL-1997 351.00 10-JUL-1997 355.25   212.5
    14   MW   SELL   30-SEP-1997 389.25 03-OCT-1997 394.75 -275.0
    15   MW   SELL   28-OCT-1997 393.50 18-NOV-1997 380.00   675.0
    16   MW   SELL   25-NOV-1997 383.00 28-NOV-1997 388.00 -250.0
    17   MW   SELL   17-FEB-1998 367.25 20-FEB-1998 371.75 -225.0
    18   MW   SELL   17-MAR-1998 379.75 30-MAR-1998 384.75 -250.0
    19   MW   SELL   07-APR-1998 366.00 14-APR-1998 367.00   -50.0
    20   MW   BUY   15-SEP-1998 328.50 30-SEP-1998 341.25   637.5

  # Wins= 7 # Loses= 13 Largest Win= $2162.5 Largest Loss= $-900 Ahead= $2712.5

```
O_   19R x 7C                                        19-OCT-1998 1:09 Page 1

     Historic single contract trades from 27-APR-1993 to 15-NOV-1994

0     1 MKT  2 B/S  3 Idate      4 Price  5 Odate      6 Price   7 W/L

-----------------------------------------------------------------------
  1    O_     SELL   27-APR-1993   145.00  07-JUN-1993   139.25    287.5
  2    O_     SELL   18-MAY-1993   138.75  26-MAY-1993   138.75      0.0
  3    O_     SELL   26-OCT-1993   135.25  10-NOV-1993   140.25   -250.0
  4    O_     SELL   26-OCT-1993   135.25  04-NOV-1993   134.00     62.5
  5    O_     SELL   23-NOV-1993   137.50  09-DEC-1993   139.25    -87.5
  6    O_     SELL   14-DEC-1993   135.00  17-DEC-1993   134.25     37.5
  7    O_     SELL   04-JAN-1994   135.25  07-JAN-1994   136.75    -75.0
  8    O_     SELL   18-JAN-1994   137.00  17-MAR-1994   133.75    450.0
  9    O_     SELL   15-FEB-1994   128.50  22-FEB-1994   135.25    -50.0
 10    O_     SELL   22-FEB-1994   135.25  14-MAR-1994   131.75    175.0
 11    O_     SELL   29-MAR-1994   133.00  12-MAY-1994   119.75    912.5
 12    O_     SELL   12-APR-1994   118.50  19-APR-1994   116.50    100.0
 13    O_     SELL   19-APR-1994   116.50  26-APR-1994   122.25    -37.5
 14    O_     SELL   03-MAY-1994   116.25  11-MAY-1994   118.00    -87.5
 15    O_     SELL   07-JUN-1994   119.00  13-JUN-1994   123.25   -212.5
 16    O_     SELL   28-JUN-1994   121.00  18-JUL-1994   117.25    187.5
 17    O_     SELL   05-JUL-1994   112.25  08-JUL-1994   117.75   -275.0
 18    O_     SELL   18-OCT-1994   128.50  27-OCT-1994   128.75   -137.5
 19    O_     SELL   15-NOV-1994   125.25  07-DEC-1994   121.50    637.5

# Wins= 10 # Loses= 9 Largest Win= $912.5 Largest Loss= $-275 Ahead= $1637.5
```

```
FC  22R x 7C                              19-OCT-1998 11:17 Page 1

     Historic single contract trades from 06-JUL-1993 to 29-SEP-1998

0    1 MKT  2 B/S  3 Idate     4 Price  5 Odate     6 Price  7 W/L

--------------------------------------------------------------------------
 1    FC     BUY    06-JUL-1993   86.225  16-JUL-1993   85.825    -200.0
 2    FC     BUY    27-JUL-1993   86.400  24-SEP-1993   85.350    -262.5
 3    FC     SELL   15-NOV-1994   74.775  17-NOV-1994   74.675      50.0
 4    FC     SELL   22-NOV-1994   74.675  08-DEC-1994   74.175     250.0
 5    FC     SELL   29-NOV-1994   72.525  01-DEC-1994   73.325    -400.0
 6    FC     SELL   17-JAN-1995   73.150  23-JAN-1995   73.975    -412.5
 7    FC     SELL   31-JAN-1995   72.550  08-MAR-1995   69.675    1275.0
 8    FC     SELL   03-OCT-1995   64.400  05-OCT-1995   65.175    -387.5
 9    FC     SELL   21-NOV-1995   64.725  01-DEC-1995   65.150    -212.5
10    FC     SELL   12-DEC-1995   63.500  05-FEB-1996   57.650    2000.0
11    FC     SELL   19-DEC-1995   63.375  08-JAN-1996   59.125    1200.0
12    FC     SELL   20-FEB-1996   56.925  22-FEB-1996   57.950    -512.5
13    FC     SELL   23-JUL-1996   61.275  25-JUL-1996   61.750    -237.5
14    FC     SELL   13-AUG-1996   62.725  16-AUG-1996   63.300    -287.5
15    FC     SELL   24-SEP-1996   63.600  30-SEP-1996   65.750    -487.5
16    FC     SELL   10-DEC-1996   65.975  12-DEC-1996   66.525    -275.0
17    FC     SELL   03-JUN-1997   77.150  11-JUN-1997   77.275     -62.5
18    FC     SELL   29-JUL-1997   81.075  01-AUG-1997   81.350    -137.5
19    FC     SELL   31-MAR-1998   73.325  02-APR-1998   75.575   -1125.0
20    FC     SELL   21-APR-1998   76.550  29-APR-1998   78.325     387.5
21    FC     SELL   19-MAY-1998   76.075  03-JUN-1998   74.550     762.5
22    FC     SELL   29-SEP-1998   69.500  02-OCT-1998   69.825    -162.5

# Wins= 7 # Loses= 15 Largest Win= $2000 Largest Loss= $-1125 Ahead= $762.5
```

```
LC  22R × 7C                                      19-OCT-1998 1:09 Page 1

   Historic single contract trades from 28-SEP-1993 to 08-SEP-1998

0     1 MKT  2 B/S  3 Idate    4 Price  5 Odate     6 Price  7 W/L

----------------------------------------------------------------------
   1   LC    BUY    28-SEP-1993  73.350  08-OCT-1993   72.725   -250
   2   LC    BUY    12-OCT-1993  73.000  03-NOV-1993   72.775    -90
   3   LC    BUY    09-NOV-1993  73.550  30-NOV-1993   72.500   -600
   4   LC    BUY    07-DEC-1993  72.550  01-FEB-1994   75.225   -120
   5   LC    BUY    08-FEB-1994  74.925  14-APR-1994   72.775    100
   6   LC    BUY    14-JUN-1994  64.200  22-JUN-1994   62.850   -540
   7   LC    BUY    28-JUN-1994  63.475  24-AUG-1994   70.800    500
   8   LC    BUY    30-AUG-1994  71.300  12-SEP-1994   69.750   -620
   9   LC    BUY    05-SEP-1995  64.500  02-OCT-1995   65.725   -300
  10   LC    BUY    30-APR-1996  57.350  25-JUN-1996   64.200   2740
  11   LC    SELL   08-APR-1997  63.325  10-APR-1997   64.575   -500
  12   LC    SELL   27-MAY-1997  65.275  13-JUN-1997   64.275    400
  13   LC    BUY    23-DEC-1997  65.750  02-JAN-1998   64.950   -320
  14   LC    BUY    13-JAN-1998  65.150  02-FEB-1998   66.400   -660
  15   LC    BUY    17-FEB-1998  67.200  19-FEB-1998   65.350   -740
  16   LC    BUY    10-MAR-1998  65.200  25-MAR-1998   63.950   -500
  17   LC    BUY    31-MAR-1998  65.775  12-MAY-1998   67.025    500
  18   LC    BUY    07-APR-1998  67.725  15-APR-1998   67.825     40
  19   LC    BUY    23-JUN-1998  65.475  25-JUN-1998   64.900   -230
  20   LC    BUY    07-JUL-1998  64.300  09-JUL-1998   63.775   -210
  21   LC    BUY    04-AUG-1998  60.475  12-AUG-1998   60.600     50
  22   LC    BUY    08-SEP-1998  58.950  28-SEP-1998   61.975    270
```

Wins= 8 # Loses= 14 Largest Win= $2740 Largest Loss= $-740 Ahead= $-1080

Historic single contract trades from 30-MAR-1993 to 15-SEP-1998

0	1 MKT	2 B/S	3 Idate	4 Price	5 Odate	6 Price	7 W/L
1	LH	SELL	30-MAR-1993	54.725	01-APR-1993	56.025	-520
2	LH	BUY	22-JUN-1993	48.175	29-JUN-1993	44.875	-330
3	LH	BUY	06-JUL-1993	47.925	27-SEP-1993	47.050	1020
4	LH	SELL	08-FEB-1994	50.050	18-APR-1994	53.150	1280
5	LH	SELL	01-MAR-1994	48.975	08-MAR-1994	48.825	60
6	LH	SELL	26-APR-1994	51.025	11-MAY-1994	49.725	520
7	LH	BUY	12-JUL-1994	44.250	15-AUG-1994	40.325	220
8	LH	BUY	06-SEP-1994	39.075	08-SEP-1994	38.600	-190
9	LH	BUY	13-SEP-1994	38.750	15-SEP-1994	37.575	-470
10	LH	BUY	01-NOV-1994	34.100	04-NOV-1994	33.400	-280
11	LH	BUY	06-DEC-1994	35.075	06-JAN-1995	37.100	810
12	LH	SELL	31-JAN-1995	39.650	22-FEB-1995	38.750	360
13	LH	SELL	18-APR-1995	44.025	25-APR-1995	44.050	-10
14	LH	SELL	03-JUL-1995	45.125	10-JUL-1995	45.275	-60
15	LH	SELL	08-AUG-1995	42.900	14-AUG-1995	43.225	-130
16	LH	SELL	29-AUG-1995	44.475	31-AUG-1995	44.650	-70
17	LH	SELL	29-AUG-1995	44.475	05-SEP-1995	45.125	-260
18	LH	SELL	26-SEP-1995	46.150	29-SEP-1995	46.600	-160
19	LH	SELL	19-DEC-1995	49.675	22-DEC-1995	50.250	-230
20	LH	SELL	26-DEC-1995	50.300	28-DEC-1995	50.075	90
21	LH	SELL	02-JAN-1996	47.075	11-JAN-1996	46.125	380
22	LH	SELL	28-MAY-1996	58.625	02-JUL-1996	54.500	420
23	LH	SELL	28-MAY-1996	58.625	03-JUN-1996	58.800	-70
24	LH	SELL	18-JUN-1996	55.250	24-JUN-1996	56.300	-420
25	LH	SELL	20-AUG-1996	53.550	09-SEP-1996	53.800	-100
26	LH	SELL	20-AUG-1996	53.550	26-AUG-1996	54.650	-440
27	LH	SELL	22-OCT-1996	52.100	28-OCT-1996	53.875	-710
28	LH	BUY	25-MAR-1997	73.175	14-MAY-1997	83.475	700
29	LH	SELL	29-APR-1997	83.650	01-MAY-1997	84.950	-520
30	LH	SELL	27-MAY-1997	81.850	02-JUN-1997	81.800	20
31	LH	BUY	17-JUN-1997	81.925	23-JUL-1997	79.950	360
32	LH	BUY	02-SEP-1997	70.250	09-SEP-1997	69.375	-350
33	LH	BUY	16-SEP-1997	71.725	19-SEP-1997	69.650	-830
34	LH	BUY	28-OCT-1997	61.600	07-NOV-1997	60.975	-250
35	LH	BUY	13-JAN-1998	57.900	15-JAN-1998	56.500	-560
36	LH	BUY	20-JAN-1998	57.325	04-FEB-1998	56.450	10
37	LH	BUY	17-MAR-1998	48.875	27-MAY-1998	59.025	2060
38	LH	BUY	31-MAR-1998	59.975	02-APR-1998	58.250	-690
39	LH	BUY	19-MAY-1998	61.975	21-MAY-1998	60.900	-430
40	LH	BUY	02-JUN-1998	61.600	11-JUN-1998	61.725	50
41	LH	BUY	11-AUG-1998	42.925	20-AUG-1998	43.250	130
42	LH	BUY	15-SEP-1998	41.175	13-OCT-1998	43.725	1980

Wins= 18 # Loses= 24 Largest Win= $2060 Largest Loss= $-830 Ahead= $2390

```
PB   3R × 7C                                     19-OCT-1998 1:10 Page 1

    Historic single contract trades from 21-OCT-1997 to 18-MAR-1998

0    1 MKT  2 B/S  3 Idate      4 Price  5 Odate      6 Price  7 W/L

-----------------------------------------------------------------------
1    PB     BUY    21-OCT-1997   62.600  06-NOV-1997   61.125    -590
2    PB     BUY    27-JAN-1998   48.850  06-FEB-1998   46.050   -1120
3    PB     BUY    18-MAR-1998   45.425  15-APR-1998   55.950    4210

# Wins= 1 # Loses= 2 Largest Win= $4210 Largest Loss= $-1120 Ahead= $2500
```

```
CC  30R x 7C                                    20-OCT-1998 9:47 Page 1

    Historic single contract trades from 11-MAY-1993 to 06-OCT-1998

0     1 MKT  2 B/S  3 Idate      4 Price  5 Odate       6 Price  7 W/L
------------------------------------------------------------------------
    1   CC    SELL   11-MAY-1993      910  17-JUN-1993       913    290
    2   CC    SELL   18-MAY-1993      883  20-MAY-1993       898   -150
    3   CC    SELL   29-JUN-1993      900  01-JUL-1993       939   -390
    4   CC    SELL   27-JUL-1993      930  02-AUG-1993       959   -290
    5   CC    SELL   10-AUG-1993      951  13-AUG-1993       975   -240
    6   CC    SELL   28-SEP-1993     1147  01-OCT-1993      1210   -630
    7   CC    SELL   05-OCT-1993     1204  20-OCT-1993      1170    340
    8   CC    SELL   02-NOV-1993     1109  10-NOV-1993      1178    -60
    9   CC    SELL   14-DEC-1993     1251  04-JAN-1994      1162    890
   10   CC    SELL   25-JAN-1994     1124  18-FEB-1994      1159    -40
   11   CC    SELL   01-FEB-1994     1055  04-FEB-1994      1079   -240
   12   CC    SELL   29-MAR-1994     1155  02-MAY-1994      1145    350
   13   CC    SELL   05-APR-1994     1101  08-APR-1994      1126   -250
   14   CC    SELL   19-APR-1994     1133  02-MAY-1994      1145   -120
   15   CC    SELL   07-JUN-1994     1318  13-JUN-1994      1391   -450
   16   CC    SELL   21-JUN-1994     1364  08-JUL-1994      1389   -250
   17   CC    SELL   02-AUG-1994     1463  16-AUG-1994      1488    260
   18   CC    SELL   30-AUG-1994     1356  09-SEP-1994      1348     80
   19   CC    SELL   20-SEP-1994     1345  23-SEP-1994      1381   -360
   20   CC    SELL   07-MAR-1995     1432  05-APR-1995      1338    940
   21   CC    SELL   14-MAR-1995     1345  20-MAR-1995      1356   -110
   22   CC    SELL   27-FEB-1996     1280  08-MAR-1996      1249    310
   23   CC    SELL   21-MAY-1996     1358  24-MAY-1996      1383   -250
   24   CC    BUY    14-FEB-1997     1285  04-APR-1997      1473   1880
   25   CC    SELL   29-APR-1997     1414  06-MAY-1997      1409     50
   26   CC    SELL   01-JUL-1997     1685  18-AUG-1997      1563   1620
   27   CC    SELL   22-JUL-1997     1502  28-JUL-1997      1539   -370
   28   CC    SELL   16-SEP-1997     1698  24-SEP-1997      1691     70
   29   CC    BUY    25-AUG-1998     1547  15-SEP-1998      1563    160
   30   CC    BUY    06-OCT-1998     1541  13-OCT-1998      1501   -400

# Wins= 13 # Loses= 17 Largest Win= $1880 Largest Loss= $-630 Ahead= $2640
```

KC 15R × 7C   19-OCT-1998 1:09 Page 1

      Historic single contract trades from 18-MAY-1993 to 06-OCT-1998

0   1 MKT 2 B/S 3 Idate   4 Price 5 Odate   6 Price 7 W/L

----
      1   KC   SELL   18-MAY-1993   63.30   01-JUN-1993   61.25   768.75
      2   KC   SELL   01-JUN-1993   61.25   15-JUN-1993   63.20   18.75
      3   KC   SELL   22-JUN-1993   63.35   25-JUN-1993   61.85   562.50
      4   KC   SELL   29-JUN-1993   60.60   02-JUL-1993   64.70   -1537.50
      5   KC   SELL   07-SEP-1993   78.25   09-SEP-1993   82.20   -1481.25
      6   KC   SELL   21-SEP-1993   77.10   24-SEP-1993   81.10   -1500.00
      7   KC   SELL   08-MAR-1994   78.65   30-MAR-1994   81.15   -937.50
      8   KC   SELL   29-MAR-1994   81.20   31-MAR-1994   82.20   -375.00
      9   KC   SELL   12-APR-1994   85.85   15-APR-1994   82.10   1406.25
     10   KC   SELL   26-JUL-1994   208.10   02-AUG-1994   213.40   -1987.50
     11   KC   BUY   18-JUL-1995   138.70   05-SEP-1995   149.10   3900.00
     12   KC   BUY   05-DEC-1995   105.45   15-DEC-1995   107.75   862.50
     13   KC   BUY   04-NOV-1997   144.30   06-NOV-1997   146.00   637.50
     14   KC   BUY   21-JUL-1998   108.25   08-AUG-1998   123.60   5756.25
     15   KC   BUY   06-OCT-1998   105.50   13-OCT-1998   104.15   -506.25

Wins= 8 # Loses= 7 Largest Win= $5756.25 Largest Loss= $-1987.5 Ahead= $5587.5

```
CT  32R x 7C                           19-OCT-1998 1:09 Page 1

    Historic single contract trades from 01-JUN-1993 to 14-JUL-1998

0     1 MKT  2 B/S  3 Idate     4 Price  5 Odate     6 Price  7 W/L
------------------------------------------------------------------------
 1    CT     BUY    01-JUN-1993   60.25  04-JUN-1993   60.33      40
 2    CT     BUY    06-JUL-1993   57.47  02-AUG-1993   57.89     210
 3    CT     BUY    24-AUG-1993   55.60  30-AUG-1993   54.90    -350
 4    CT     SELL   05-APR-1994   75.33  12-APR-1994   78.05   -1360
 5    CT     BUY    19-JUL-1994   71.25  01-AUG-1994   69.95    -650
 6    CT     BUY    09-AUG-1994   71.19  12-AUG-1994   69.27    -960
 7    CT     BUY    23-AUG-1994   69.23  25-AUG-1994   69.20     -15
 8    CT     BUY    30-AUG-1994   70.33  16-SEP-1994   69.24    -195
 9    CT     BUY    11-OCT-1994   68.50  07-FEB-1995   90.28   10215
10    CT     SELL   07-FEB-1995   90.28  13-FEB-1995   92.99   -1355
11    CT     BUY    15-AUG-1995   76.91  07-SEP-1995   80.42    1755
12    CT     SELL   13-FEB-1996   84.50  15-FEB-1996   85.35     -10
13    CT     SELL   05-MAR-1996   82.38  07-MAR-1996   83.86    -740
14    CT     SELL   16-APR-1996   84.05  19-APR-1996   85.34    -645
15    CT     SELL   30-APR-1996   85.12  02-MAY-1996   85.83    -355
16    CT     SELL   14-MAY-1996   82.87  24-MAY-1996   82.55     160
17    CT     BUY    16-JUL-1996   72.80  07-AUG-1996   70.00   -1400
18    CT     BUY    19-NOV-1996   74.10  30-DEC-1996   74.31     105
19    CT     BUY    22-APR-1997   72.90  07-JUL-1997   73.24    -420
20    CT     BUY    12-AUG-1997   74.79  20-AUG-1997   73.65      35
21    CT     BUY    09-SEP-1997   72.79  30-SEP-1997   71.55    -745
22    CT     BUY    21-OCT-1997   72.18  12-NOV-1997   70.47      70
23    CT     BUY    18-NOV-1997   72.08  21-NOV-1997   71.22    -430
24    CT     BUY    23-DEC-1997   67.43  09-JAN-1998   66.04    -695
25    CT     BUY    06-JAN-1998   68.49  08-JAN-1998   66.90    -795
26    CT     BUY    20-JAN-1998   66.38  22-JAN-1998   65.49    -445
27    CT     BUY    27-JAN-1998   65.21  18-FEB-1998   66.52      60
28    CT     BUY    10-FEB-1998   67.53  13-FEB-1998   66.24    -645
29    CT     BUY    03-MAR-1998   67.67  19-MAR-1998   69.33     830
30    CT     SELL   24-MAR-1998   69.36  26-MAR-1998   69.51     -75
31    CT     SELL   31-MAR-1998   67.23  16-APR-1998   65.06    1865
32    CT     SELL   14-JUL-1998   72.35  17-JUL-1998   74.08    -865

# Wins= 11 # Loses= 21 Largest Win= $10215 Largest Loss= $-1400 Ahead= $2195
```

```
LB  2R x 7C                                    19-OCT-1998 1:09 Page 1

    Historic single contract trades from 14-MAY-1996 to 11-JUN-1996

0    1 MKT  2 B/S  3 Idate      4 Price  5 Odate      6 Price  7 W/L

-----------------------------------------------------------------------
1    LB     SELL   14-MAY-1996   347.7  22-MAY-1996    357.5   -784
2    LB     SELL   11-JUN-1996   350.5  24-JUN-1996    331.3   1536

# Wins= 1 # Loses= 1 Largest Win= $1536 Largest Loss= $-784 Ahead= $752
```

```
JO  29R × 7C                                  19-OCT-1998 1:09 Page 1        .

     Historic single contract trades from 02-FEB-1993 to 31-MAR-1998

0    1 MKT  2 B/S  3 Idate      4 Price  5 Odate      6 Price  7 W/L
-----------------------------------------------------------------------
 1    JO    SELL   02-FEB-1993    69.00  11-FEB-1993    67.85     172.5
 2    JO    SELL   20-APR-1993    89.50  04-MAY-1993    94.25    -165.0
 3    JO    SELL   08-JUN-1993   109.95  15-JUN-1993   107.40     382.5
 4    JO    SELL   20-JUL-1993   116.20  22-JUL-1993   118.75    -382.5
 5    JO    SELL   12-OCT-1993   129.25  12-NOV-1993   112.60    2947.5
 6    JO    SELL   30-NOV-1993    97.15  03-DEC-1993   101.00    -577.5
 7    JO    BUY    26-APR-1994   102.65  06-MAY-1994   100.30    -352.5
 8    JO    SELL   22-NOV-1994   105.25  02-DEC-1994   104.95      45.0
 9    JO    SELL   27-DEC-1994   116.35  01-FEB-1995   104.10    1837.5
10    JO    SELL   10-JAN-1995   101.50  13-JAN-1995   108.30   -1020.0
11    JO    SELL   25-APR-1995   111.40  02-MAY-1995   106.90     675.0
12    JO    SELL   14-NOV-1995   121.40  16-NOV-1995   123.10    -255.0
13    JO    SELL   12-DEC-1995   119.40  09-JAN-1996   122.40     187.5
14    JO    SELL   14-MAY-1996   117.35  17-MAY-1996   123.50    -922.5
15    JO    BUY    04-JUN-1996   122.25  11-JUN-1996   119.15    -465.0
16    JO    BUY    30-JUL-1996   115.15  03-SEP-1996   107.10    -352.5
17    JO    SELL   11-FEB-1997    79.90  18-FEB-1997    78.70     180.0
18    JO    SELL   11-MAR-1997    81.55  13-MAR-1997    83.30    -262.5
19    JO    SELL   01-APR-1997    76.15  03-APR-1997    77.05    -135.0
20    JO    SELL   08-APR-1997    72.80  14-APR-1997    75.65    -427.5
21    JO    SELL   29-APR-1997    74.95  02-MAY-1997    76.20    -187.5
22    JO    SELL   27-MAY-1997    79.85  28-JUL-1997    75.35    1102.5
23    JO    SELL   10-JUN-1997    76.80  12-JUN-1997    77.00     -30.0
24    JO    SELL   08-JUL-1997    75.25  15-JUL-1997    74.50     112.5
25    JO    SELL   23-SEP-1997    69.25  25-SEP-1997    73.75    -675.0
26    JO    SELL   14-OCT-1997    67.15  05-NOV-1997    74.50      37.5
27    JO    SELL   30-DEC-1997    85.85  08-JAN-1998    81.70     622.5
28    JO    SELL   10-FEB-1998    96.55  20-FEB-1998   100.50    -592.5
29    JO    SELL   31-MAR-1998   104.05  06-APR-1998   101.05     450.0
```

Wins= 13 # Loses= 16 Largest Win= $2947.5 Largest Loss= $-1020 Ahead= $1950

Historic single contract trades from 27-SEP-1994 to 06-OCT-1998

0	1 MKT	2 B/S	3 Idate	4 Price	5 Odate	6 Price	7 W/L
1	SB	SELL	27-SEP-1994	12.45	29-SEP-1994	12.56	-123.2
2	SB	SELL	31-JAN-1995	14.12	03-FEB-1995	14.35	-257.6
3	SB	BUY	09-MAY-1995	11.54	11-MAY-1995	11.18	-403.2
4	SB	BUY	22-OCT-1996	10.63	30-OCT-1996	10.47	-22.4
5	SB	BUY	12-NOV-1996	10.38	03-DEC-1996	10.27	-123.2
6	SB	BUY	10-DEC-1996	10.35	10-JAN-1997	10.64	324.8
7	SB	BUY	04-FEB-1997	10.44	12-MAR-1997	10.77	392.0
8	SB	SELL	29-APR-1997	11.03	12-MAY-1997	11.04	-11.2
9	SB	SELL	05-AUG-1997	11.61	07-AUG-1997	11.58	33.6
10	SB	SELL	12-AUG-1997	11.51	15-AUG-1997	11.86	-392.0
11	SB	SELL	02-SEP-1997	11.70	02-OCT-1997	11.87	392.0
12	SB	SELL	02-SEP-1997	11.70	11-SEP-1997	11.56	156.8
13	SB	SELL	16-DEC-1997	11.93	20-MAR-1998	9.88	2296.0
14	SB	BUY	05-MAY-1998	8.53	26-MAY-1998	8.56	33.6
15	SB	BUY	12-MAY-1998	9.35	15-MAY-1998	9.09	-291.2
16	SB	BUY	16-JUN-1998	7.60	21-JUL-1998	8.51	784.0
17	SB	BUY	11-AUG-1998	9.05	13-AUG-1998	8.71	-380.8
18	SB	BUY	29-SEP-1998	7.53	02-OCT-1998	7.35	-201.6
19	SB	BUY	06-OCT-1998	7.27	08-OCT-1998	7.27	0.0

Wins= 9 # Loses= 10 Largest Win= $2296 Largest Loss= $-403.2 Ahead= $2206.4

Note: Individual contract data were used in this study to accurately track the performance. In position trading, longer-term positions must be rolled from one contract month to the next due to expiring contracts. This process is called a *rollover* and simply involves exiting the expiring month and taking the same position in the next lead month. Rolling occurred during this historical study, and occasionally there were differences in prices between expiring contracts and the new contract months. Profits or losses in expiring contracts were also rolled into the new contract. The profit or loss shown by trade may not always equate to the difference between the two prices shown (entry and exit) because there may have been a difference in price at the time the contract was rolled. See the following example:

- Trader enters short January soybeans at 5.00. Stop is set at 5.40 (a $2,000 per contract risk) in January.
- Market moves against trader to 5.30 but trader is not stopped out and must roll.
- Trader rolls into March contract, which is trading 20 cents lower than January at 5.10.
  —Trader adjusts stop to 5.20 basis March. Total potential loss is still set at $2,000.
- Market moves 10 cents against trader to 5.20 basis March and trader is stopped out.

Note: The 30 cent loss was carried forward into the March contract, which was trading 20 cents lower than the January at the time the trader rolled. The trader entered January at 5.00 and sustained a 30 cent (–$1,500) loss prior to rolling into March at 5.10. The trader then sustained an additional 10 cent loss in the March, bringing the total loss to $2000 and stopping the trader out at 520 basis the March contract.

The back-testing program would handle this trade and report results as follows:

Mkt	B/S	Idate	Price	Odate	Price	W/L
S_	Sell	1/2/95	5.00	1/19/95	5.20	–2000

where: Mkt   = Market
        B/S   = Buy/Sell
        Idate = In date
        Odate = Out date
        W/L   = Win/Loss

Risk-per-Trade Table A

Using the 10 percent rule (for accounts ranging from $5,000 to $99,000), traders should not take on a trade that exposes more than 10 percent of their capital at a given time. Following is a 10 percent maximum risk reference guide for various size accounts (*Note:* Traders who do not have the appropriate amount of risk capital based on this table should not take trades exceeding that risk level.):

Minimum Account Size ($)	10 Percent Max Risk ($)
2,500	250
5,000	500
10,000	1,000
15,000	1,500
17,500	1,750
20,000	2,000
25,000	2,500
30,000	3,000
50,000	5,000

Risk-per-Trade Table B

For larger accounts, the risk per trade should be well below the 10 percent threshold, which reflects maximum capital at risk ranging from 8 percent down to 5 percent:

Reduce Risk for Large Accounts ($)	Percent Risk = 8, 7, 6, 5 Percent ($)
100,000	8,000
200,000	14,000
500,000	30,000
1,000,000	50,000

Index

A

Agricultural futures reporting
   levels, 151
Australian dollar futures, 45, 52

B

Bearish markets, 52, 62, 70–71
British pound trade example,
   138–139
Bullish markets, 52, 61, 63–64,
   70–71

C

Carrying charges, 63
Charts, technical, 49–51
Closing stops, 65–66, 74–75
Collective combined position, 32
Commercial bull markets, 63–64,
   71
Commercial history graphs, 57–58
Commercial Open Interest Graphs,
   68–69
Commercial traders. *See also*
   Net-commercial positions
   consumer trading behavior,
   9–10
   historical performance, 59–62